# Post-Butt
# The Power of the Image

Melani De Luca

## Oh dear derriere!
**Charlotte Van Buylaere**

For a very long time man has been fascinated by those round, mushy cheeks, that shape an appealing and sensual line at the back of our bodies. They swing, twerk, seduce, muffle and protect. Some are obstruent, while others only emit a trump. Their popularity is growing, and their meaning is shifting. What were once an indication of fertility, have now became the ultimate image of female empowerment. Where 2nd wave feminists were focused on the liberation of their breasts, post-feminism is all in for the buttocks. Instagram belfies circle the globe while carrying a clear message that declares: 'We are in control of our bodies, how it is represented, and we love our buttocks!'

Historically, there has always been an enduring interest in the derriere. Early examples of this curiosity include the Greek Venus Callipyge and the soft buttocks of Proserpina, which were masterly sculpted by Bernini out of white marble. Yet an emphasised butt only really became fashionable in the West around 1870 when the bustle – a wire framed and cushioned underskirt – replaced the crinoline or hoop skirt. This fashion trend happened only a few decades after a group of men had forced the South-African women Saartjie Baartman on a European tour, during which they exhibited her exotic morphology as a showcase attraction. Baartman embodied a general fascination for exotic 'things', which went hand in hand with the great colonial expansion in the second half of the 19th century.

The current bootyfication trend stems from the Afro-American hiphop culture, in which female rappers relate their sexual appetites and conquests in the same manner as many men do, (Bonnette, 2015, p 84). Some black female rappers were inspired by the Combahee River Collective, which was a group of black lesbian feminists that was founded in 1974. These women stated that they were more aligned with a feeling of solidarity with black men, than with the issues acknowledged by white feminism. The need for autonomy and personal body control became a key point within black feminist politics, and emerged from a long history of slavery and sexual oppression. Rights like the freedom of sexual choice and birth control were played at for a much higher stake in black communities than those within the European sexual revolution.

In the background of these cultural and historical events, one can witness bootyfication within the female hiphop culture. However, the popularisation of this counter culture ended up being the catalyst for body positivism in Western pop culture. It didn't take long for media companies to consume this new trend: commodifying feminism by co-opting a positive body message in advertisements. Brands such as Dove, American Apparel and lingerie brand Aerie replaced supermodels on their posters with 'average' women, claiming that these ads would fight for common beauty standards. But is this really what they're doing? The posters may not show super-thin models, but the image is still constructed by a perfect (often seducing) pose, professional lighting, make-up and photoshop. Instead of getting rid of beauty standards, they are transferring them onto everyday girls under the guise of accepting who you are, or want to be. This is where marketing strategies meet the neoliberal ideology; it is not sufficient to just be yourself, but rather you have to make yourself. And therefore, products and clothes are the necessary adornments to give expression to your own fictitious brand. Unfortunately feminism in the 21st century became much more a part of individual branding, than a movement for solidarity and human activism.

Within the sometimes precarious ideology of post-feminism and the way it's consumed by neoliberal thoughts, the post-butt may induce a reunification of a younger generation of feminists. Exploring the different aspects and histories of twerking, belfies and artistic representations, this book digs deeper into the significance of the buttocks as a current icon within popular media.



References

Bonnette L.M., Pulse of the People: Political Rap Music and Black Politics, University of Pennsylvania Press, 2015

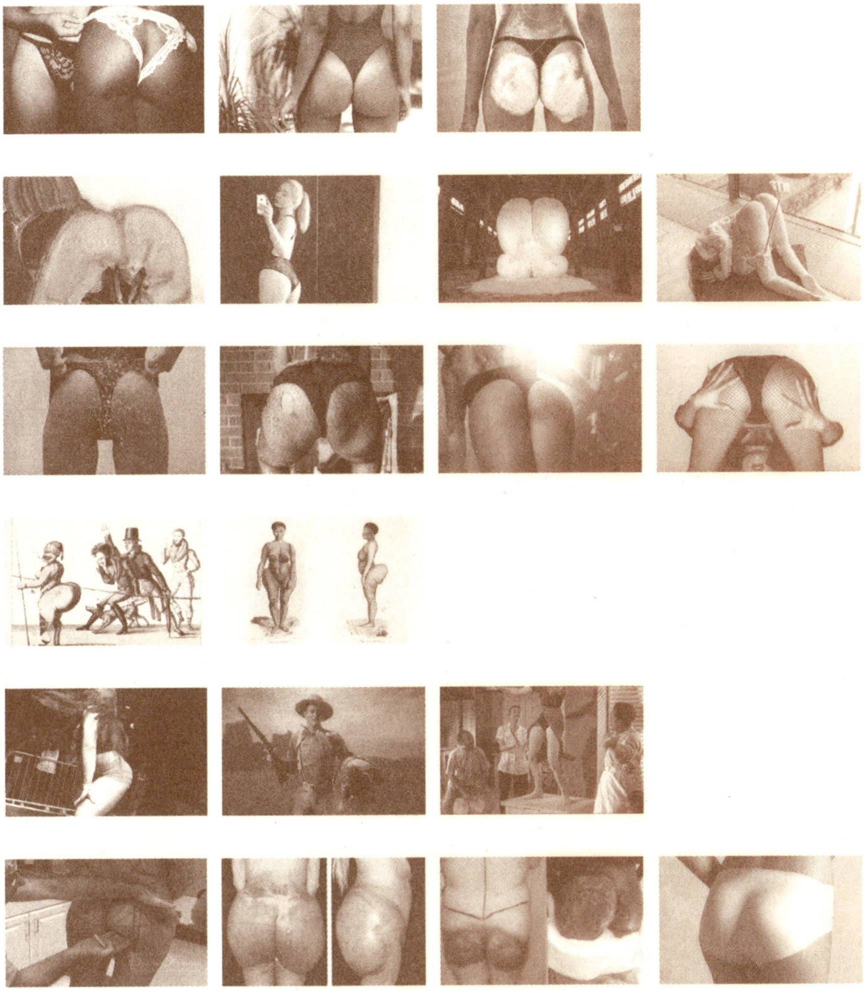

# Introduction

Nudity is nothing new, but in today's visual culture it has permeated so deep that it's in danger of being taken for granted. The nude images coming out of pop and internet culture are incredibly provocative with the amount of flesh they expose. Despite the seemly graphic content of these images, they're not actually classified as porn. The line between porn and not porn is in continuous flux; as if every new image uploaded onto a platform wants to break a new barrier and shift the existing border. The perception of an image often changes over time, thanks to this more naked skin has been conquered and new body parts are being explored. The décolleté lost its fascination and since the late 90s society has moved on to a new body part: the buttocks. The image of a women with a posterior has become a totem of our time. Thanks to song lyrics, music videos, photography, magazine covers, articles, TV series, pornography, social networks, and fitness culture; the buttocks have become a focus point in today's cultural imagery. A phenomenon that has reached the masses, and one that has been spread mainly through the internet.

The adoption of the butt as the focal point of the female body is a political statement, it's a sign of the integration of different cultures and their beauty ideals into Western society. It also acts as a form of revenge for the often marginalised, like African, Caribbean, and Queer cultures.
The new power given to the buttocks empowers these subgroups and legitimises their aesthetics and makes them a new beauty ideal. The era of the buttocks presents a meaning that contains – amongst other things – the history of African tribes and of colonised countries. This meaning is always shifting between cultures, historical contexts, communities and subcultures.

The re-interpretation of those meanings through the mediation of images establishes a link between image and culture. The visual language itself does not only reflect the world as it is already, but at the same time it's producing a new cultural meaning through representing it. Through this the boundaries between image and reality are becoming blurred.

The buttocks are strictly related to visual culture and the way information, meaning, and pleasure are sought by the consumer. What started as the promotion of the African shape and a healthier body type, was then appropriated by mass culture and with it its meaning. While for many people the buttocks reflect a lifestyle connected to sport and Instagram photography, the pictures shown often exaggerate reality. With the increasing production of images the relationship between image and reality has become complex. The sociologist Erving Goffman speaks of "hyperritualizing", this phenomena is when the social use of images takes a separate, almost autonomous path of development, that then goes on to a whole new significance. There is no single relation between image and meaning, as every image has its own realm of possible meanings. The interpretation of the image always depends to a large extent on the observer. Images function in a subcultural context and they create meaning for that specific subculture. A relevant question is if the distinction of image and reality can still be maintained? This publication will focus on today's visual culture and the relationship between the image, its consumer, and its producer. It'll analyse the process of the origins of the images as well as their influence and re-interpretation. Photography works through the objectification of things. However the thing in this case will be the human body and its varied collection of different sized extremities. Its inherent changeability is what makes it the perfect target; allowing the camera to focus on specific parts highlights aspects of our cultures that could otherwise go unnoticed. The butt is an example that shows a paradoxical situation. It stands for homosexuality as well as for femininity. It, we might argue, is a genderless object. Since the definition of 'Gender' in the Oxford dictionary is no longer current "Either of the two sexes (male and female)", this blurry border between genders has created the perfect conditions for the rise of the butt. The butt has also helped create a stronger image of the 'bombshell', the classical curvy woman. Taking this into consideration the research concentrates mostly on the effects and consequences the butt has had on the 'supposedly female' body.

The natural butt has exhausted its cycle of original meaning intended in hip-hop in the early 90s. It's created a phenomenon that consumes itself mainly through the production and reinterpretation of images; leading us to a visual culture with content far from its initial intentions of promoting a healthier body type. This form of representation has the power to influence the appearance of the body, but what are the consequences? How much has the image been integrated into our lives and how much do we depend on it?

This publication investigates the contemporary power of the image and its influence on human lives as well as the incorporation of the images into every day situations.

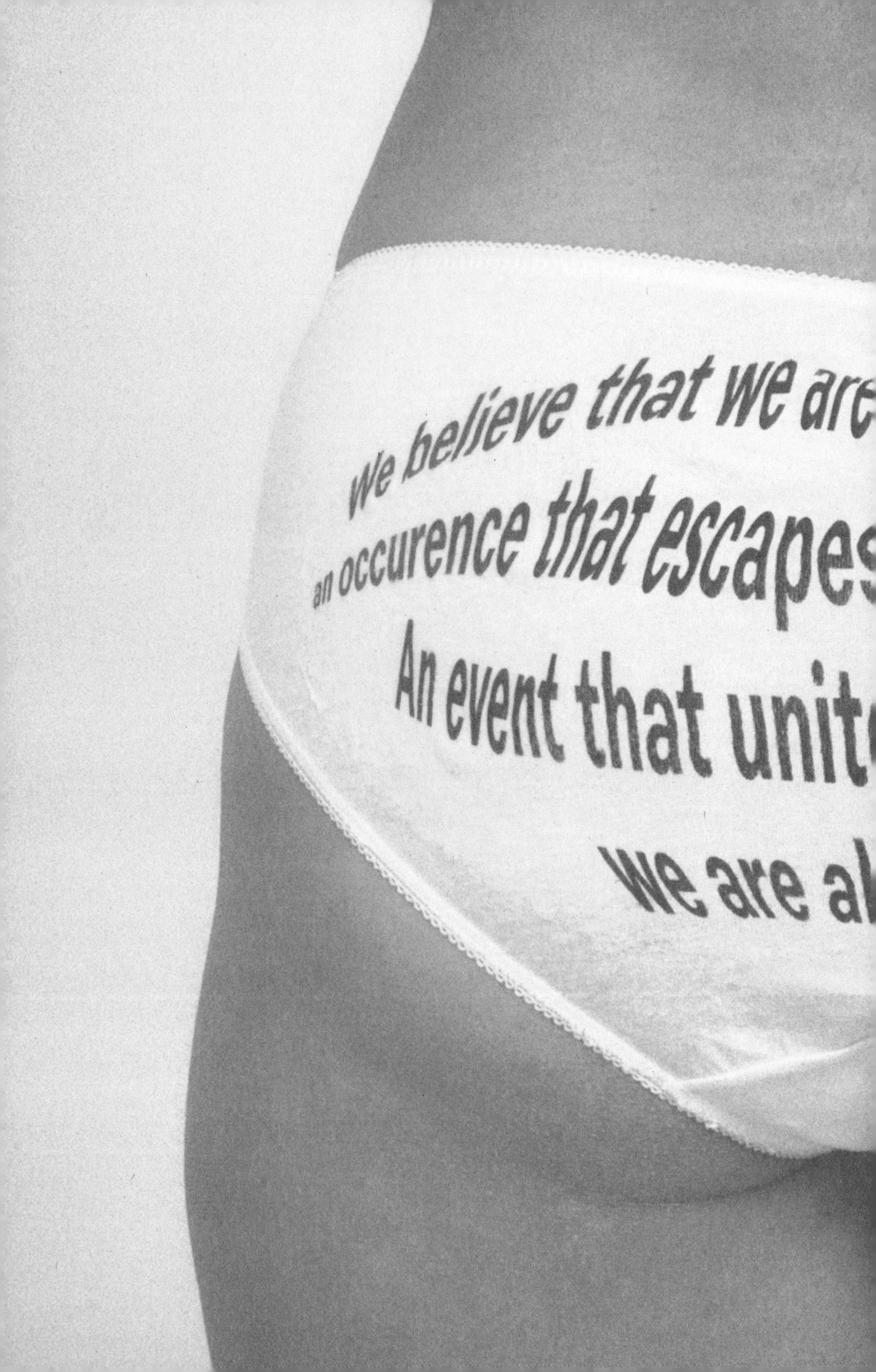

We believe that we ar
an occurence that escapes
An event that unit
we are al

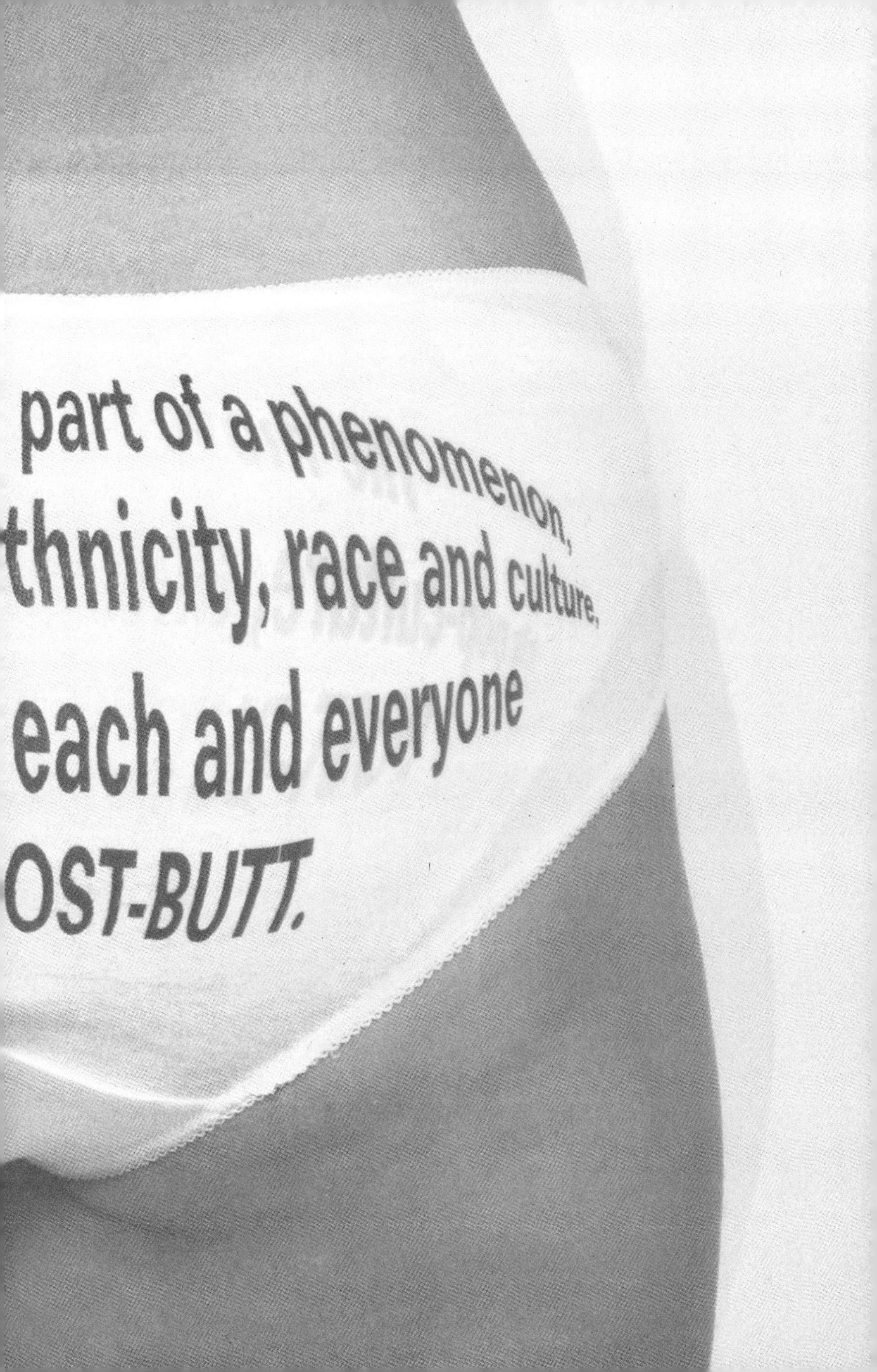

part of a phenomenon,
thnicity, race and culture,
each and everyone
OST-*BUTT.*

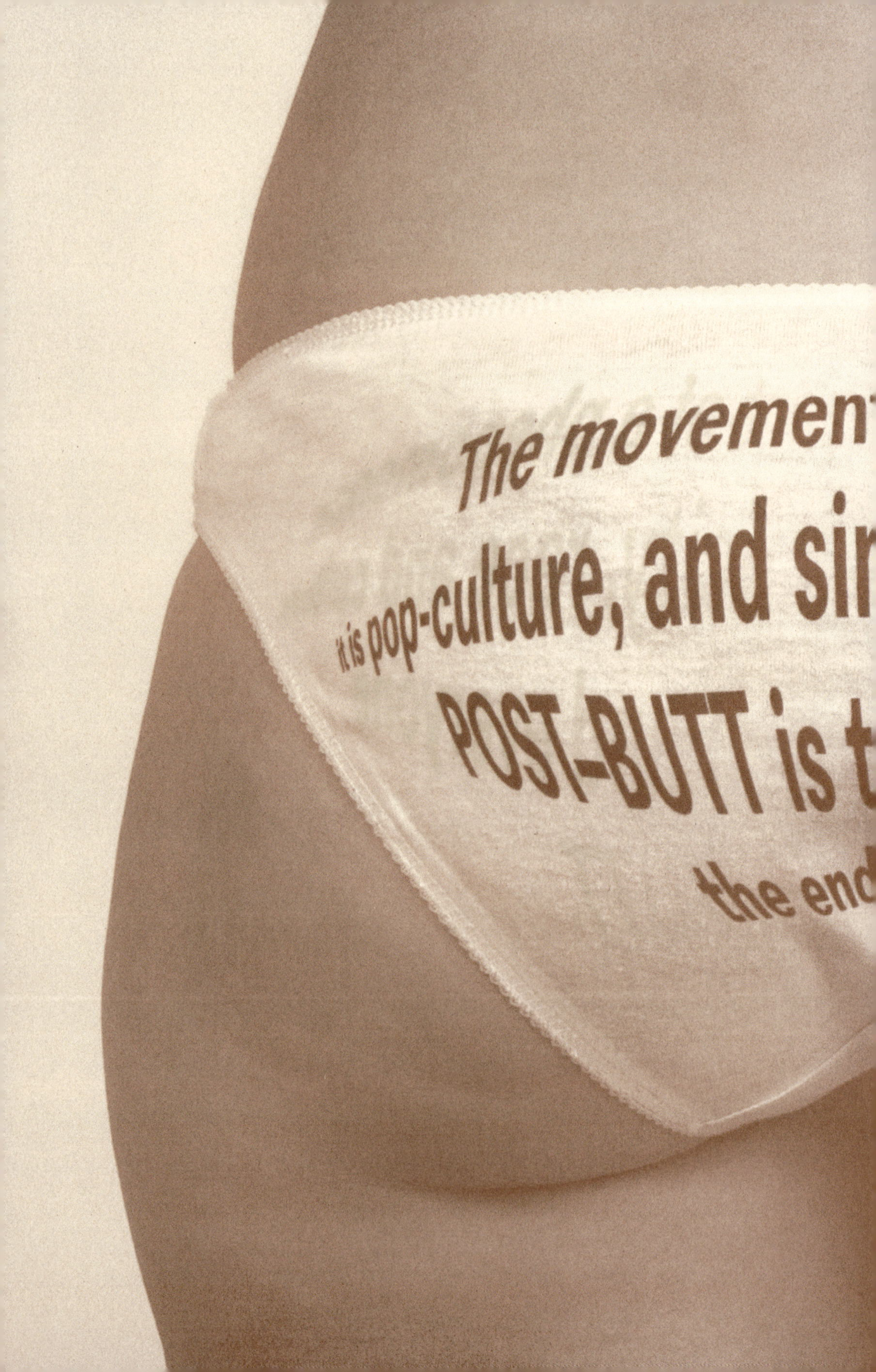

The movement
it is pop-culture, and sir
POST-BUTT is t
the end

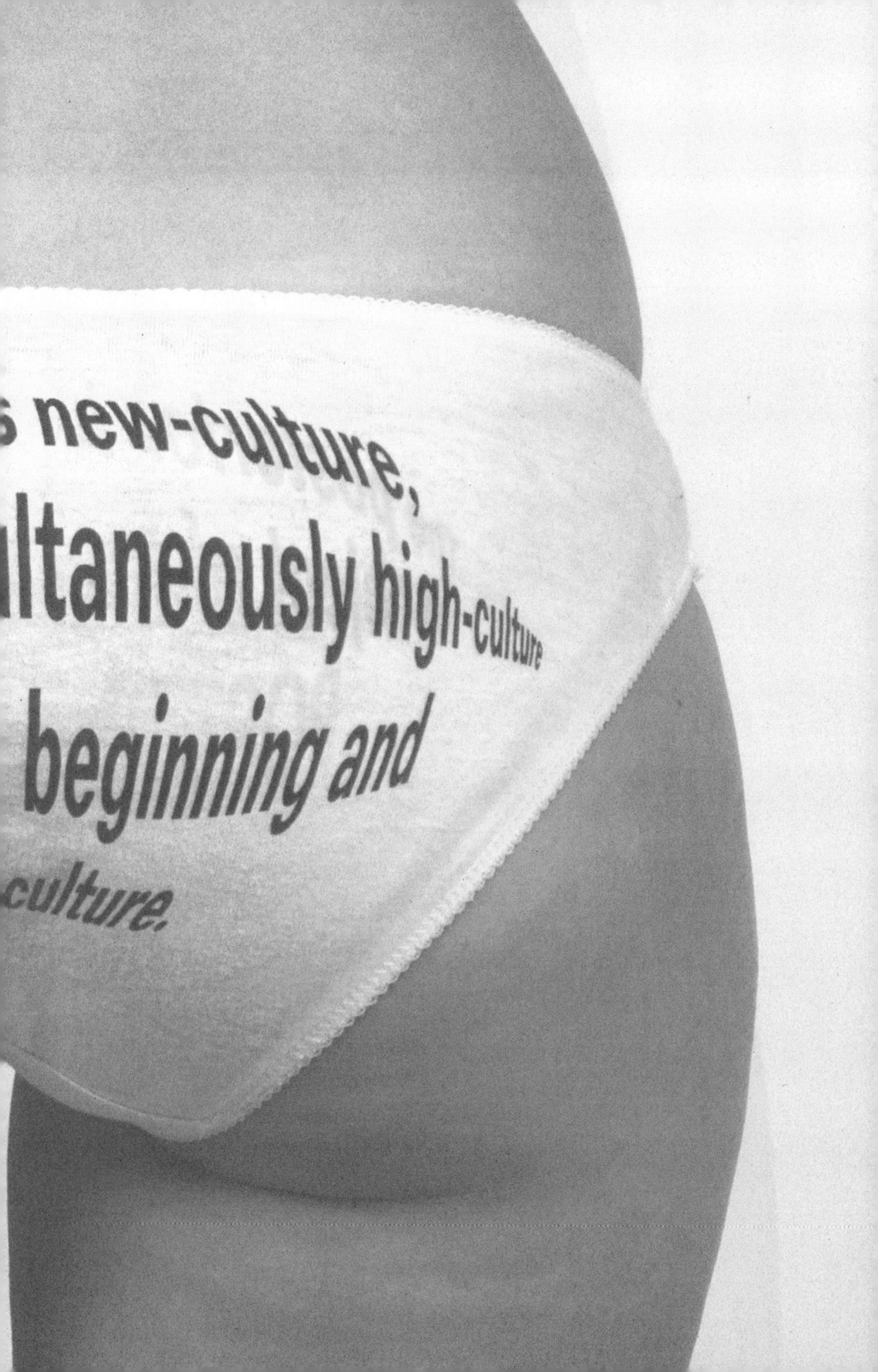

s new-culture,
ultaneously high-culture
beginning and
culture.

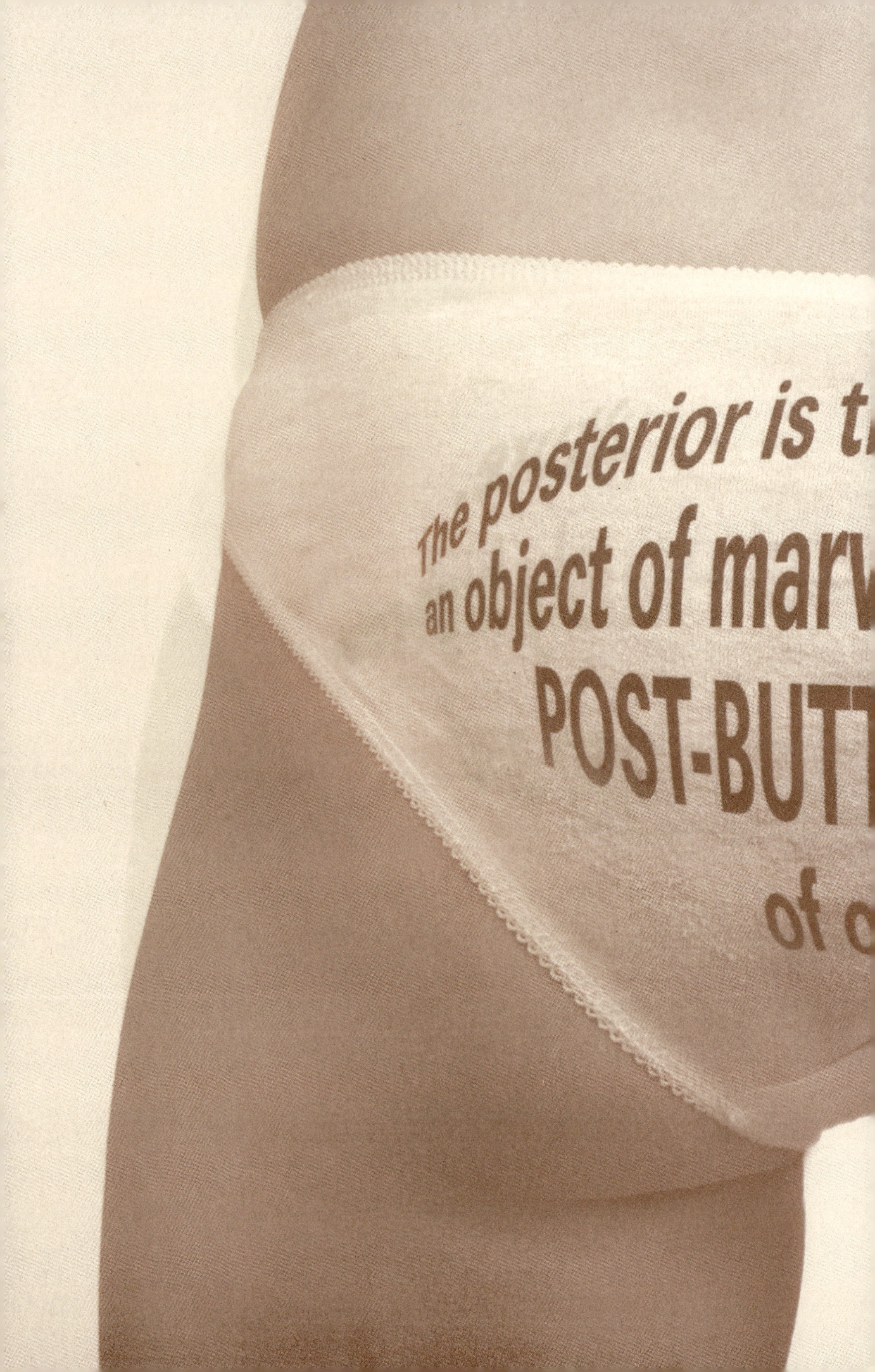

The posterior is t
an object of marv
POST-BUTT
of o

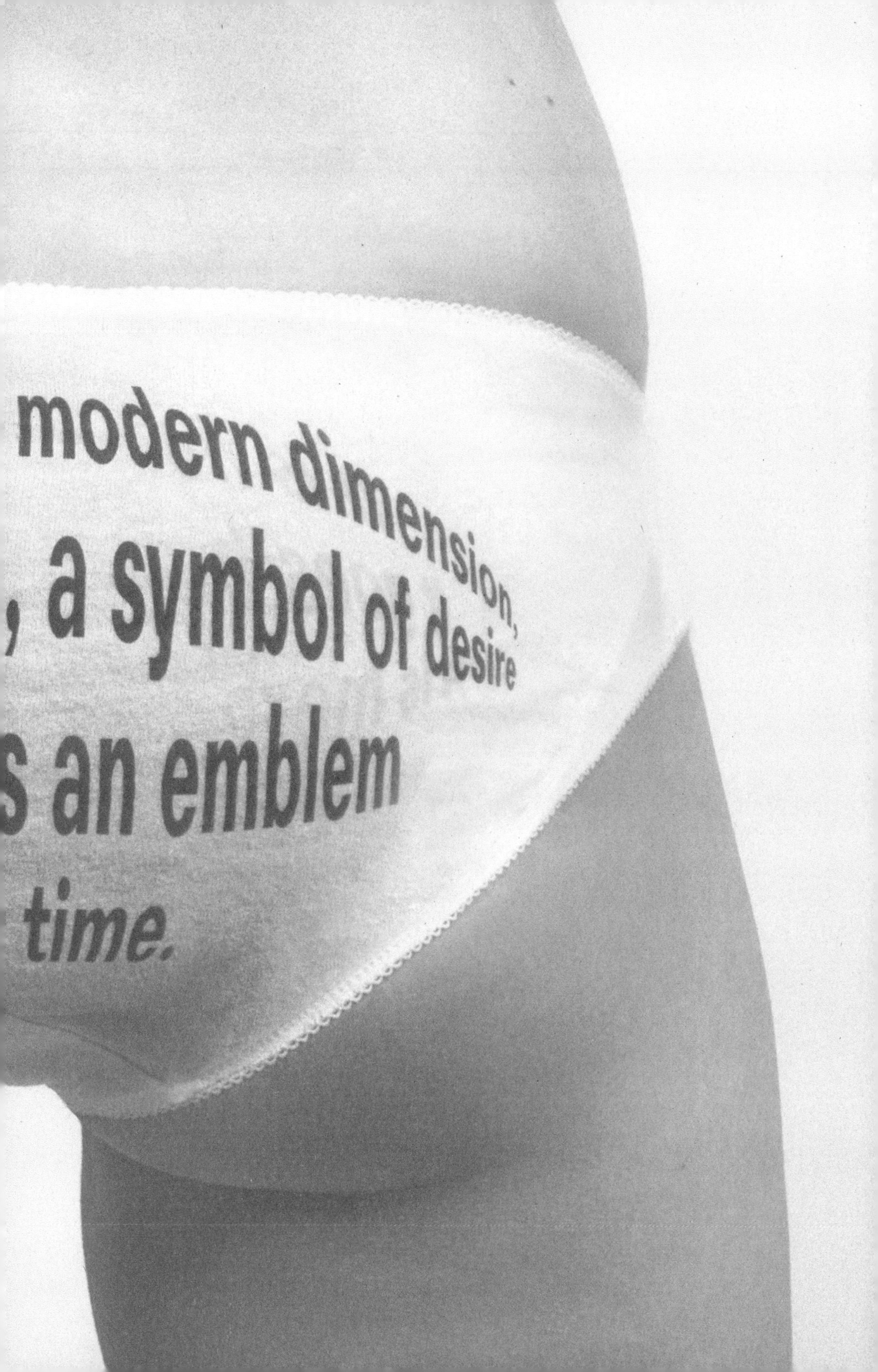

modern dimension,
, a symbol of desire
s an emblem
*time.*

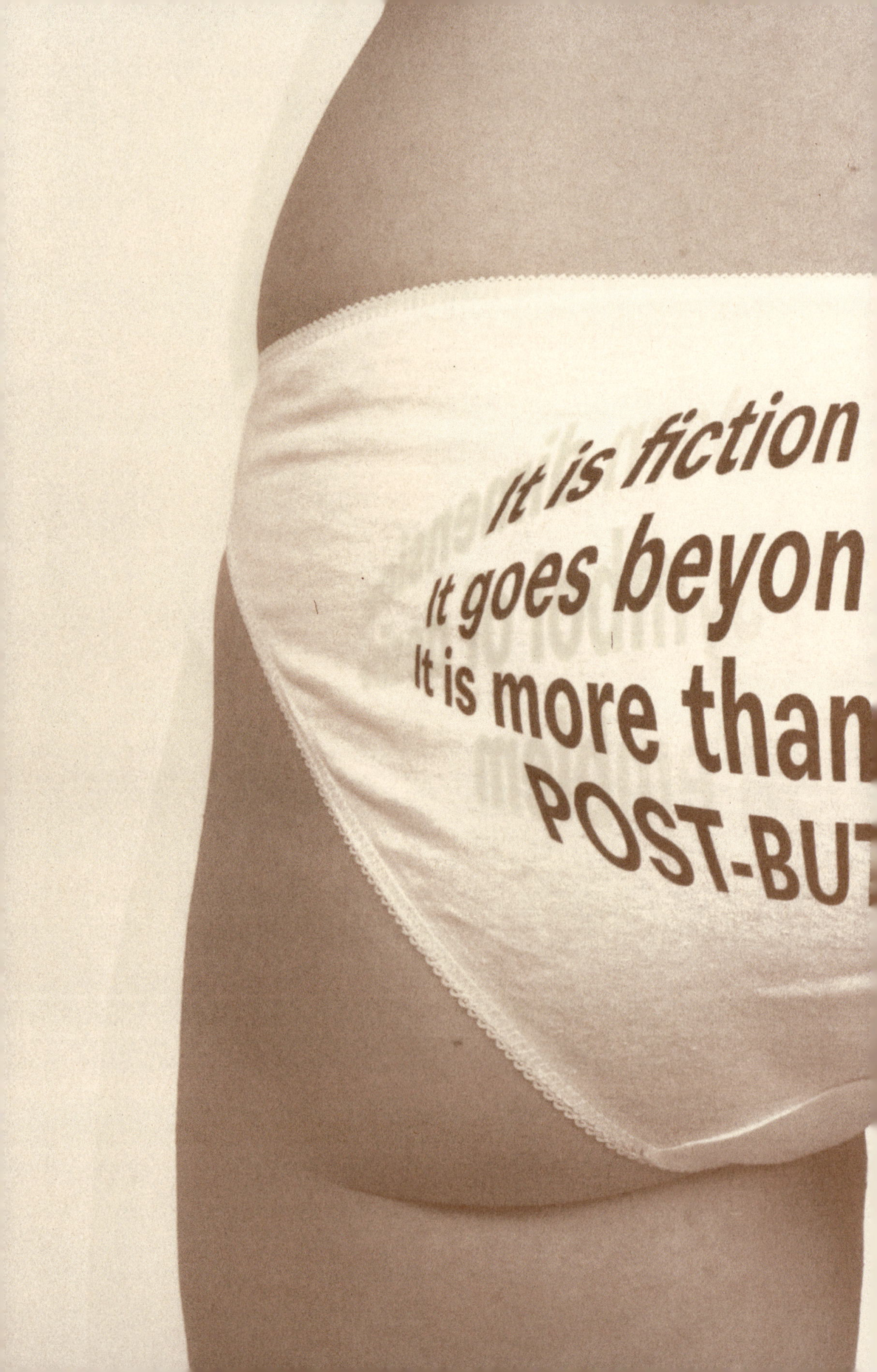

It is fiction
It goes beyon
It is more than
POST-BUT

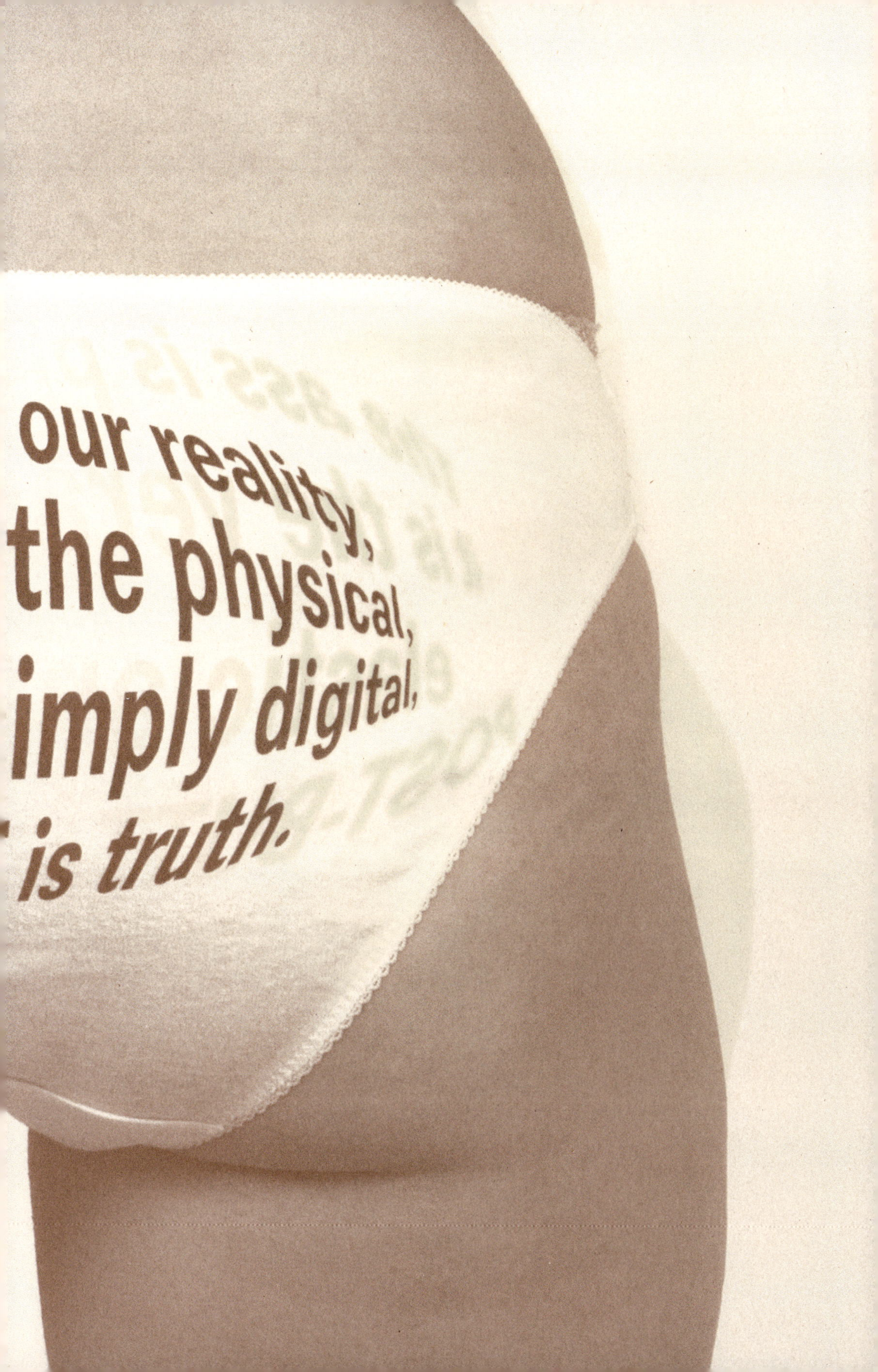

our reality,
the physical,
imply digital,
is truth.

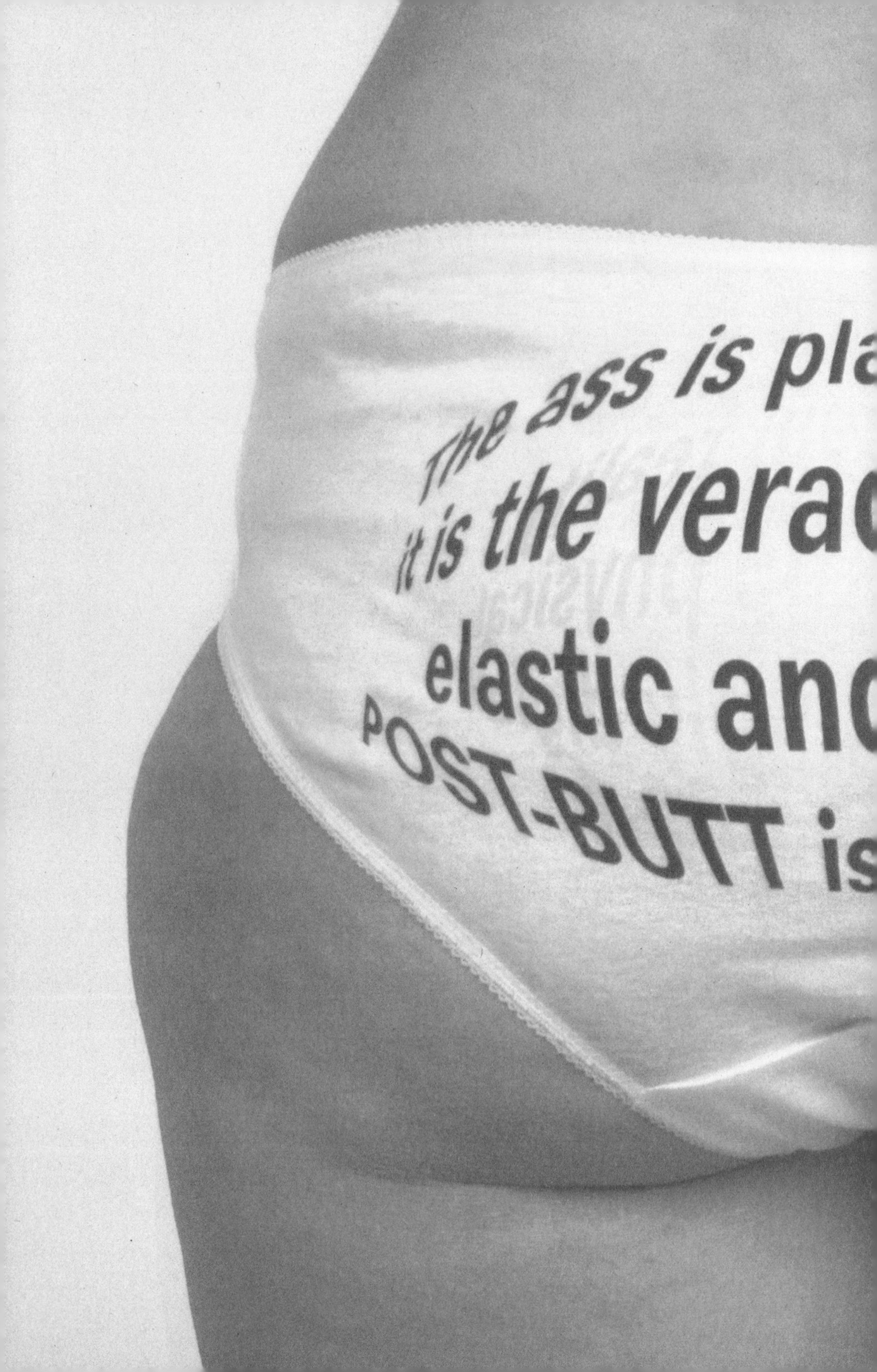

The ass is pla
it is the verac
elastic and
POST-BUTT is

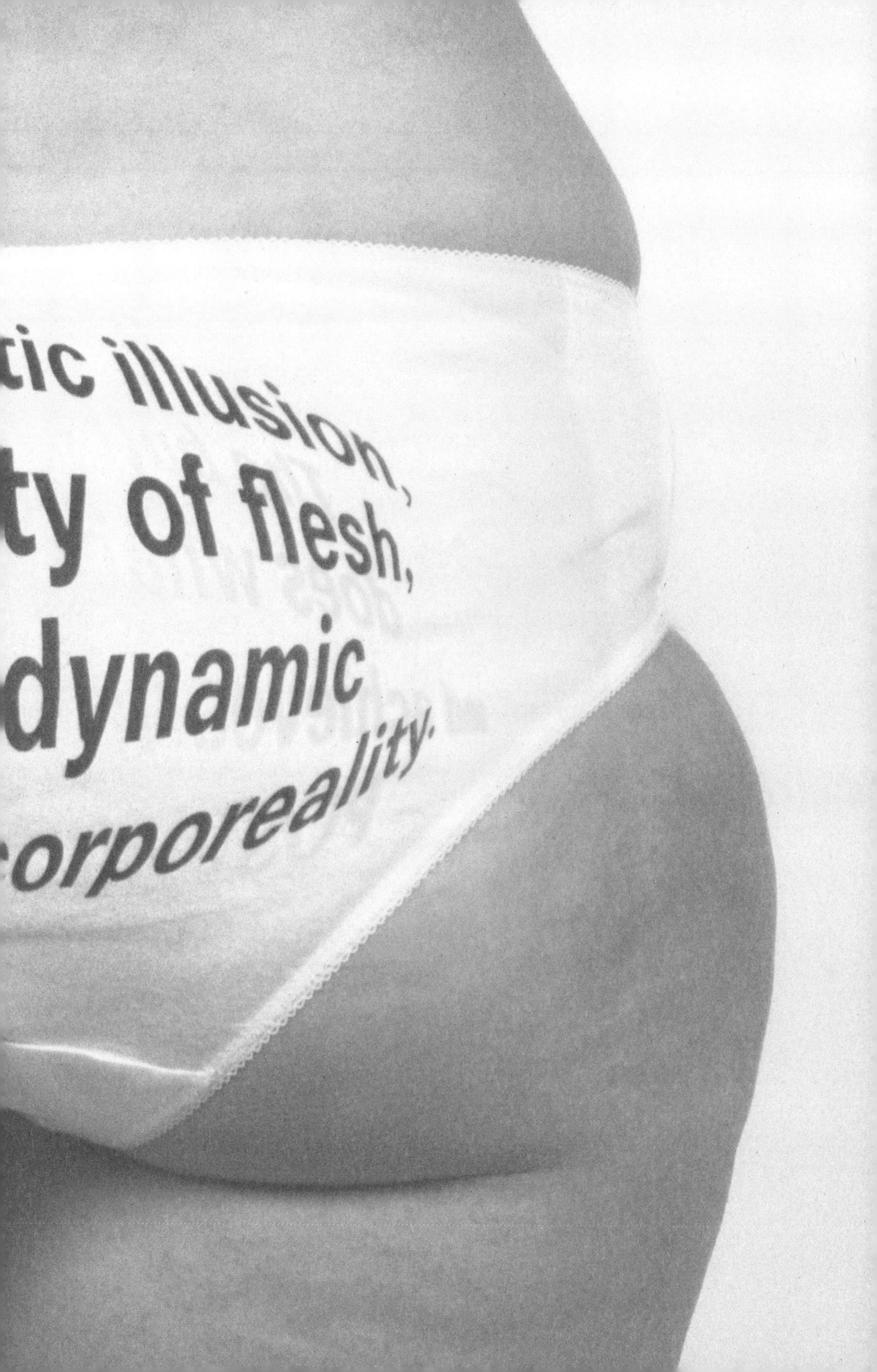

tic illusion,
ty of flesh,
dynamic
corporeality.

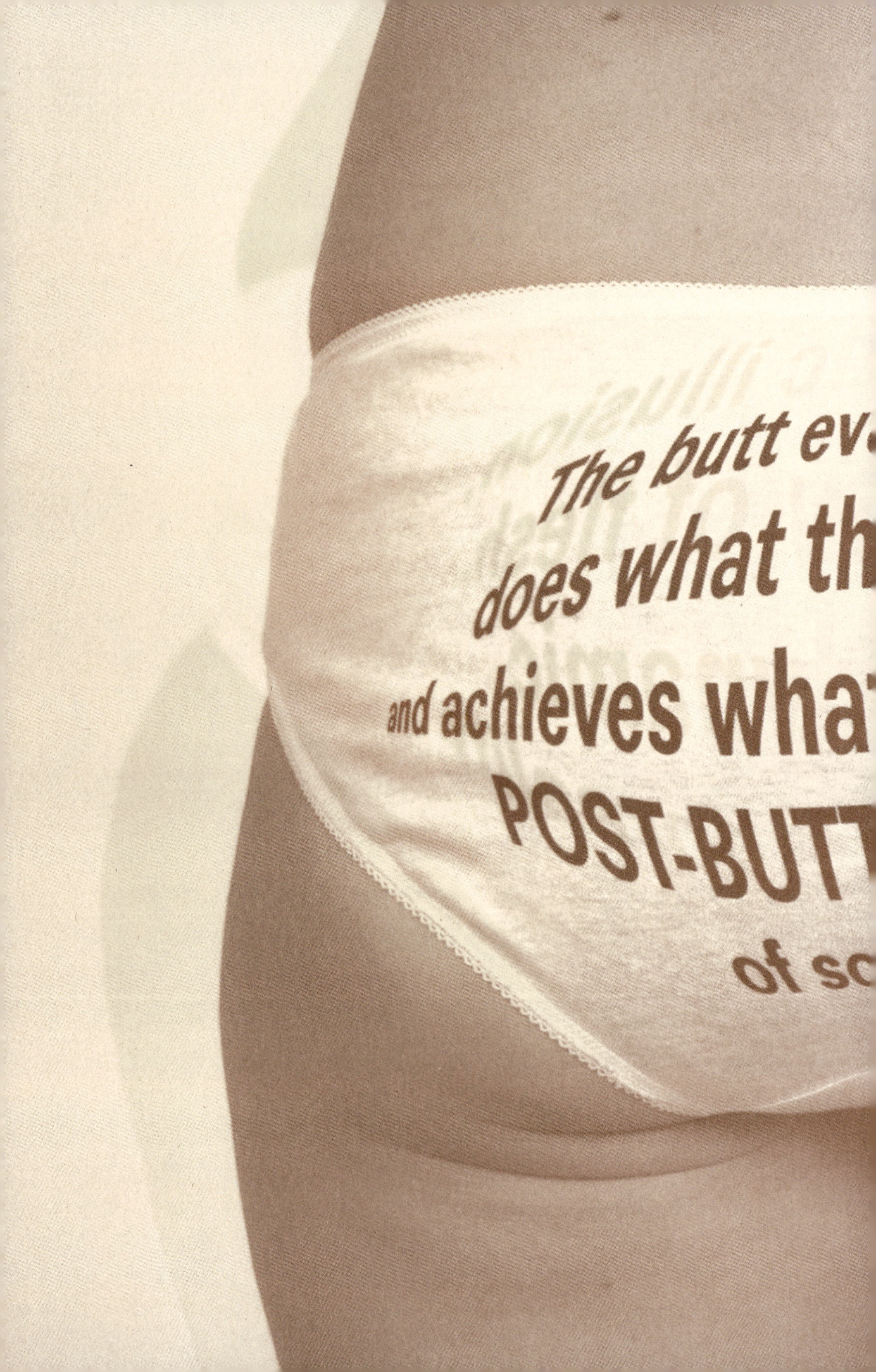

The butt ev
does what th
and achieves wha
POST-BUTT
of sc

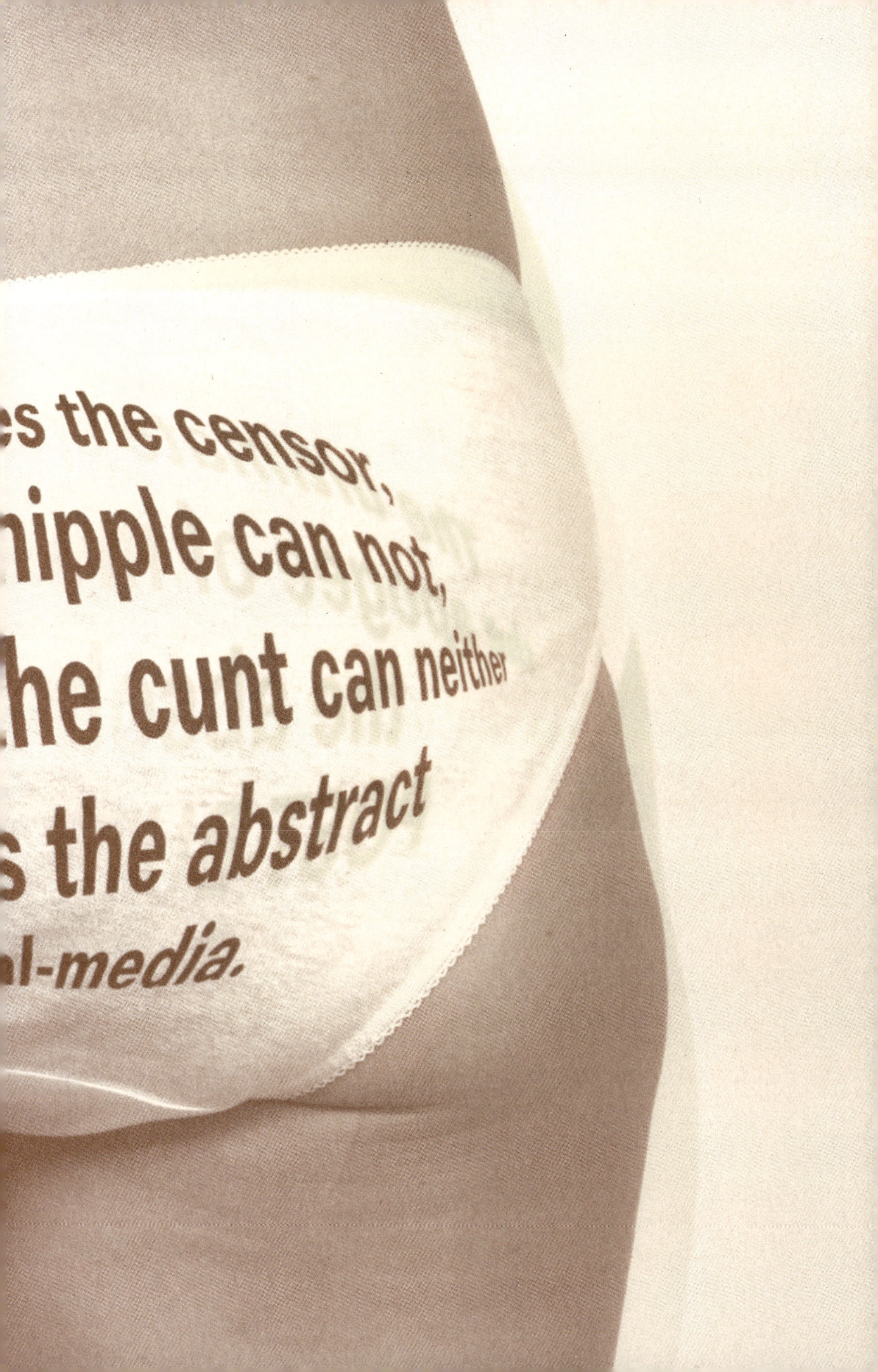

es the censor,
nipple can not,
he cunt can neither
s the *abstract*
al-*media.*

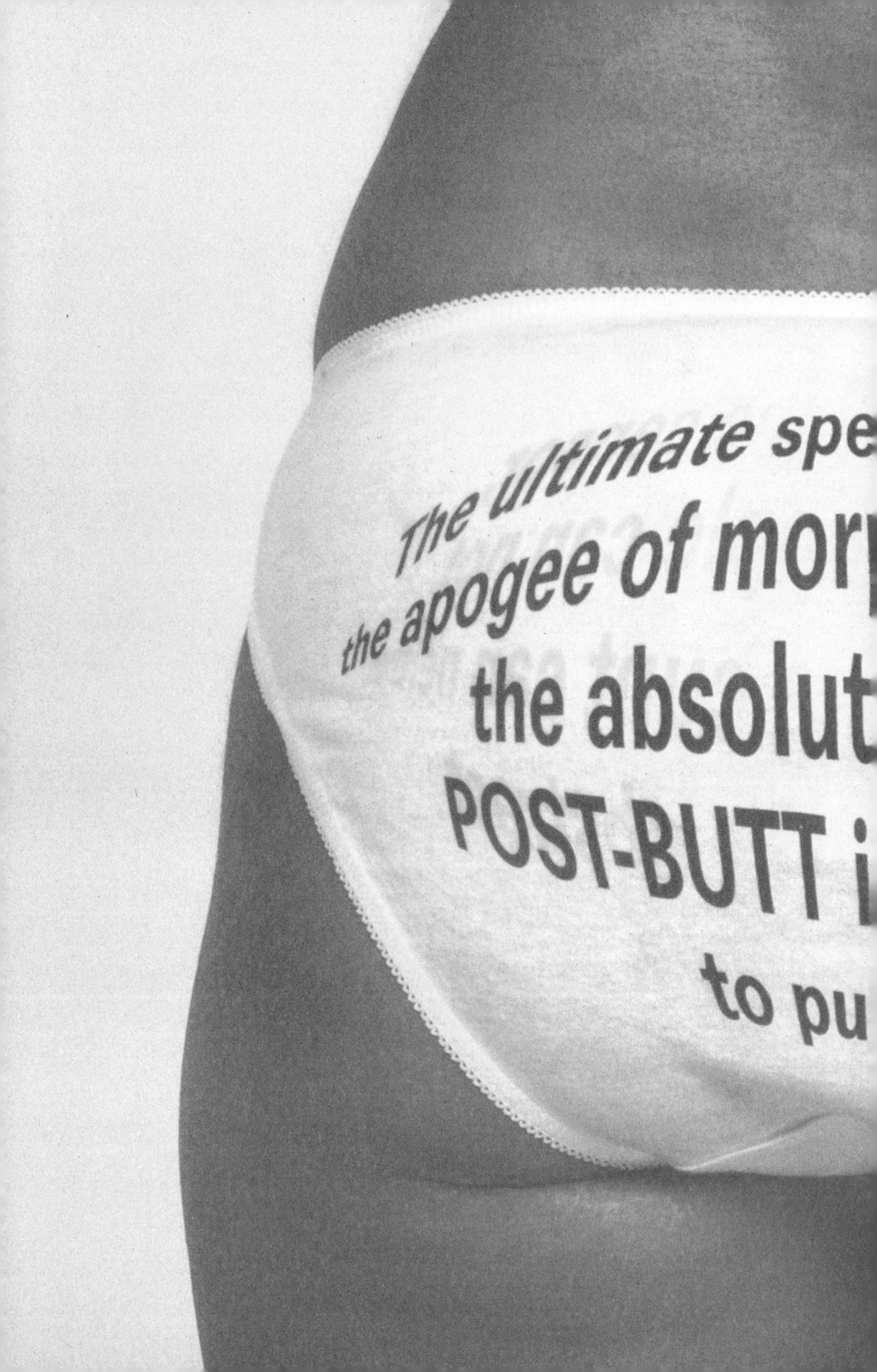

The ultimate spe
the apogee of mor
the absolut
POST-BUTT i
to pu

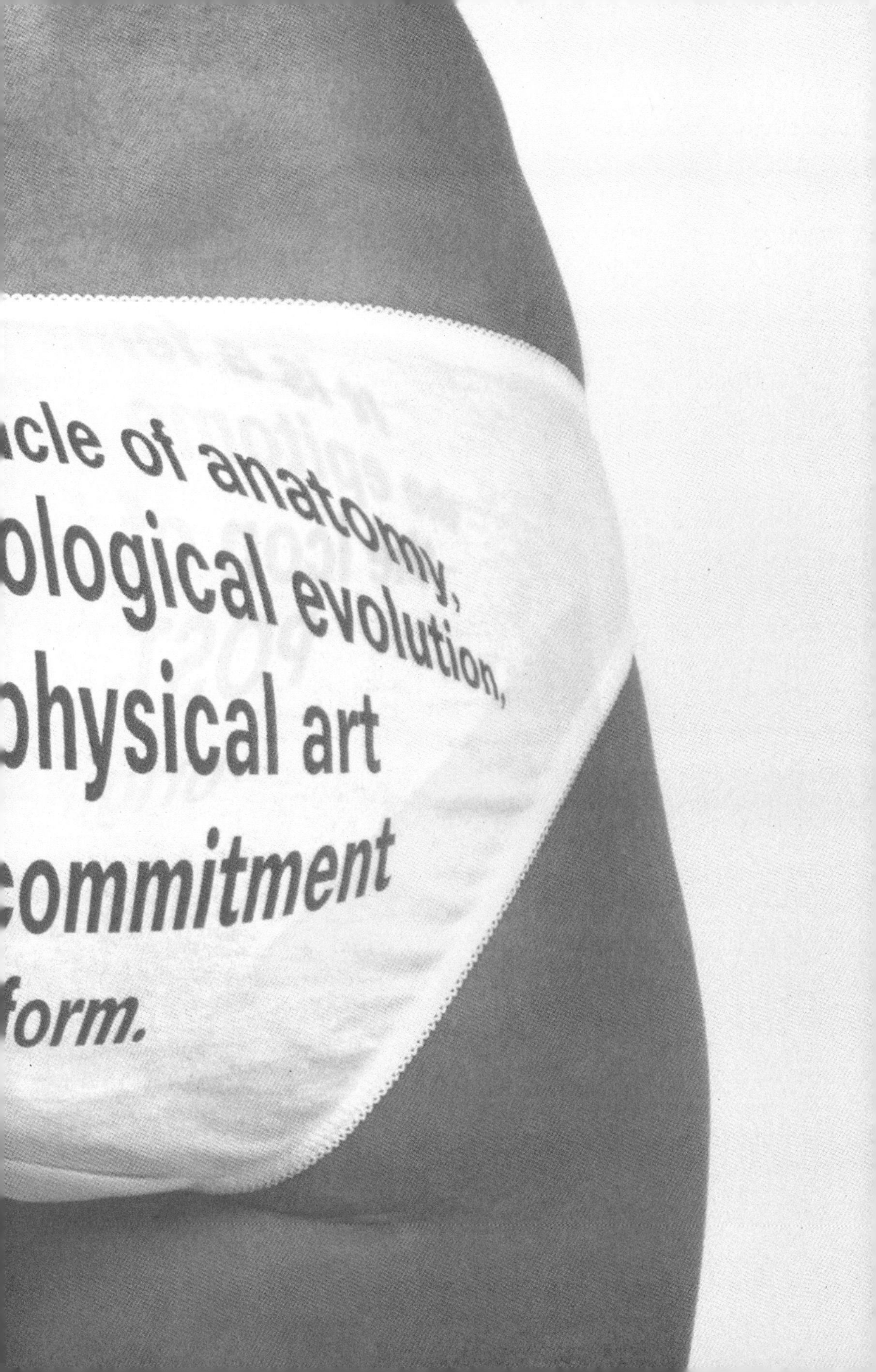

acle of anatomy,
ological evolution,
physical art
commitment
form.

It is a femini
the epitome of
the icon of fe
POST-BU
origina

**movement,**
**minine power,**
**nine fertility**
***is the***
***non.***

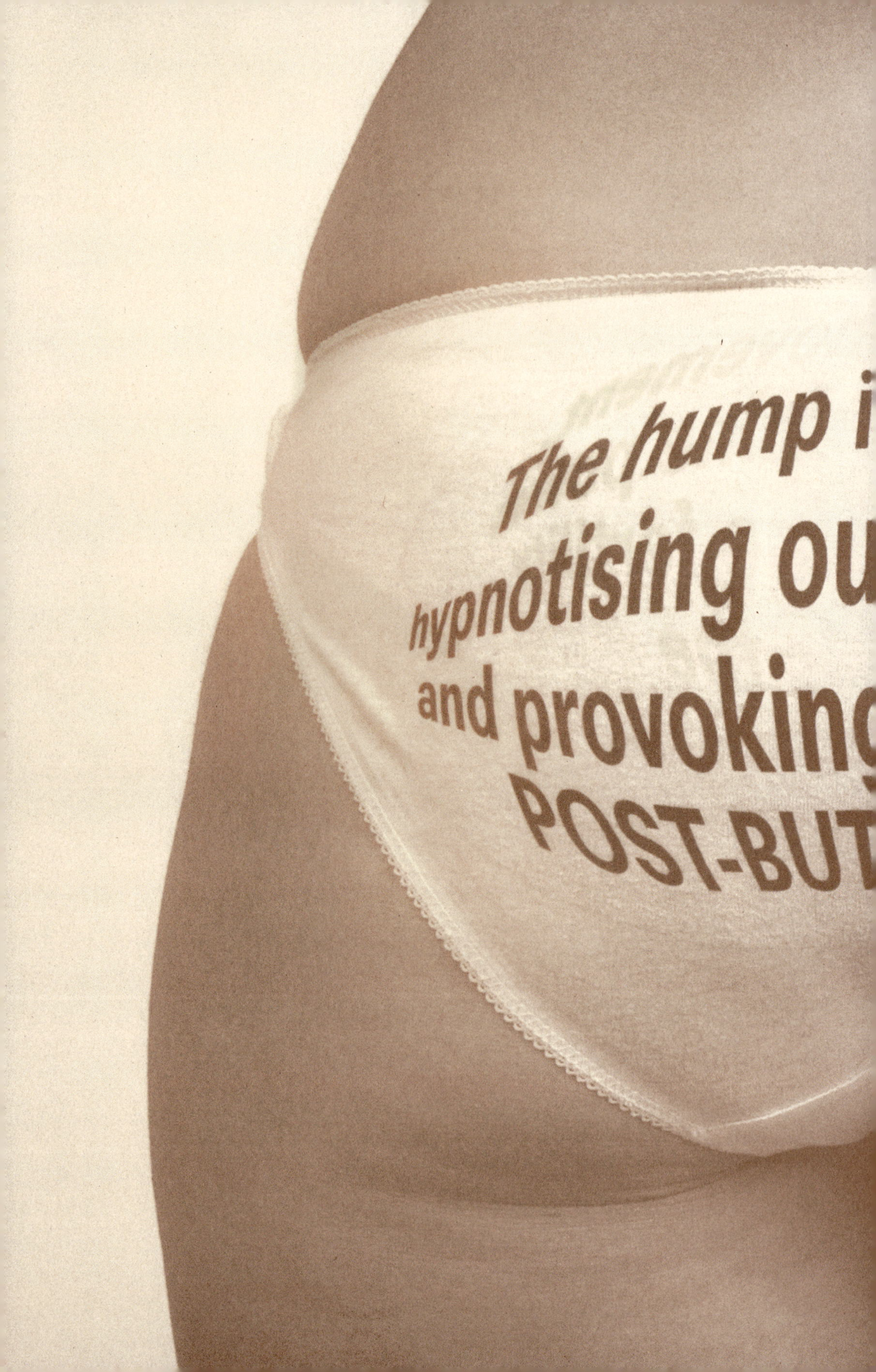

The hump i
hypnotising ou
and provoking
POST-BUT

n our DNA,
visceral needs,
our primal lust
is creation.

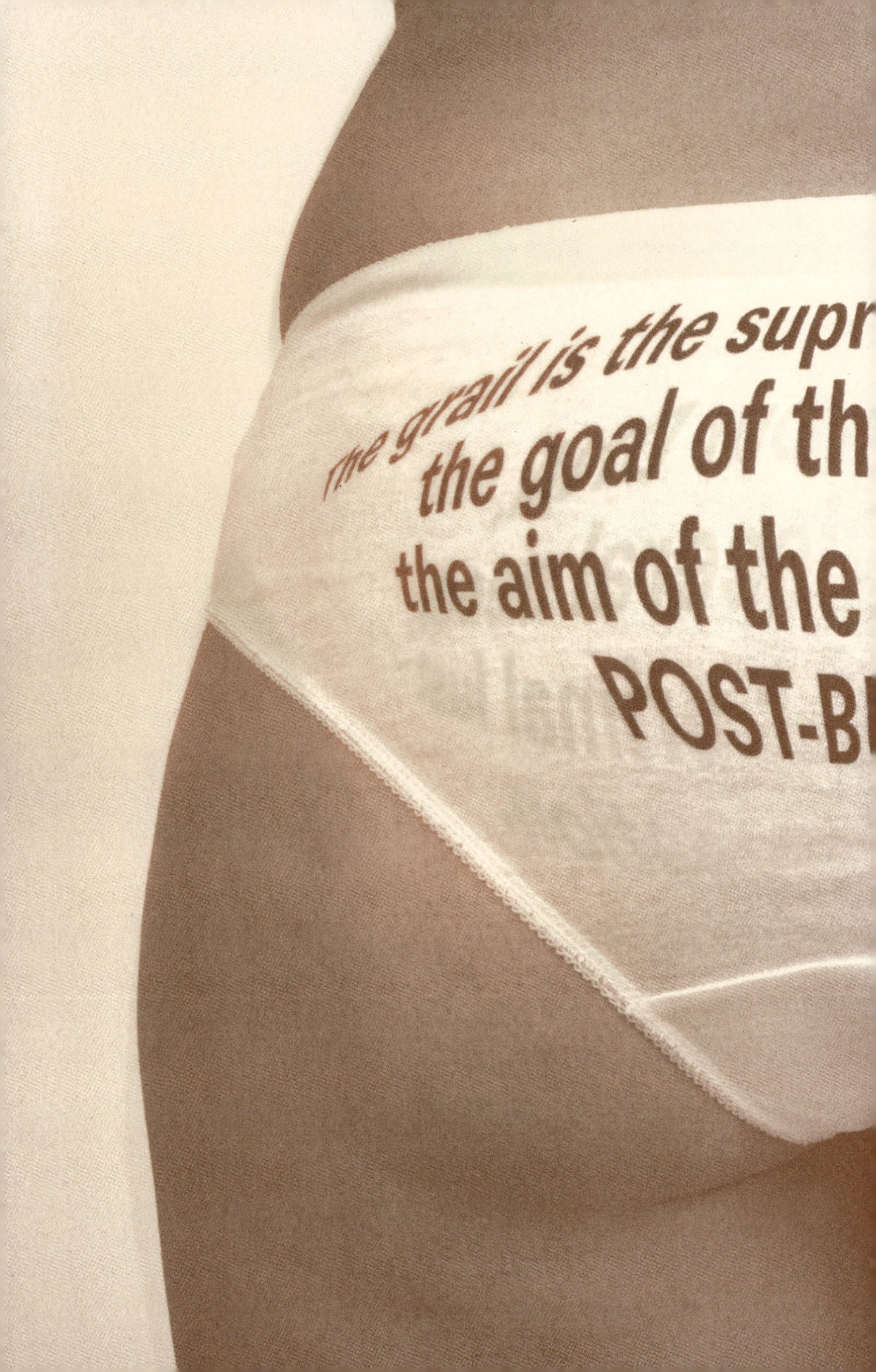

The grail is the supr
the goal of th
the aim of the
POST-B

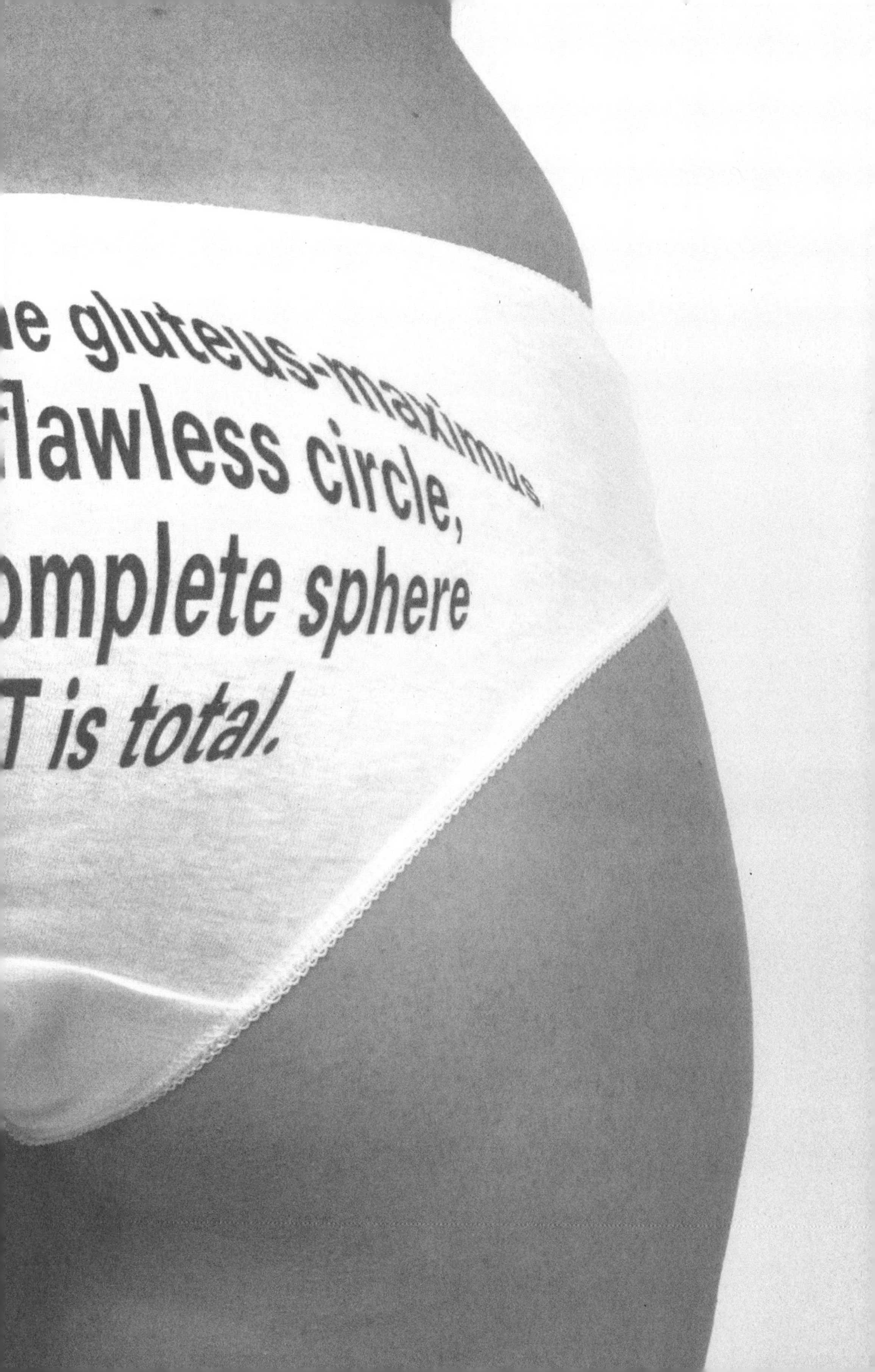

e gluteus-maximus.
flawless circle,
omplete *sphere*
*T is total.*

# Instagram Overview

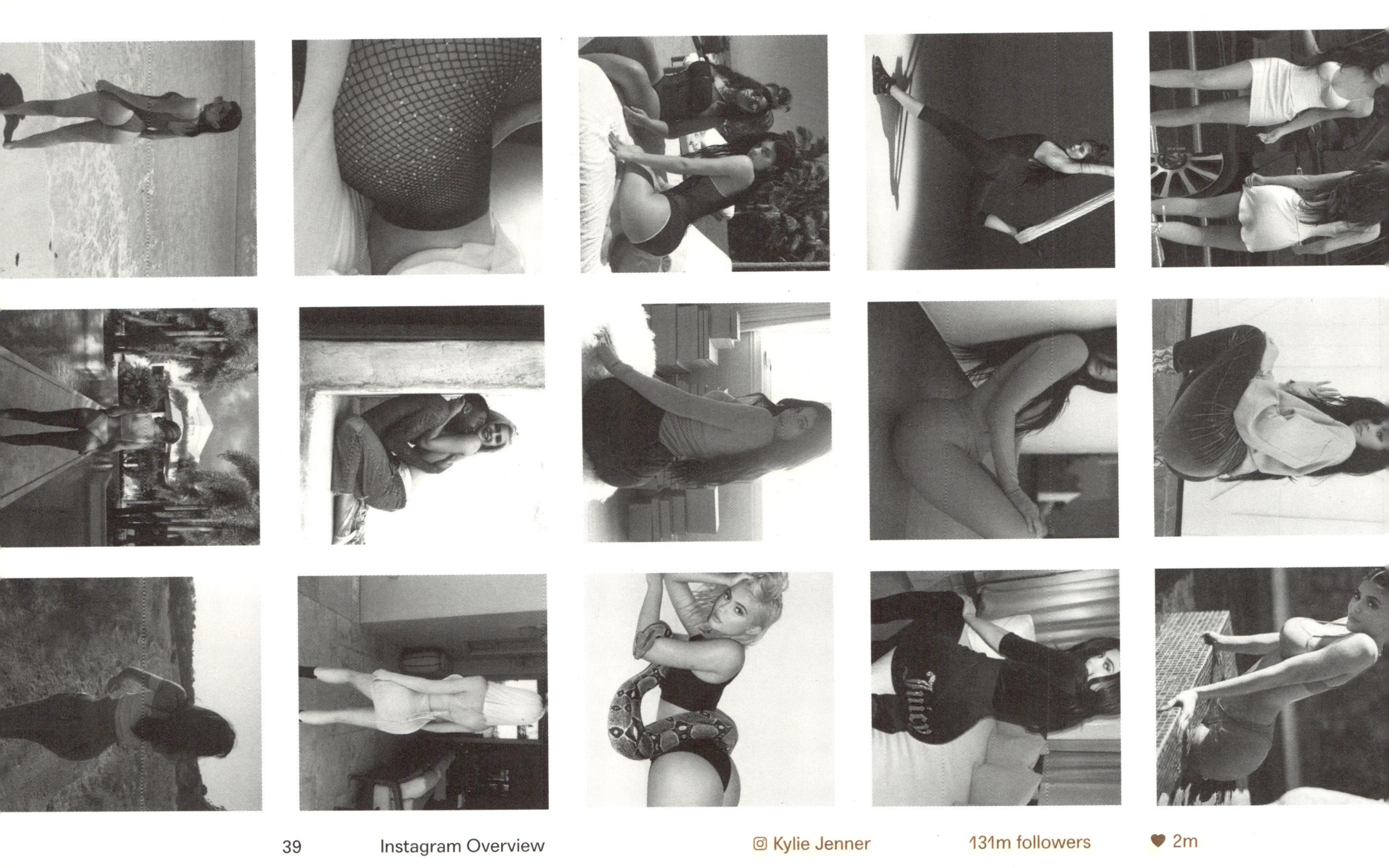


Kylie Jenner 131m followers ♥ 2m

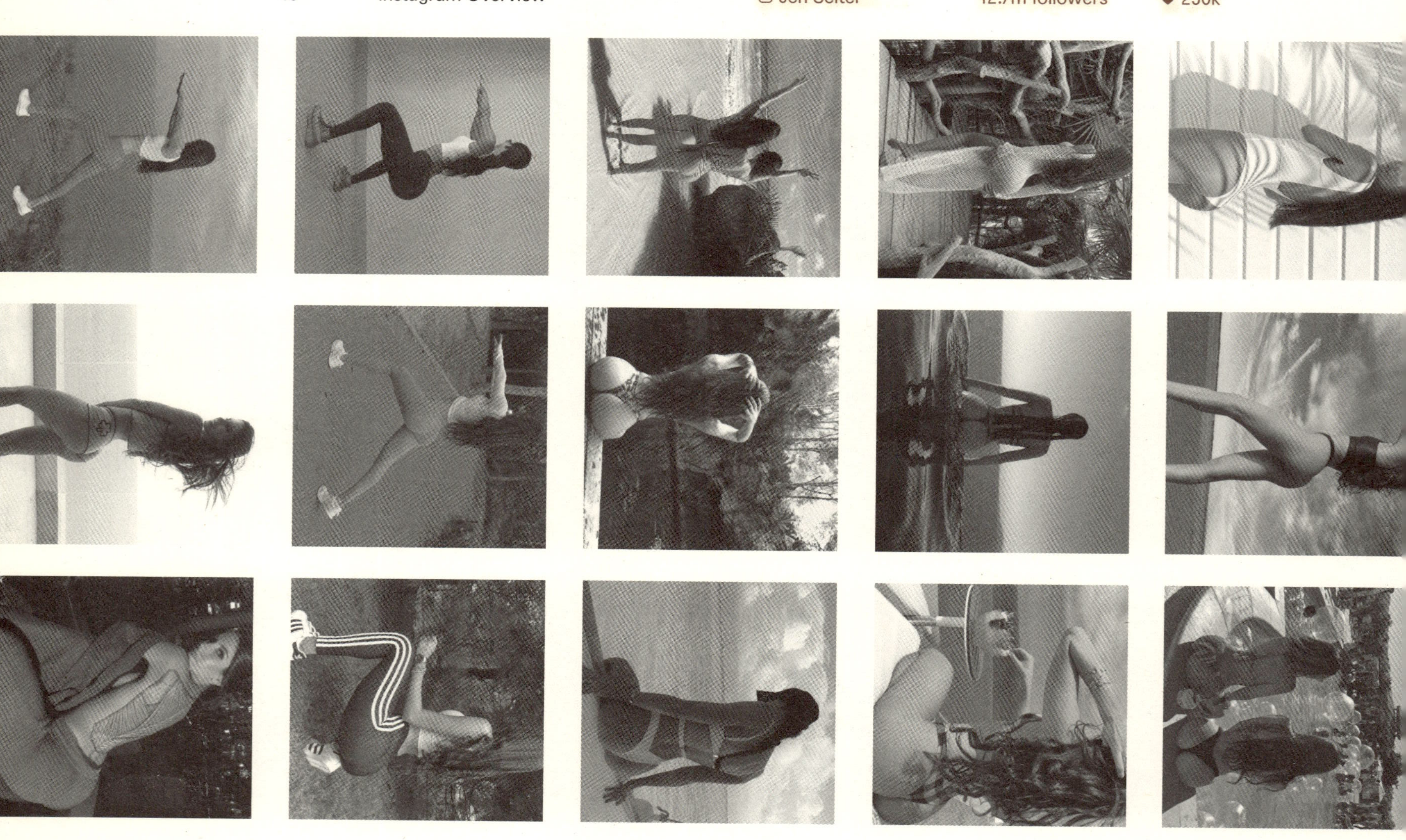

Victoria's Secret 65.6 m followers ♥ 500k

Terry Richardson 1.1m followers ♥ 20K

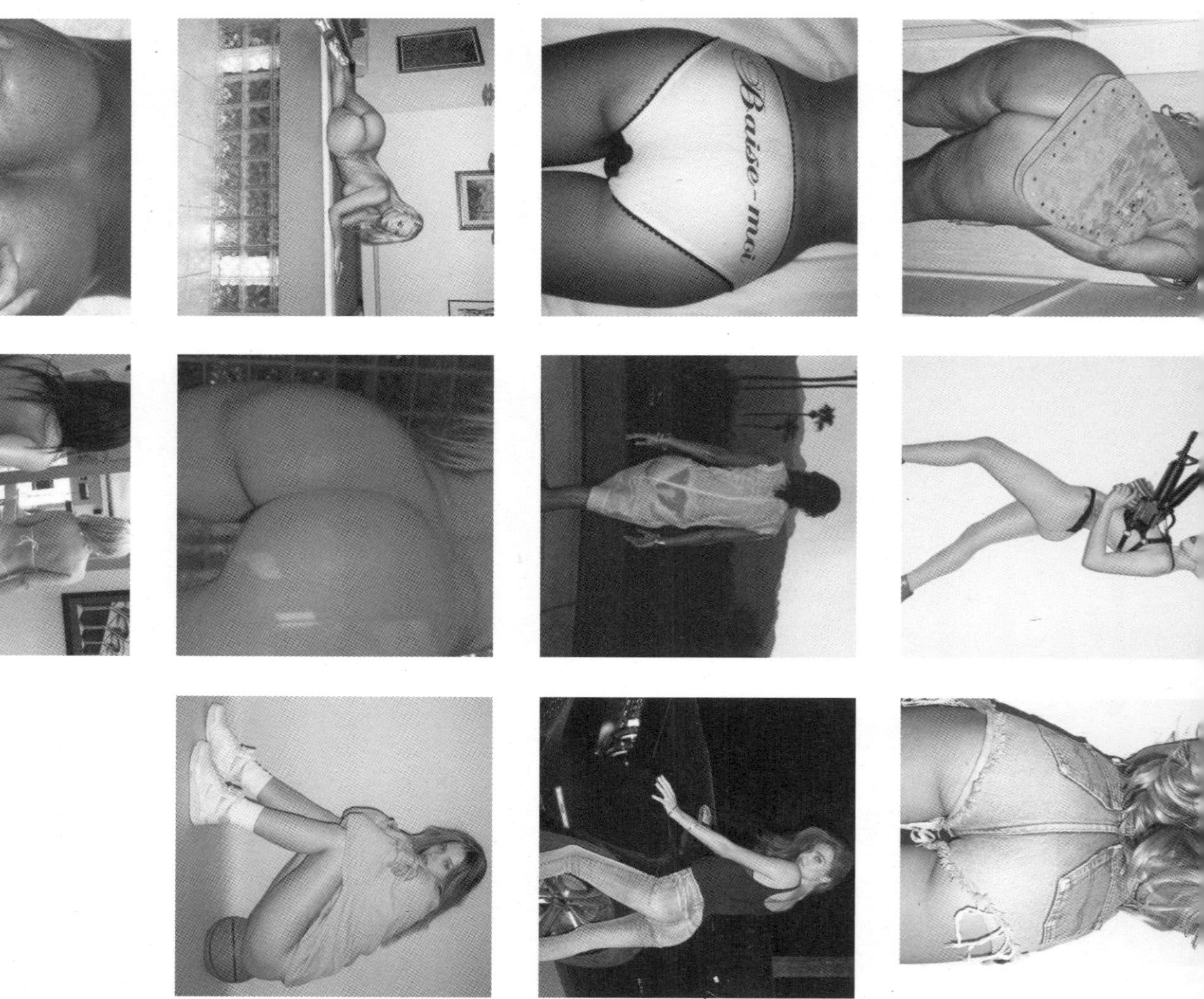

Butt Snorkeler 358k followers ♥ 4.500

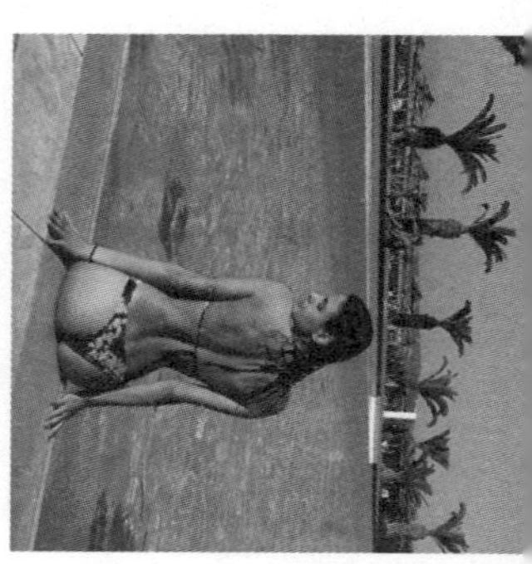

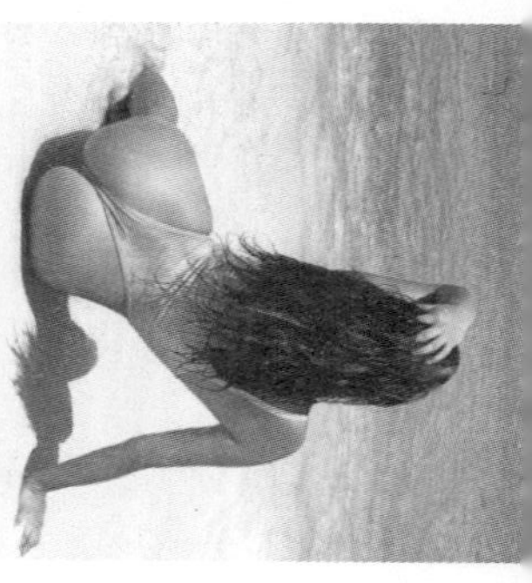

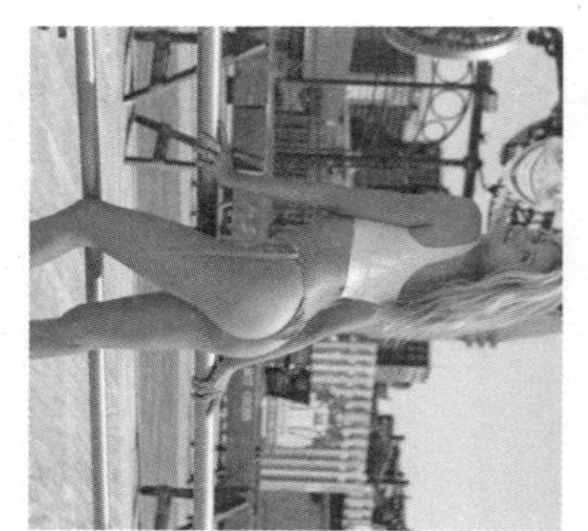

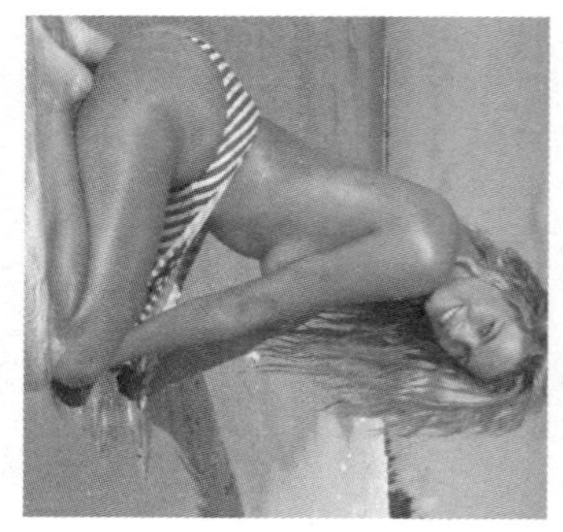

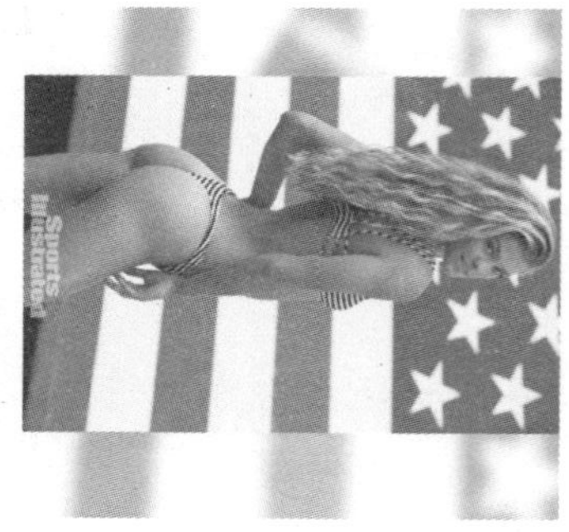
Sports Illustrated

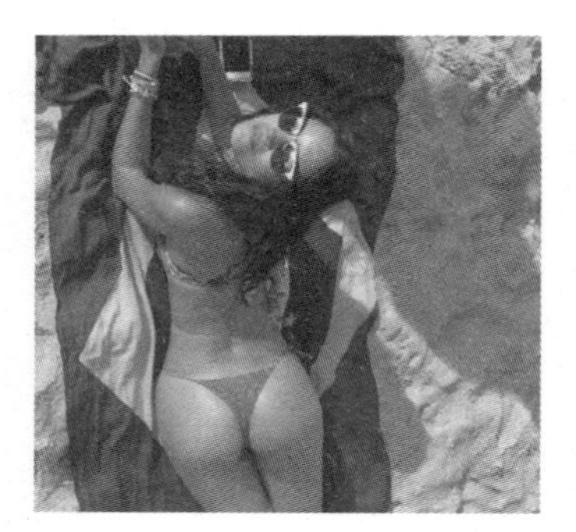

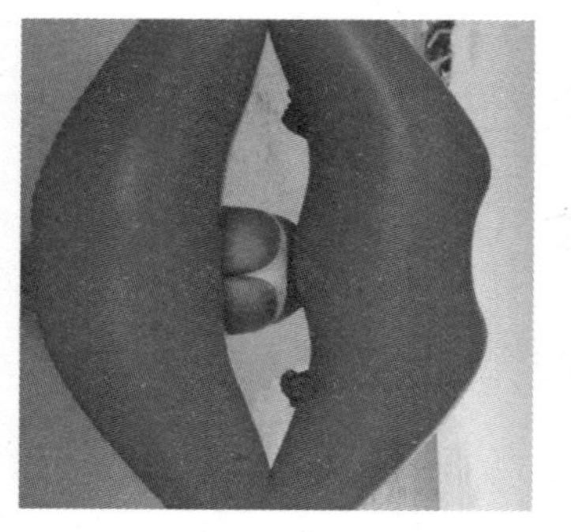

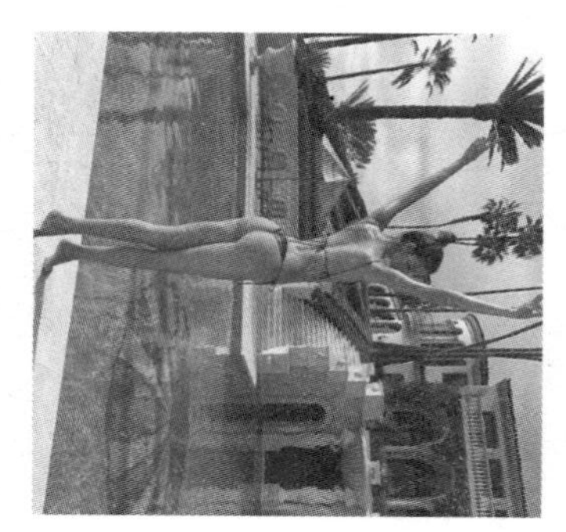

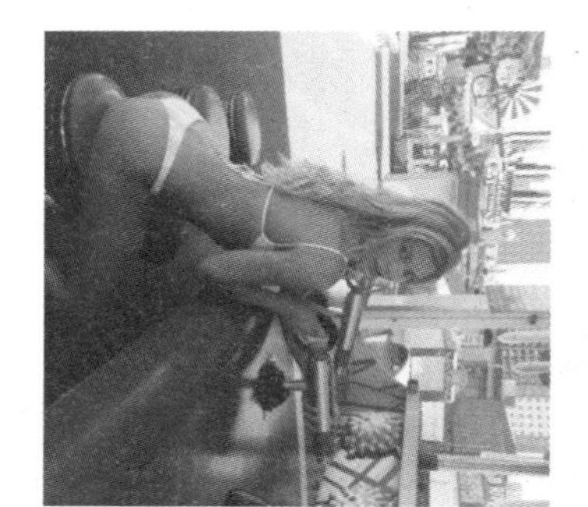

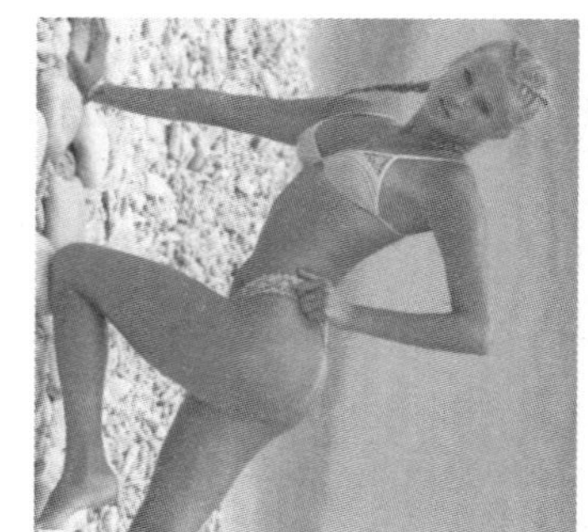

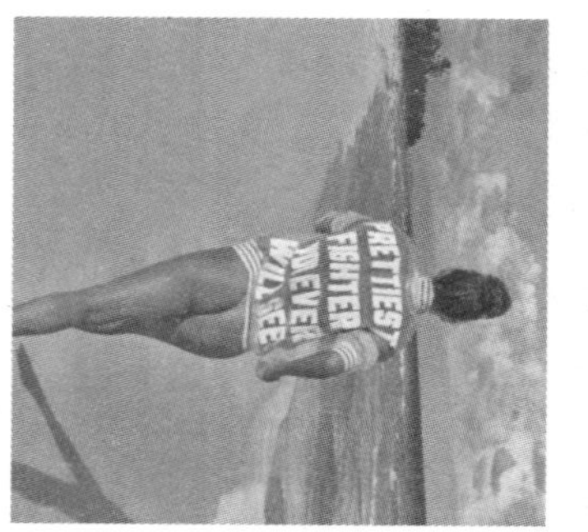
PRETTIEST
FIGHTER
EVER
WILL SEE

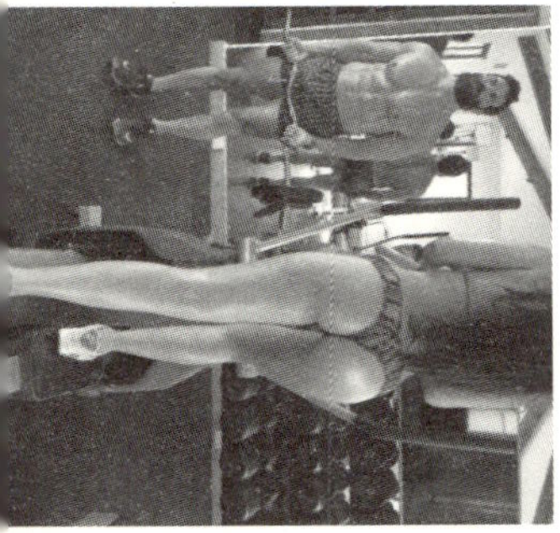

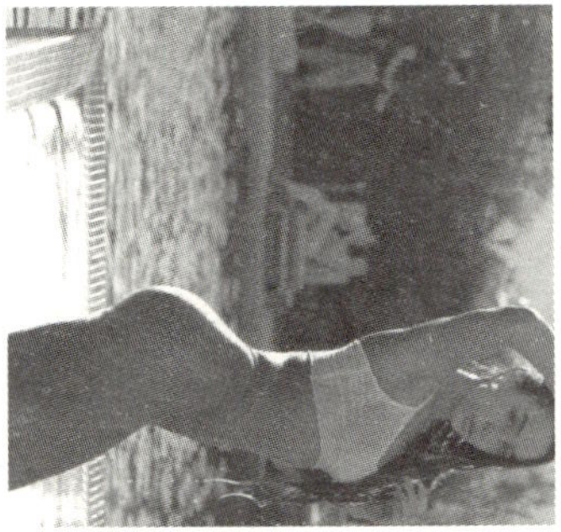

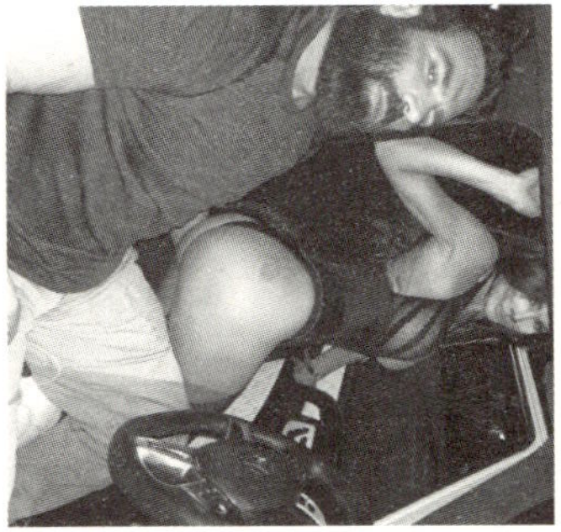

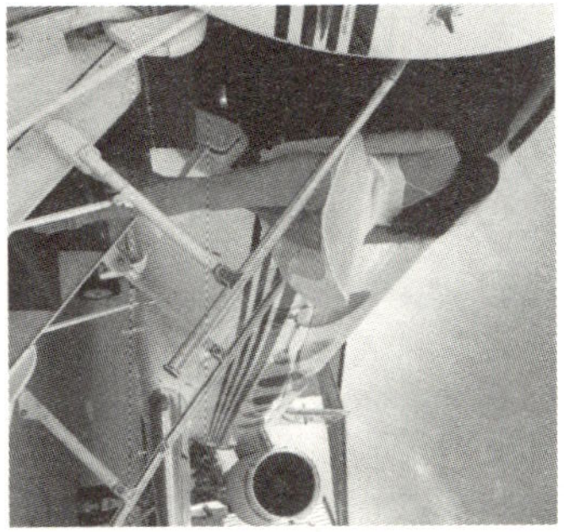

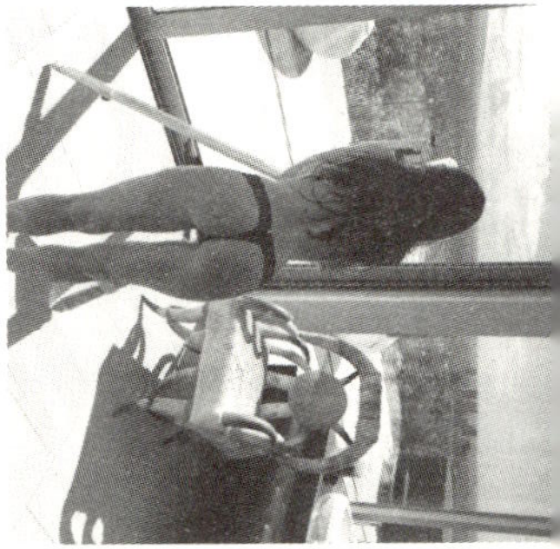

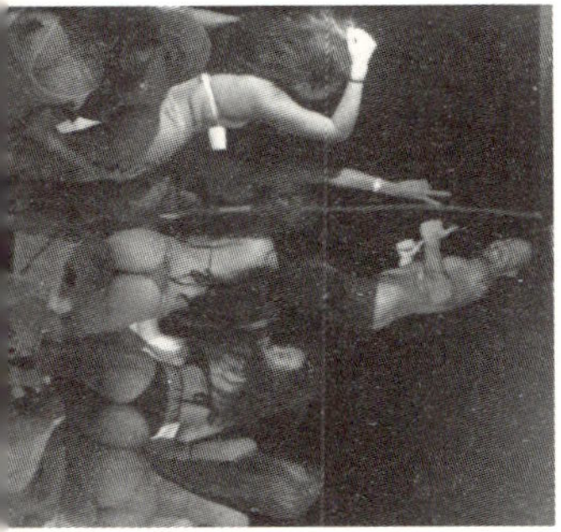

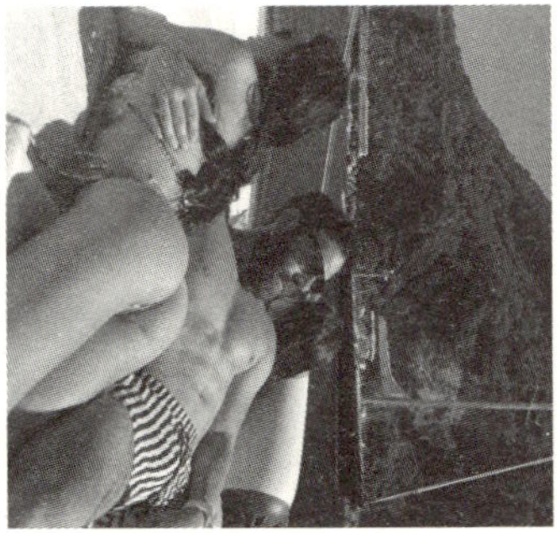

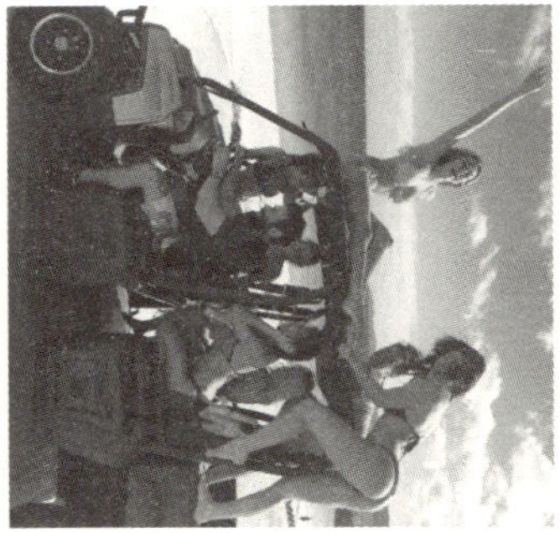

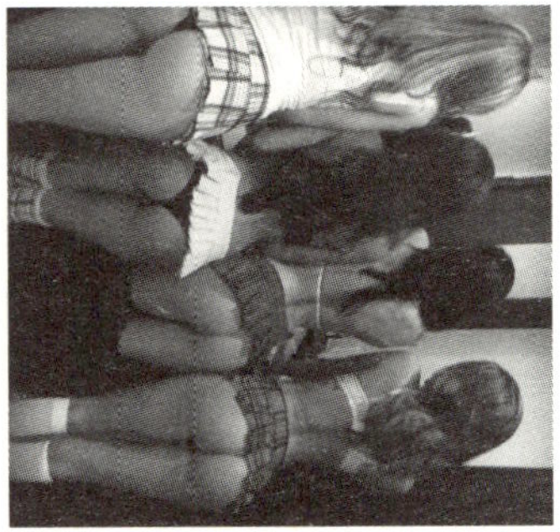

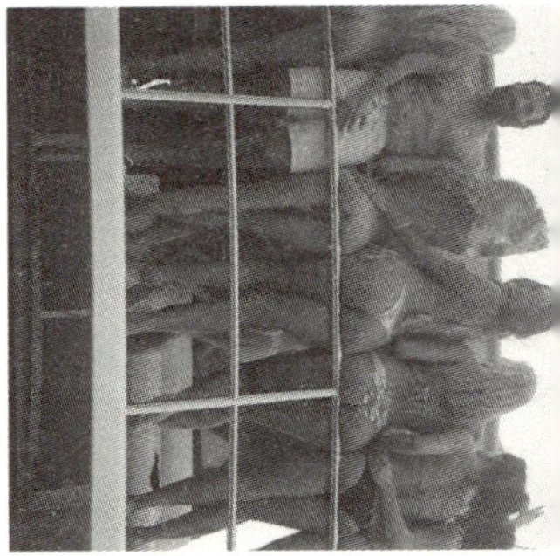

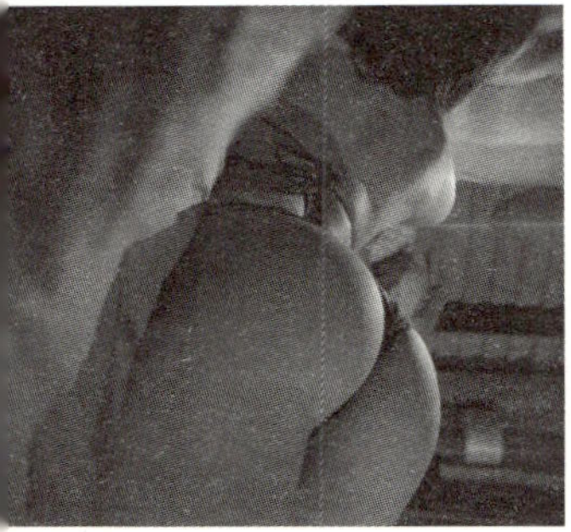

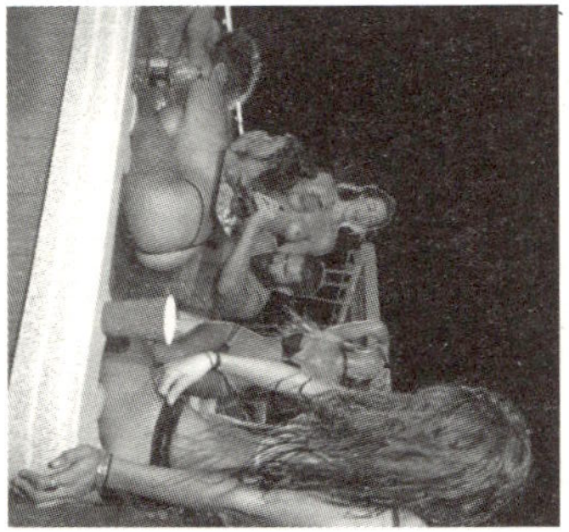

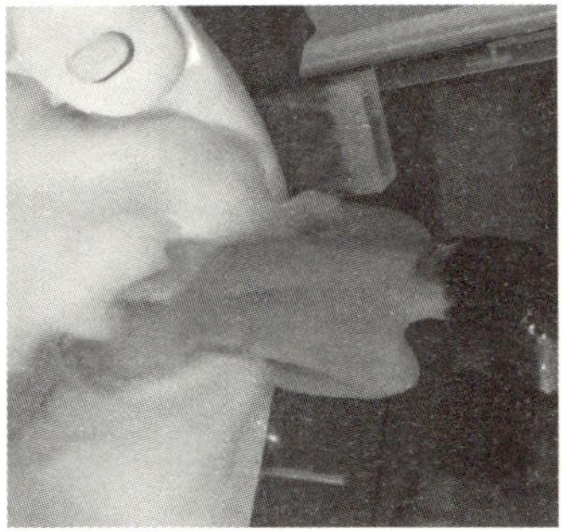

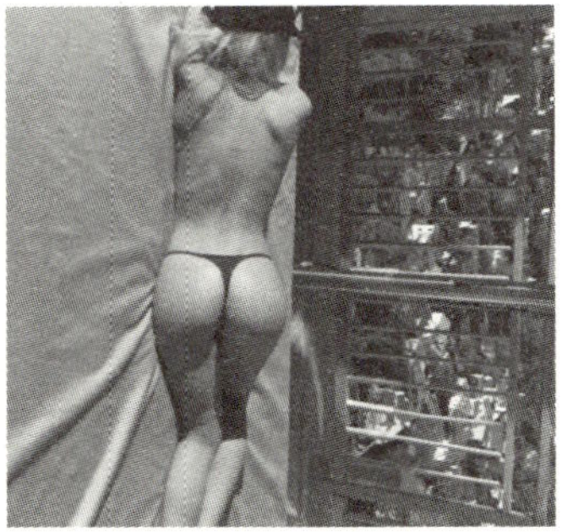

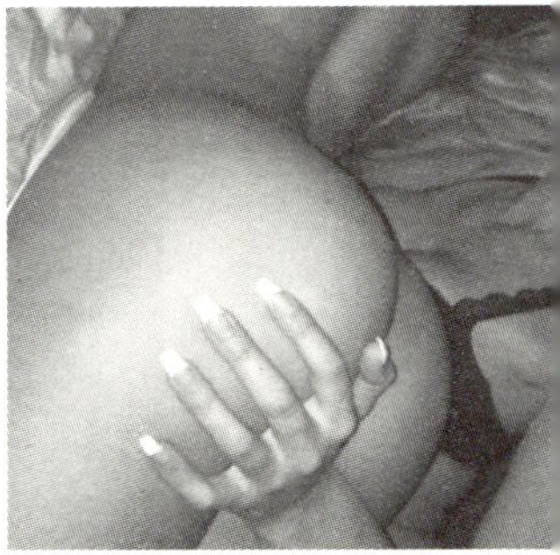

Dan Bilzeria 26.5m followers ♥ 380k

Nicki Minaj 102m followers ♥ 900k

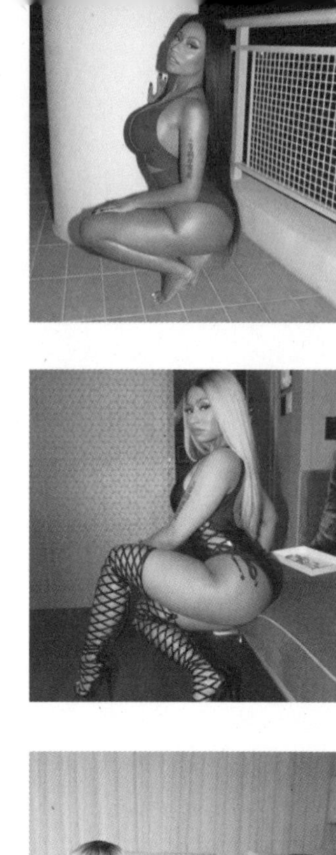

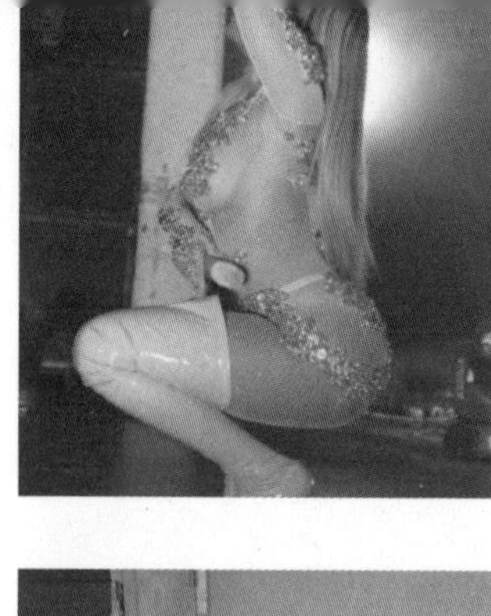

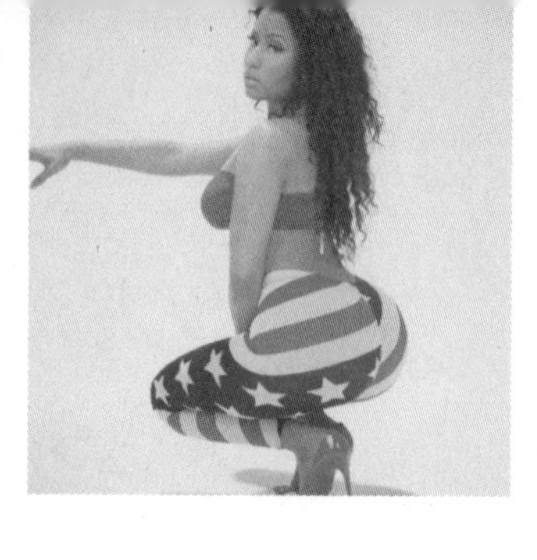

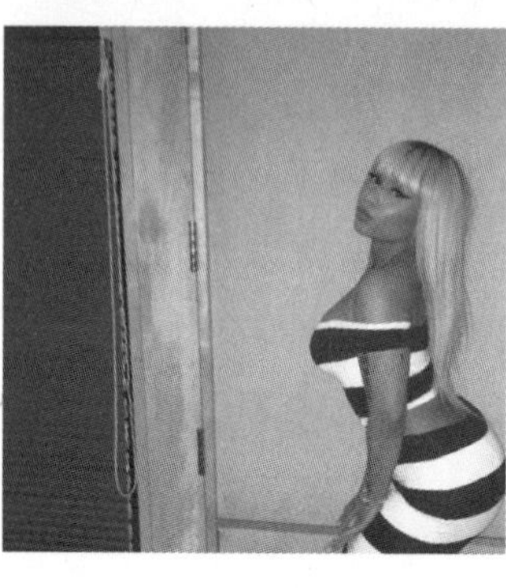

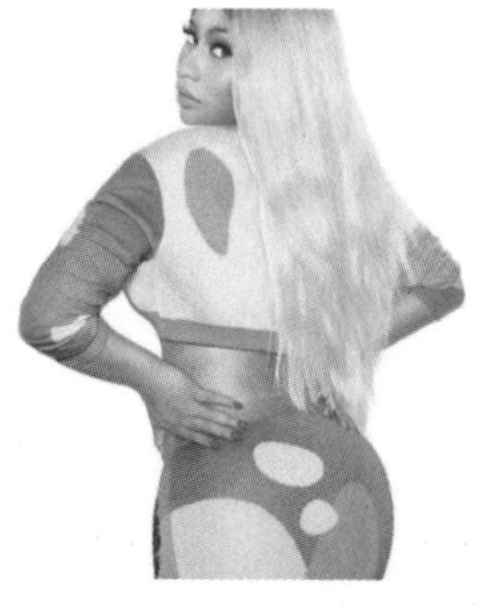

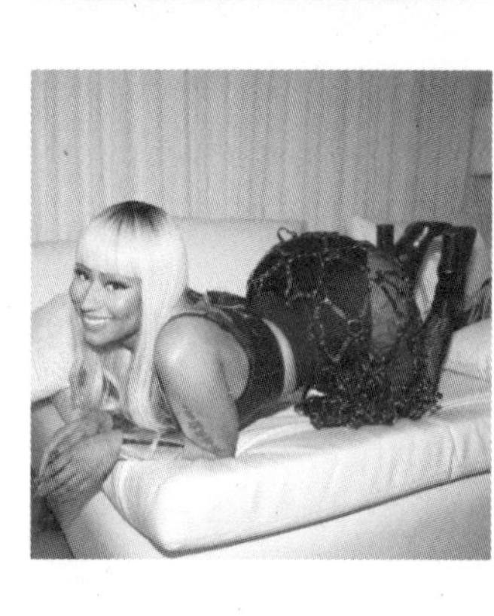

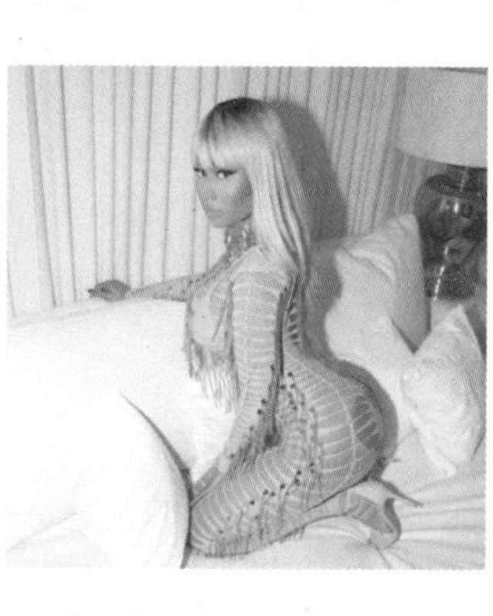

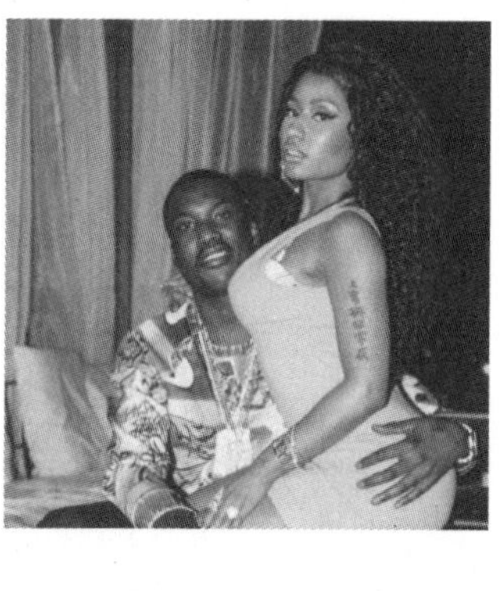

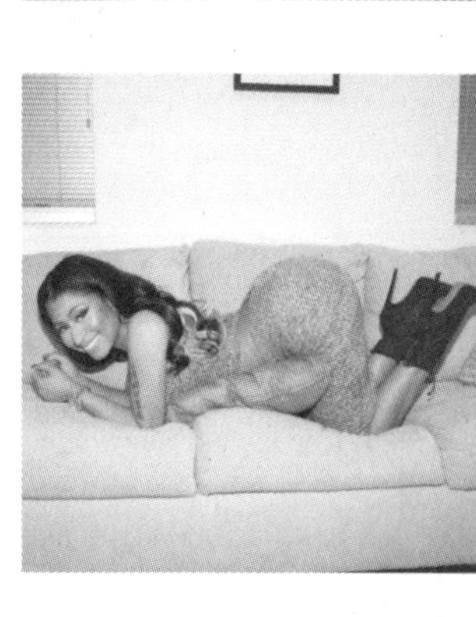

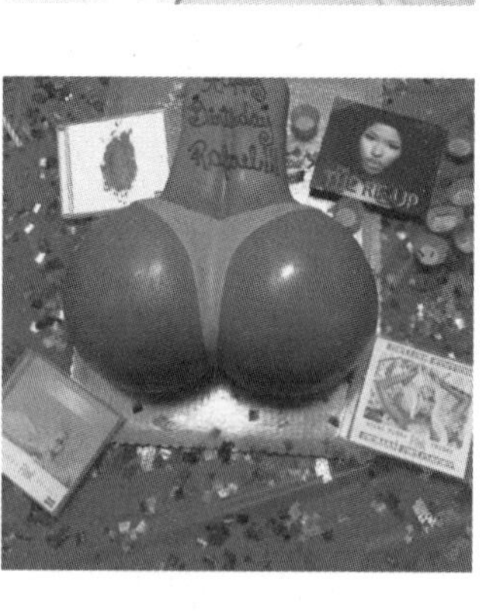

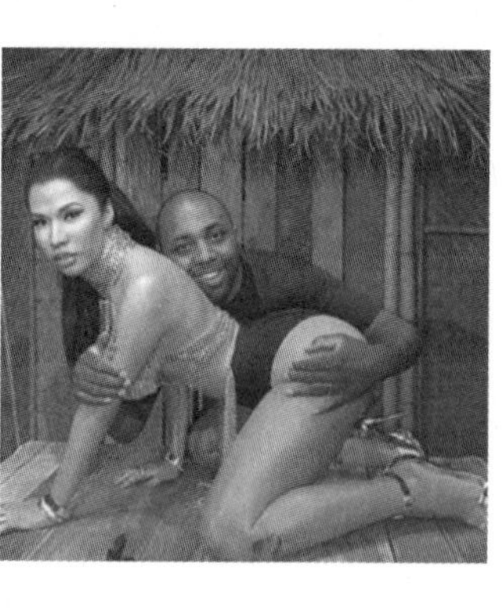

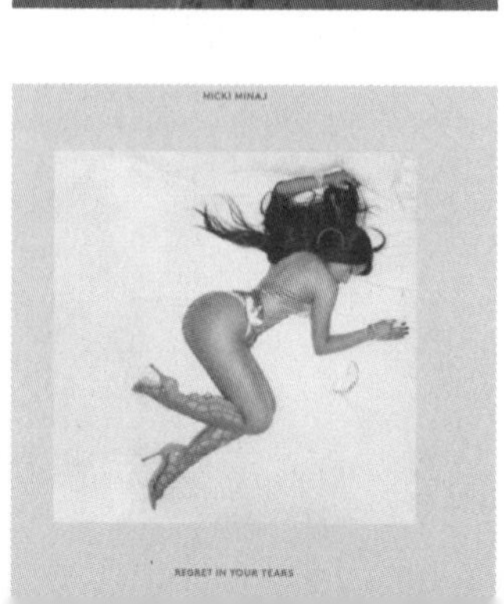

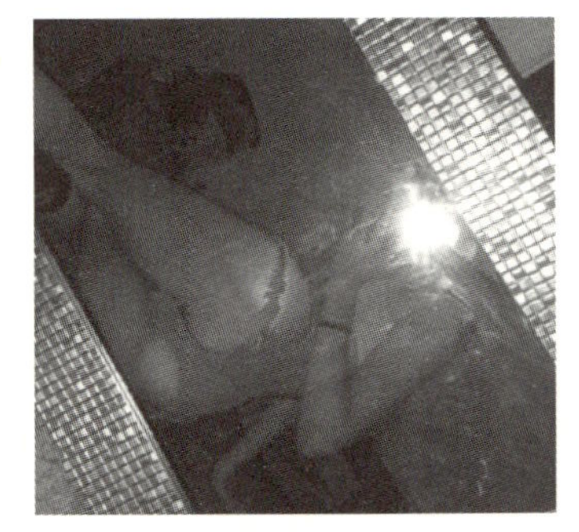
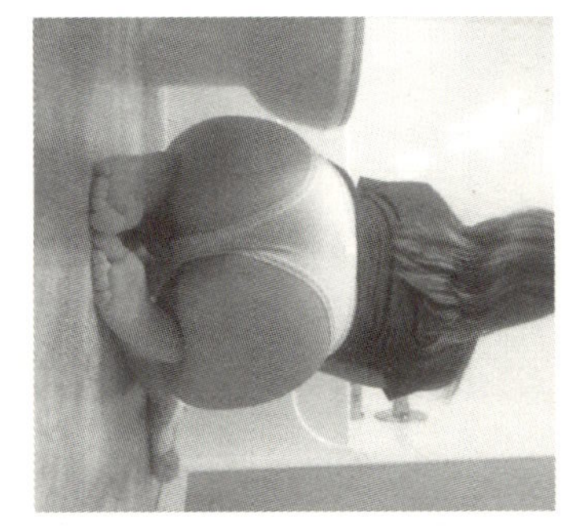
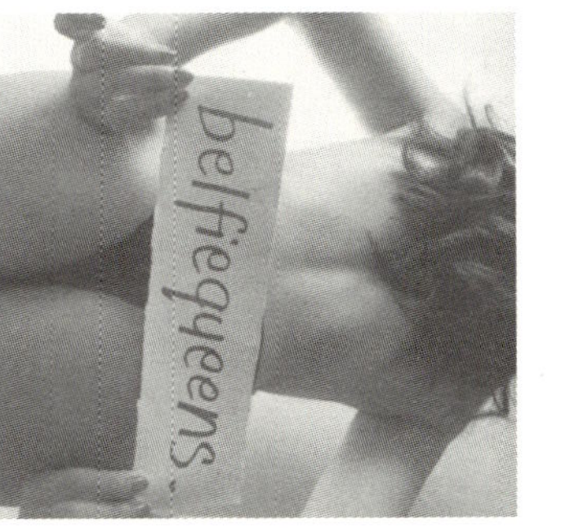

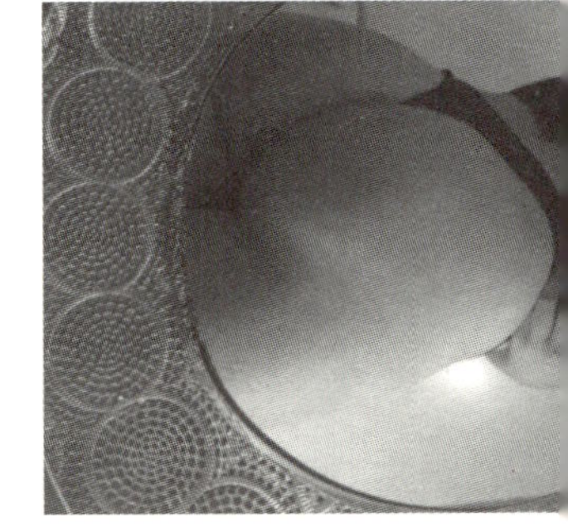
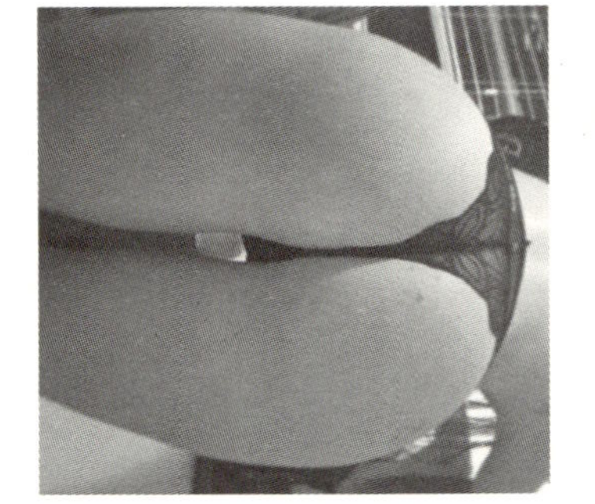
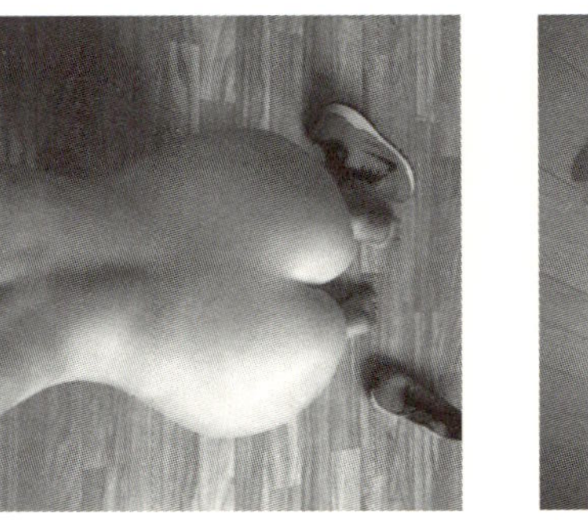
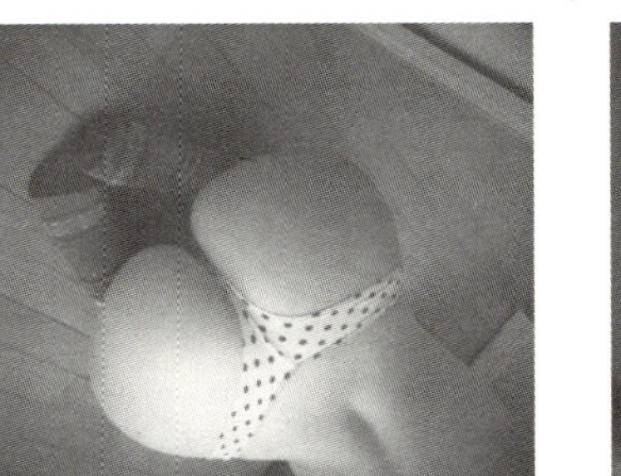
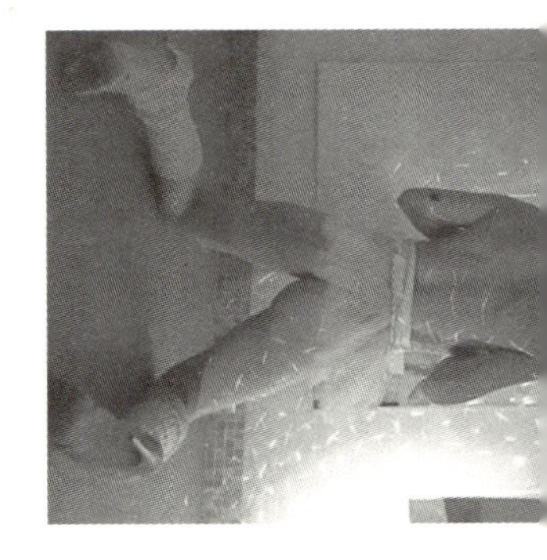
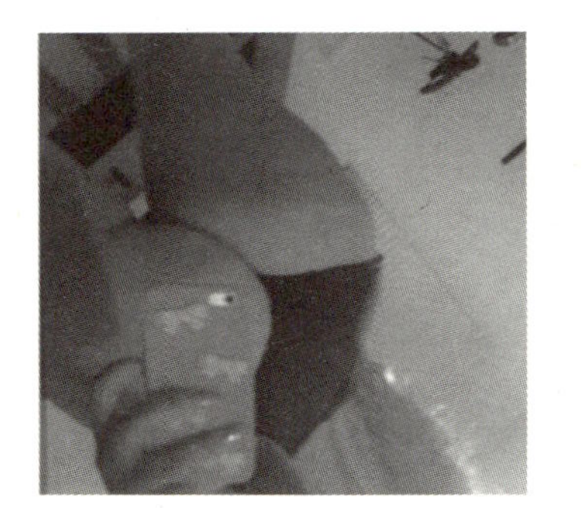
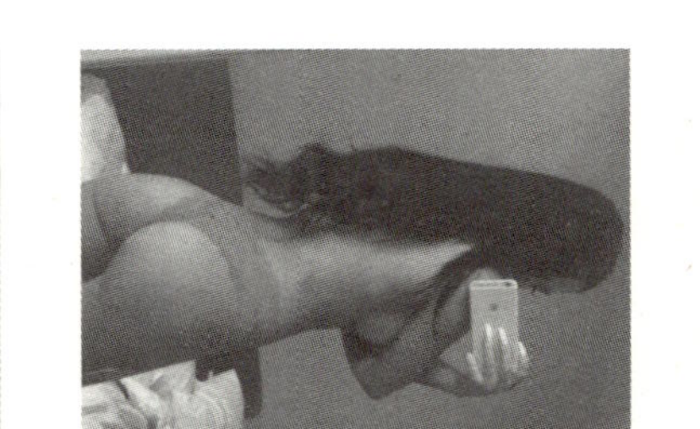



Belfie Queens 5.994 followers ♥ 60

# Pornography, Art and Museums

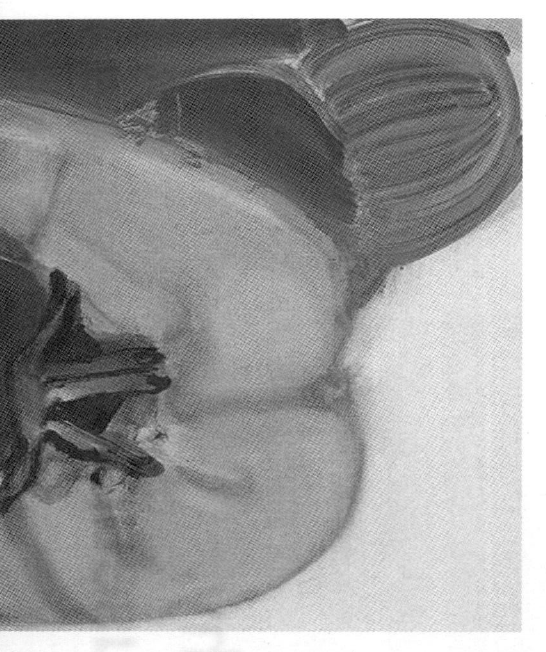

Marlene Dumas, Fingers 1999

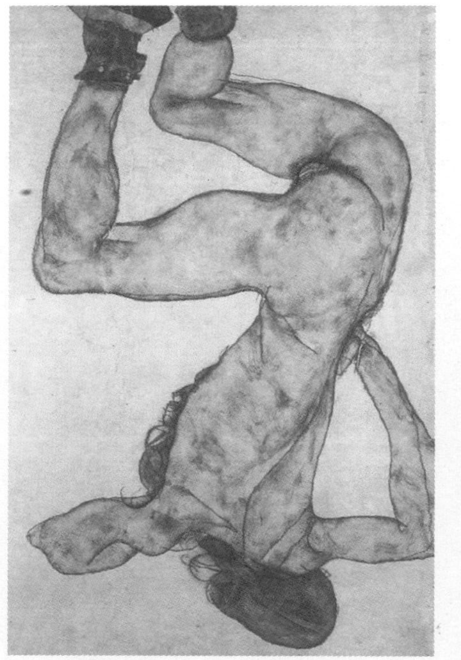

Egon Schiele,
Bended Female Nude, 1917

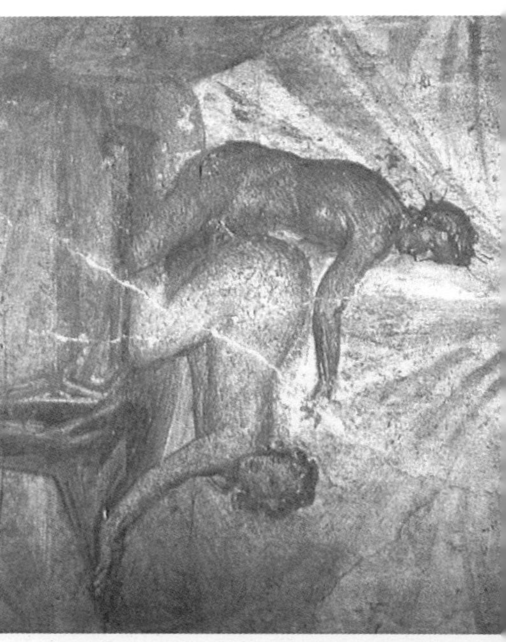

Pompeii frescoes 79 AD

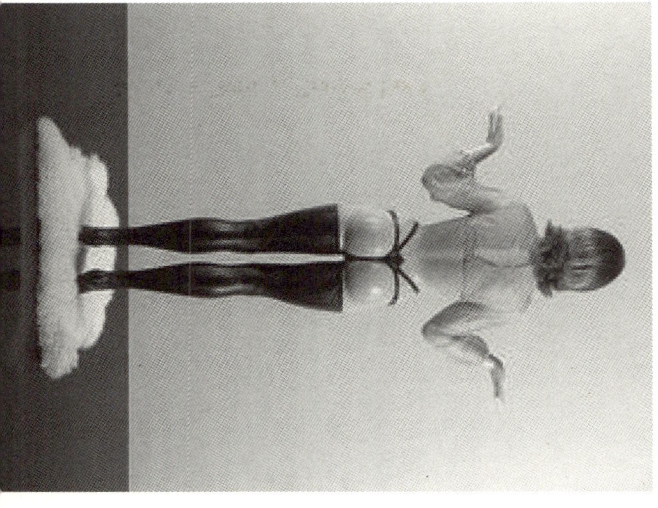

Allen Jonesr, Hat Stand 1969

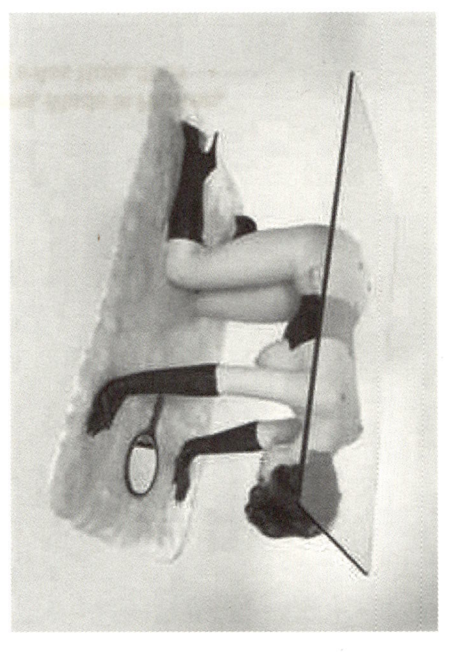

Allen Jones, Table, 1969

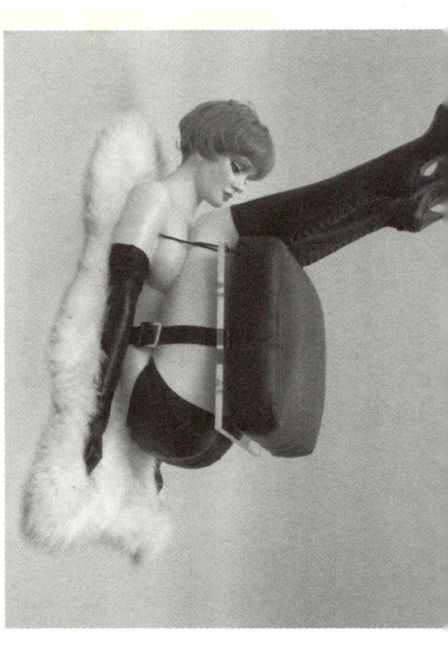

Allen Jones, Chair, 1969

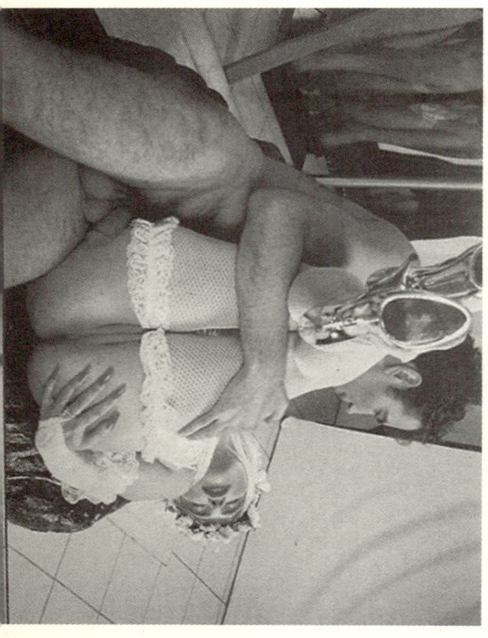

Jeff Koons, Made in Heaven,
Ilona's Ass Hole, 1991

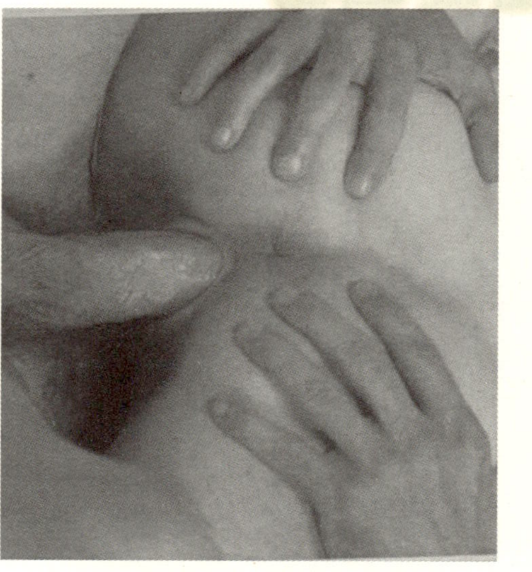

Jeff Koons, Made in Heaven,
Ilona's Ass Hole, 1991

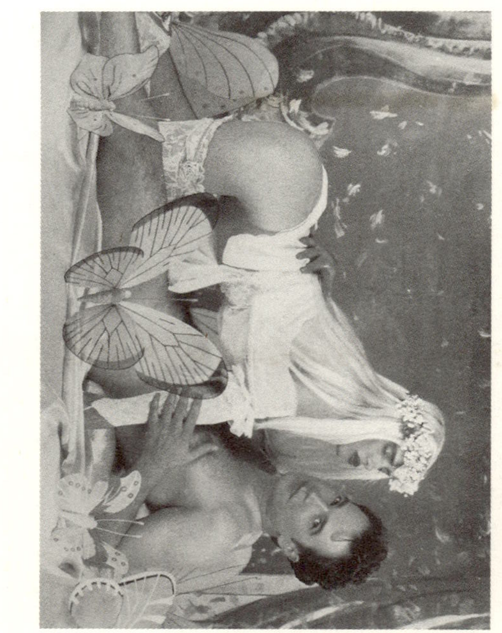

Jeff Koons, Made in Heaven,
Ilona on Top, 1990

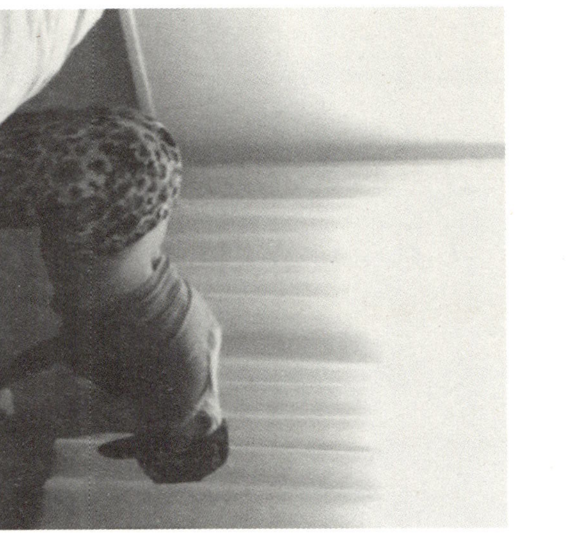

Amalia Ulman, Excellence & Perfections, 2014

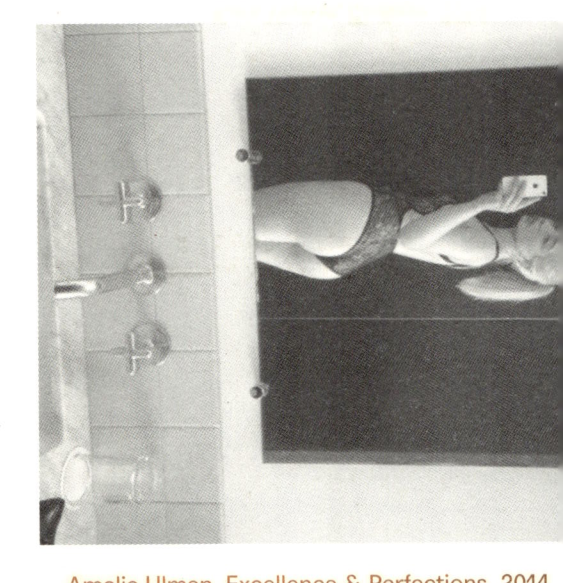

Amalia Ulman, Excellence & Perfections, 2014

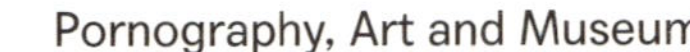

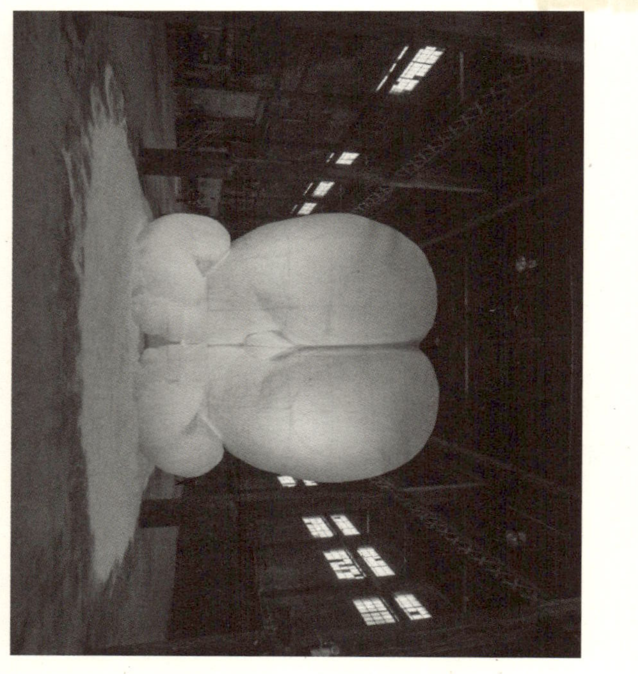

Kara Walker, Sugar Baby, 2014

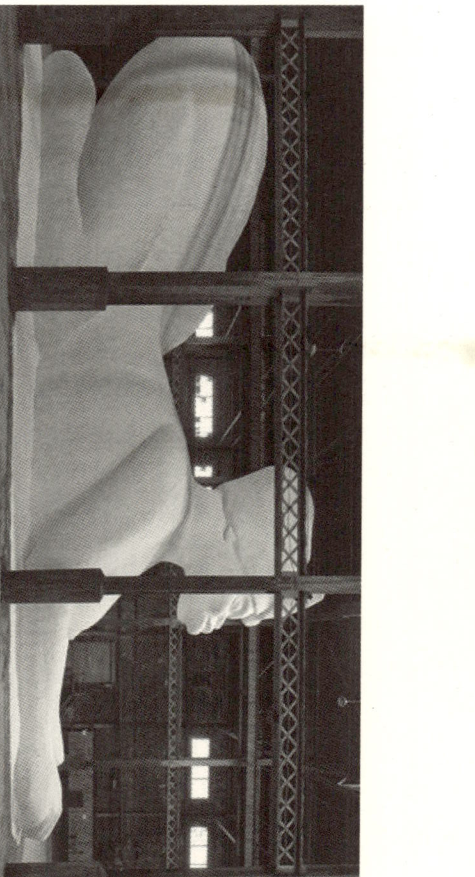

Kara Walker, Sugar Baby, 2014

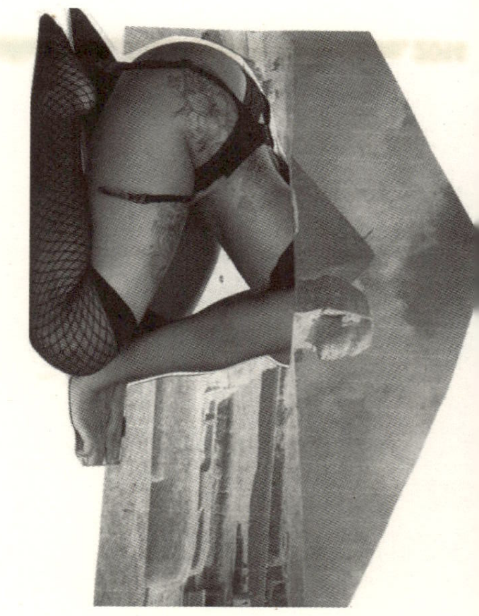

Kara Walker, Collage, 2014

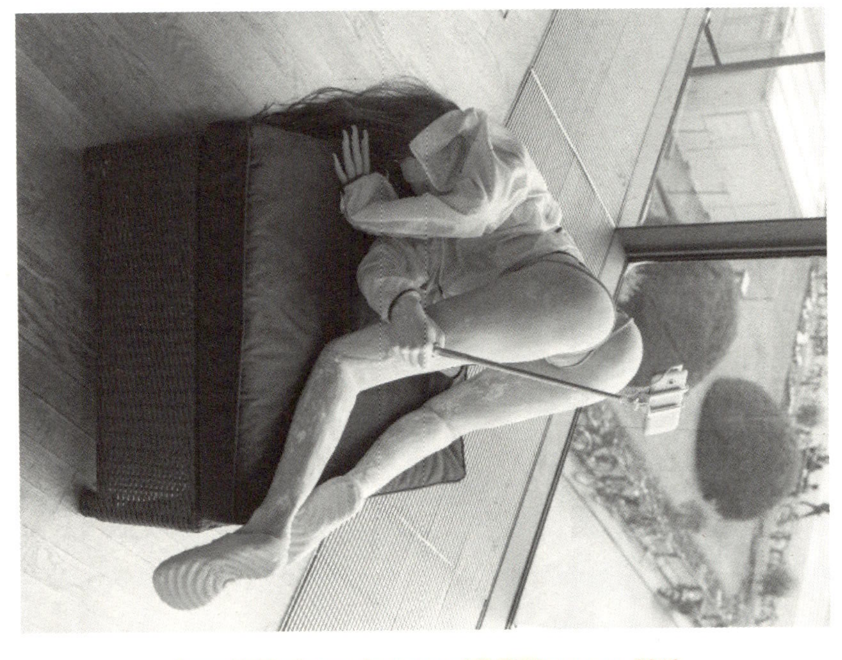

Anna Uddenberg, Journey of Self Discovery, 2016

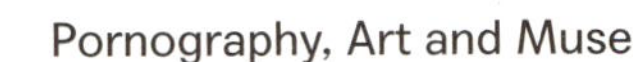

The distinction between erotic art and pornography is often not very clear and is still a topic of debate. Nevertheless these two categories cross over more that most would think, causing scandals and discussion within the art world along the way. Art represents a mirror to the culture of its time, and since the Western attitude towards sex is becoming more open and accepted by society; its art then contains more of it.

The word pornography has its root in the Greek language – *Pornographos* from *porne:* prostitute and *graphein:* writing – means writing about prostitutes. But the contemporary notion of pornography in modern European vernacular derives from different historical events. Partly responsible for this is a story that was unearthed by the excavations at Pompeii. Among many of the ancient city's cultural habits was an open predilection towards sexuality. This openness was not usual among the European cultures of the eighteenth century and caused a minor scandal at the time. The archaeological digs revealed pictures and sculptures of naked animals and human bodies as well as oversized male genitalia. These erotic images were not only part of the brothels but were embedded in the whole city, and revealed a completely different appreciation of the body and sexuality. (fig. 1) The finds were classified around 1800 by the administration and public authorities and it was decided that they could not be seen without supervision. The material became the Secrete Collection of the Bourbon Museum in Naples, also known as the Secret Museum. Only upper-class man were allowed to see the collection. Women, children or members of the lower classes were not allowed to enter this part of the museum.

fig. 1

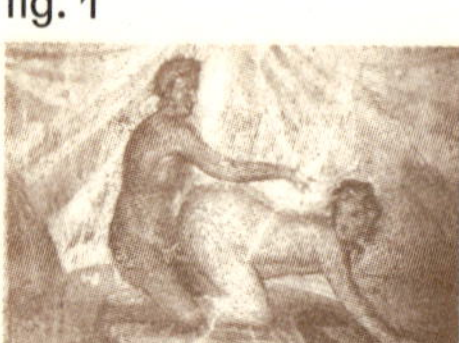

The world Pornography started to refer to the content of the Secret Museum and the 1864 edition of Webster's Dictionary defined pornography as "licentious paintings employed to decorate the walls of rooms sacred to Bacchanalian orgies, examples of which exist in Pompeii." The collection only opened to the public in April of 2000 after authorisation was given by the National Education Ministry in Rome.
The finds are now displayed in the Secret Cabinet of the National Archaeological Museum of Naples. Although there is no longer any kind of censorship, children under the age fourteen can only visit that particular section if accompanied by an adult. The historian Walter Kendrick took this example to define pornography in the modern Western society. He argues that pornography emerged as a tool to control public space and traces limits between visibility and the public. Pornography is also not made only out of images but of political architectures, it becomes a definition of what is acceptable and what can be visible to a larger public. The centralisation of the distribution of images is today no longer possible. Giving mass media and the individual private use of it, we are dealing with a completely different system that empowers individuals.

In his essay "On the Ethical Distinction between Art and Pornography" Brandon Cooke suggests that the term 'pornographic' is pejorative, while the term 'erotic' is neutral or approving. "Contemporary art criticism has often cast art with sexual content as being in the business of 'critique', or 'interrogation', or 'questioning'." He focuses on Allen Jones' *Chair* (fig. 2) which is a life size sculpture of a woman lying on her back, with her legs pressed to her chest and her feet in the air. She is dressed only in a pair

fig. 2

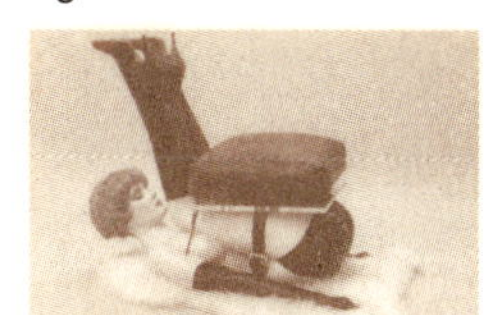

of leather gloves, shorts and boots, with a leather set cushion strapped to the back of her thighs. *Chair* and its companion pieces *Table* and *Hat Stand* (fig. 3 – 4) are sculptures that use furniture as their subject. Yet their appearance is sexually provocative was clearly intended. Sometimes an artwork is an appropriate object of ethical criticism, and sometimes so is an item of pornography. According to Cooke there is no categorical ethical distinction between art and pornography.

fig. 3

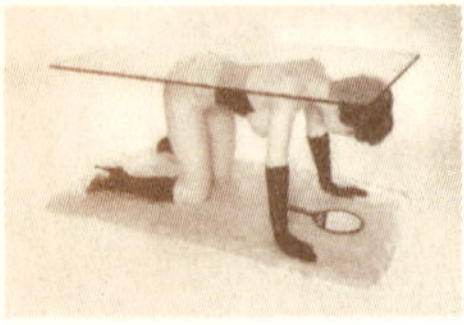

fig. 4

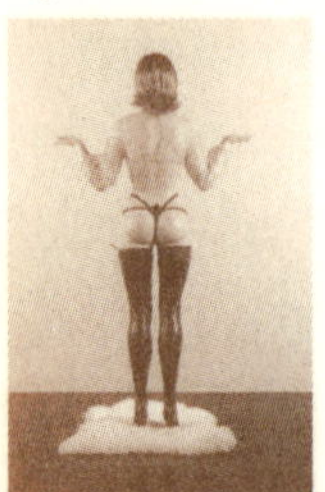

In an article for the Tate Modern, art director Lily Bonesso writes about the increasing liberal Western society in which the distribution of porn and products of sex industry are becoming more commonplace. She argues that James Joyce saw his novel Ulysses banned for 10 years due to 'explicit' passages, and Egon Schiele served jail time for producing erotic drawings, yet we now see sex becoming a relevant and provocative conversation within contemporary art.
The Guardian[1] speaks of prostituting everything, including art, when referring to artist Marlene Dumas' studies taken from mass produced pornographic images. Dumas stated in 1986: "At the moment my art is situated between the pornographic tendency to reveal everything and the erotic inclination to hide what it's all about".

1. G. Greer, 'Marlene Dumas's paintings of nudes and kids are always unsettling. Go girl!' The Guardian, 22.08.2010 (accessed 10.01.2017).

Another strongly discussed art work is Jeff Koons' *Made in Heaven.* (fig. 5) The photography series he made with former porn star Cicciolina, bares all, and leaves nothing for our fantasies. Susan Sontag in *The Pornographic Imagination,* argues that "there is a considerable gain in truth if pornography as an item in social history is treated quite separately from pornography as a psychological phenomenon. A minor but

fig. 5

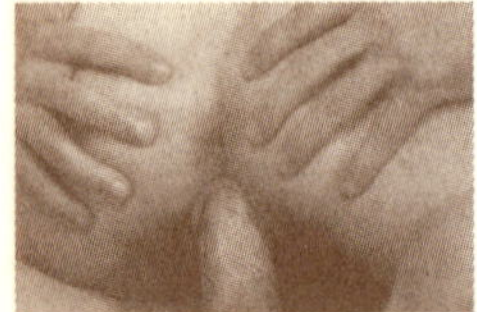

interesting modality or convention within the arts".[2] She explains that pornography is treated as a social psychological phenomenon, yet some pornographic material is important work for the arts as well. She continues by saying that "Pornography yields more than the truths of individual nightmares. It does generate a vision of the world that can claim the interest of those who are not *erotomanes*[3]".[4] With all this talk of pornography within art, it's inevitable that the buttocks start to emerge like two fleshy islands in a sea of ambiguity. The posterior has appeared countless times in frescos and nudes, and has been subsequently reinterpreted for each new epoch. Looking at some contemporary works of art it is possible to notice that the butt has been used as a tool for criticism and to make bold political statements.

2, 4. S. Sontag, Styles of Radical Will, The Pornographic imagination, New York, Picador USA 2002, p. 205

3. Erotomania: [mass noun] Excessive sexual desire. Oxford Dictionary.

In 2014 Kara Walker, presented her exhibition *A Subtlety or the Marvellous Sugar Baby*, at the Domino Sugar Factory in Brooklyn. She created a massive, sugar coated female figure that was reminiscent of an ancient Egyptian sphinx. The sculpture's intended function was to act as a reference to slavery. With this piece she is telling the story of a building that was constructed in the 19th century and used for storing raw sugar, or as Kara Walker herself called it: "A cathedral to industry". The whole exhibition is concentrated around the space and about the demolition of the space after it. That's why the sculpture itself was coated in sugar, making it a very temporal piece which allowed the audience to literally see it melting during the exhibition. Even though the statue has a clear reference to the sphinx, it is a figure of a black woman with a huge emphasis on the behind. (fig. 6) Almost two-thirds of the piece is made out of booty. The New York Times wrote:

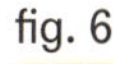

fig. 6

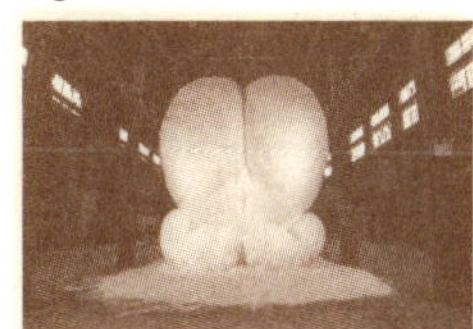

"From the back this dome turns into a perfect heart shape, buttocks whose cheeks protect a vulva that might almost be the entrance to a temple or cave. A powerful personification of the most beleaguered demographic in this country – the black woman – shows us where we all come from, innocent and unrefined."

Amalia Ulman is a young Argentinian artist and author of *Excellence & Perfections,* (fig. 7) an art work that she performed on Instagram by uploading mostly preening selfies taken on her iPhone. With this series of photographs she documented her attempt to be an "It girl" in Los Angeles, every photograph was well studied and inspired by stereotypes of how young woman presented themselves online. Amalia's project was more entwined with sex than it first seemed since she also worked as an escort – "For me, sex work wasn't like a dark thing to do, or an empowering thing to do either. I was just buying time for myself to think"[4].Not surprisingly in the first picture of the series – also in many others – she was showing her behind. While online it ensured many followers and helped increase her popularity, in the art world it had the opposite effect. Amalia reported that people starting hating her and one of her gallerists told her to stop immediately because otherwise she would not be taken seriously as an artist anymore. Amalia explained that "Suddenly I was this dumb bitch because I was showing my ass in pictures." A year and a half later in 2014 her series of 175 photographs were shown in different exhibitions in London.

fig. 7

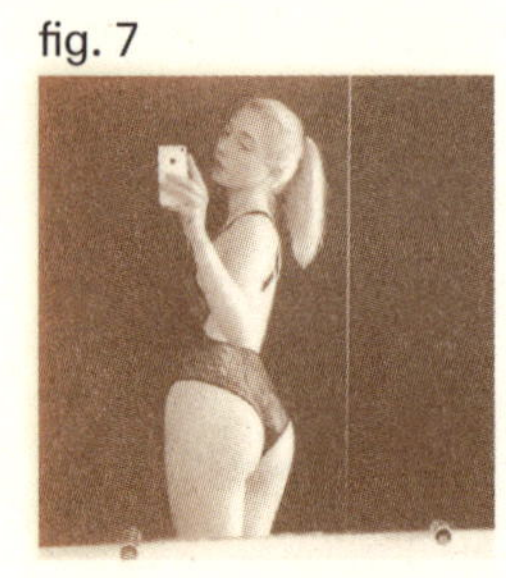

4. V. D'Alessio, 'What Does Amalia Ulman's Instagram Art Mean for Sex Workers?', Titsandsass, 18.08.2016, (accessed 14.04.2017)



Pop culture and art often mix and overlay. Within this dwells selfie culture, which presents itself as form of art too; but not only in the form of photography as it also uses sculpture as a medium. Swedish Artist Anna Uddenberg presented her series *Lady Unique # 1-3* at the 9th edition of Berlin Biennale 2016 for contemporary art. These sculptures were cast in resin and plaster and then dressed up with piercings and shoes. The point of this was to give the viewer everything that they needed to be able to feel as if they were consuming art. The stylised bodies represent a contemporary image of women, yet their hyper-feminine physique, position and accessories capture something about the way we look at ourselves.[5] Uddenberg's work plays with societal ideals and one specific piece 'Journey of Self Discovery' is dedicated to the popularity of butts as it shows a woman on her knees with a selfie stick, taking a picture of her ass. This piece clearly refers to the numerous pictures of butts circulating on the web. (fig. 8) The position of the sculpture is contorted and at the same time irritating. Several stereotypes of contemporary photography are taken into consideration for this piece. For example the face is almost completely covered by a jacket. Also the framing of the selfie is excluding every other body part except the behind. The sculpture produces a physical representation of a main stream photograph of her butt, something that's easily found on Instagram and other social networks.

5. B. Heuser, 'Twisted Femmes: Anna Uddenberg's Uncompromising Sculptures' 032c, 29.07. 2016 (accessed 10.01.2017).

fig. 8

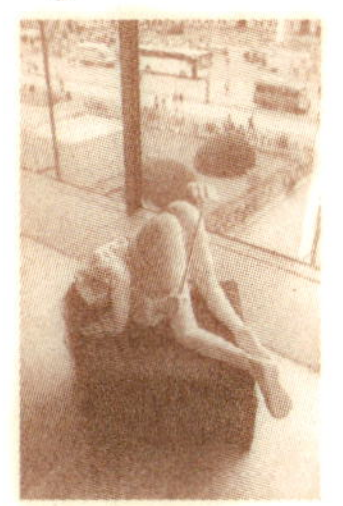

The posterior is a hybrid body part and object that's both part of the pop and internet culture, yet also intersects with pornography, politics and the art world. In a world in which visibility determines our lives and social position, it's easy to use the popularity of the buttocks to attract attention in the media. Would it be the same in the art world? Does pornographic and erotic material make art more attractive?

The acceptance of pornography is still a taboo in Western culture, even though many images in circulation – although not classified as porn – are very questionable. Nevertheless pornographic material and its aesthetics find acceptance in the art world. Maybe this is because art is a pioneer in trends, or maybe because it's a free harbour where artists can experiment and break boundaries.

# The Contemporary Image of Buttocks within Western Society

Da Butt, E.U. 1989

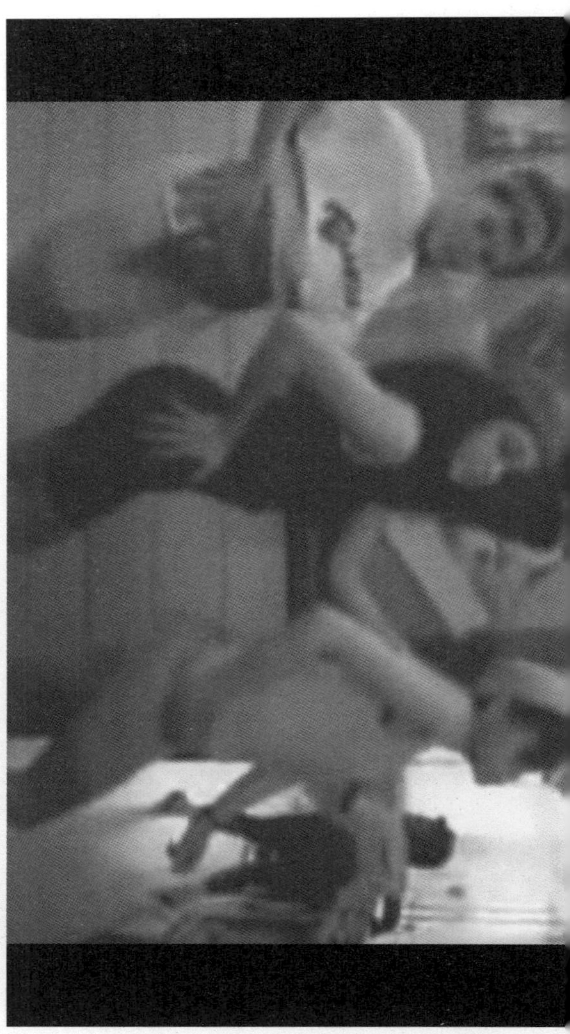

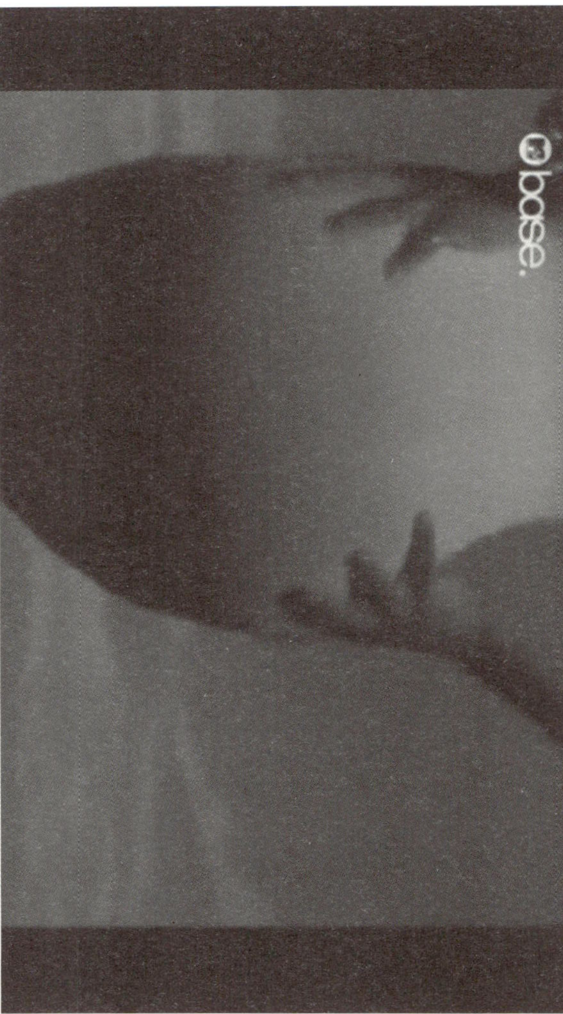


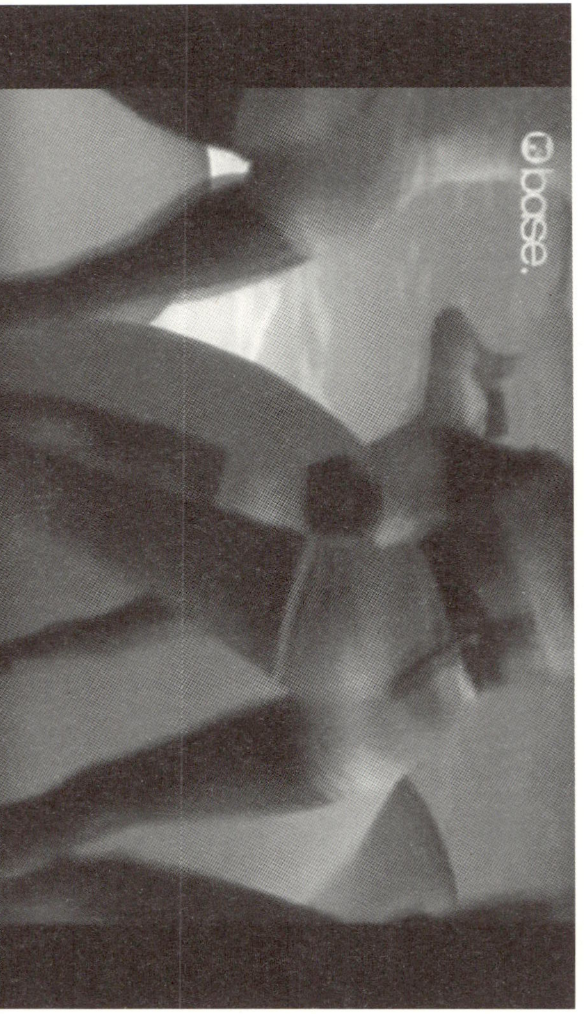


Baby Got Back, Sir Mix-a-Lot, 1992

Baby Got Back, Sir Mix-a-Lot, 1992

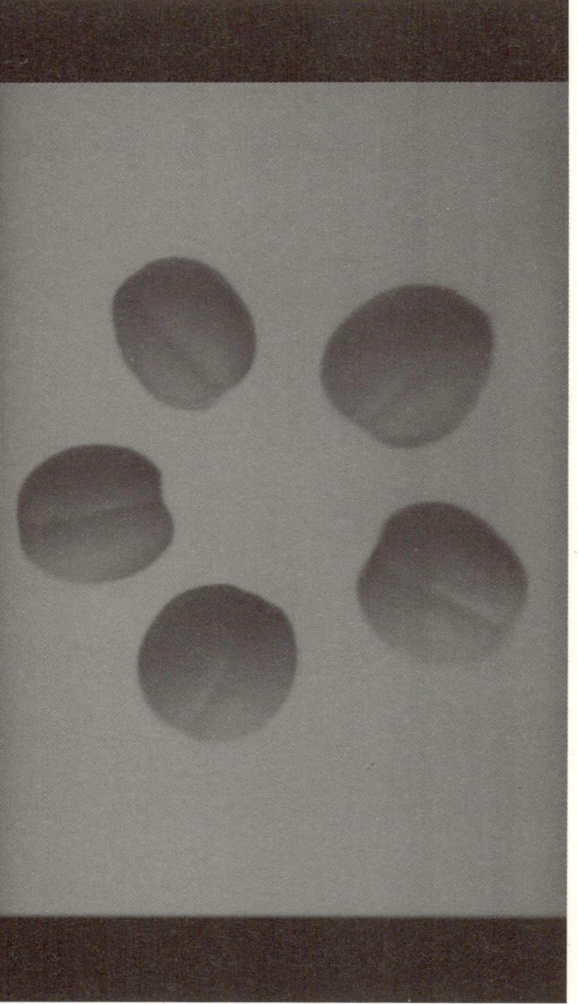

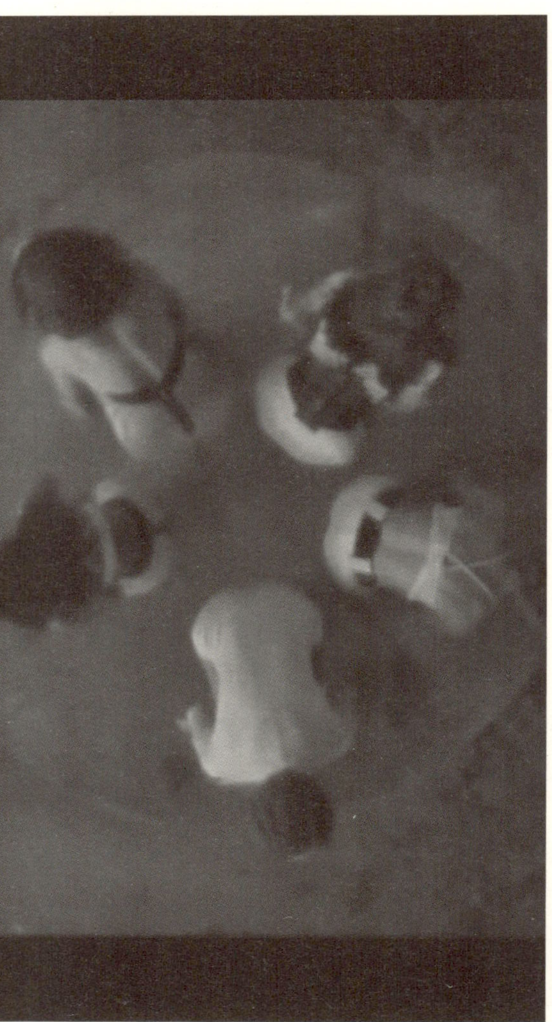

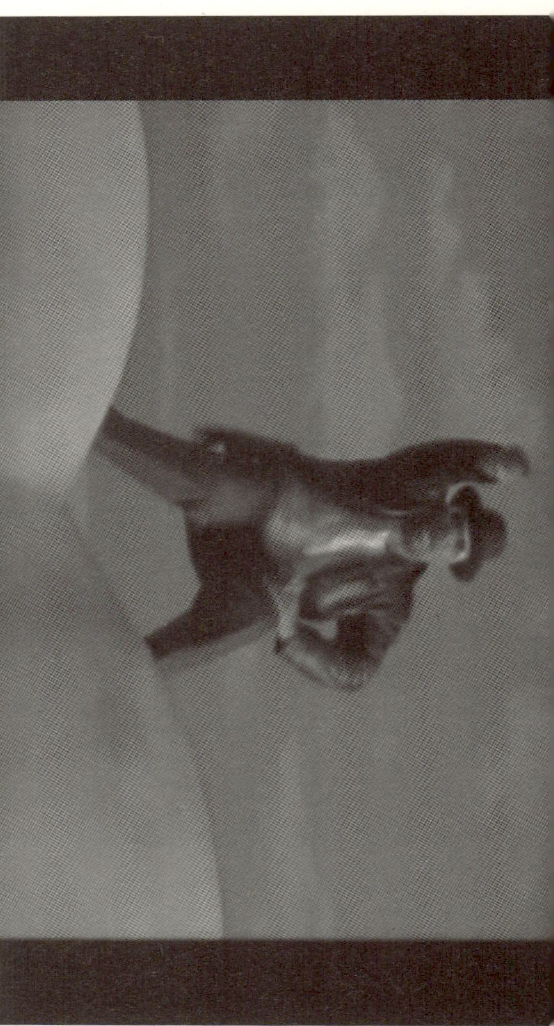

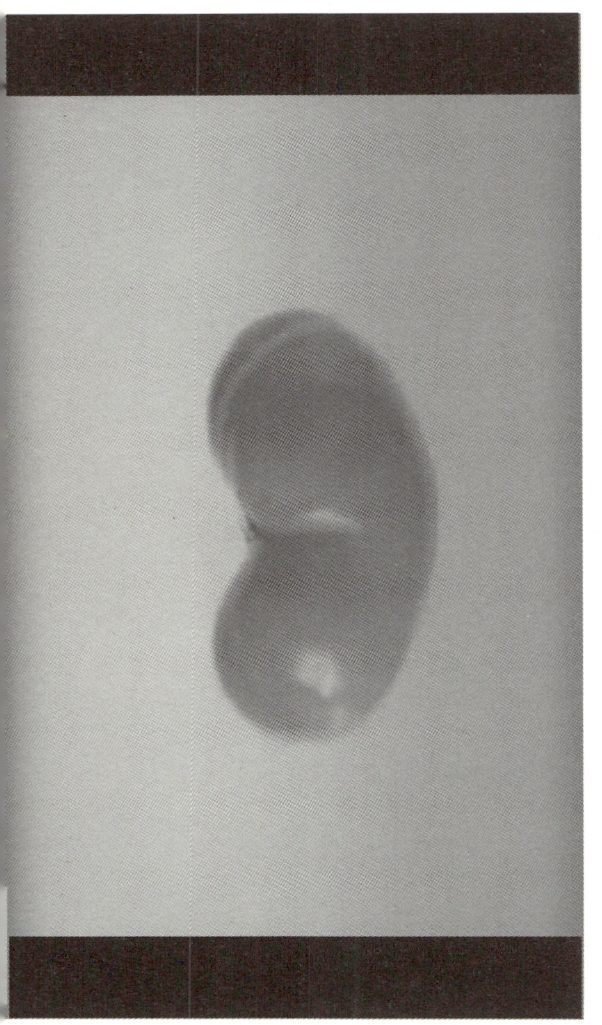

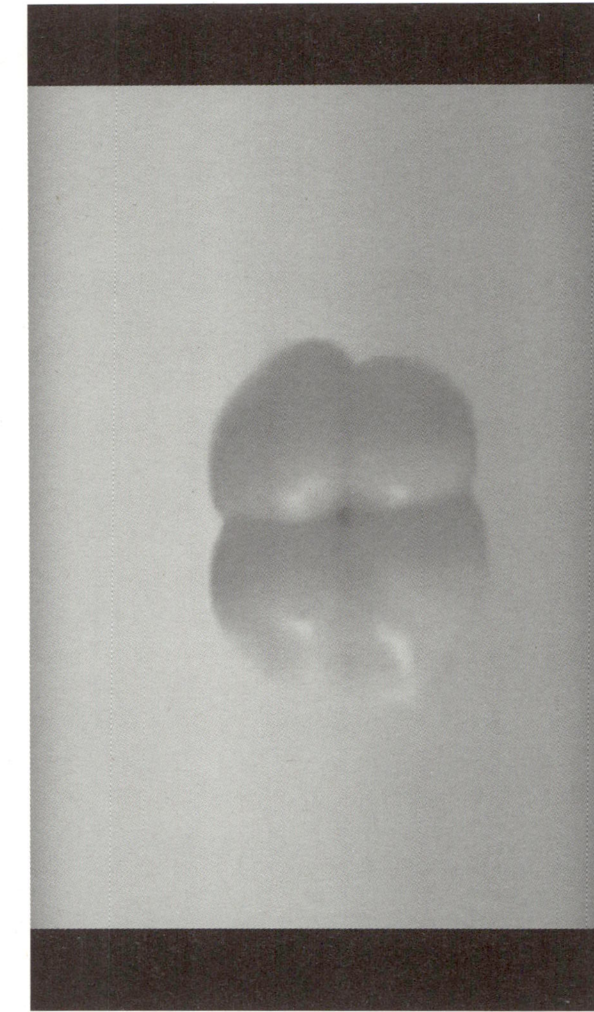



Baby Got Back, Sir Mix-a-Lot, 1992

Rumpshaker, Wreckx-n-Effect, 1992

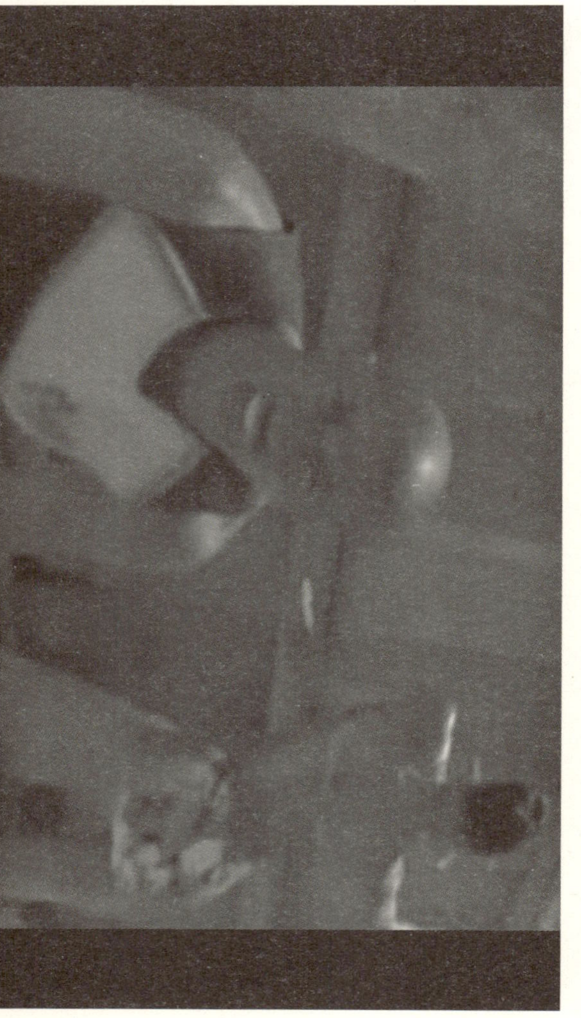

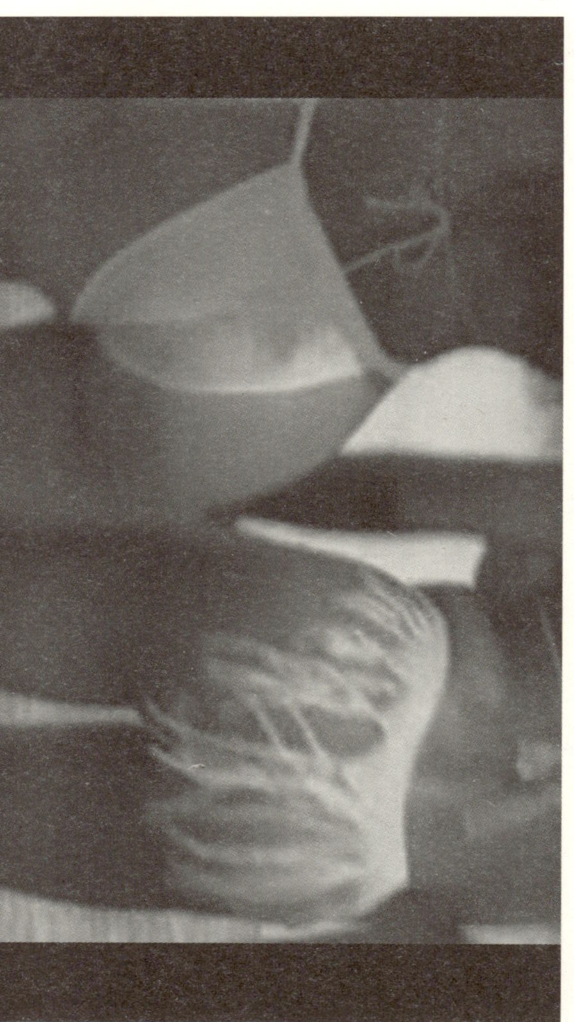

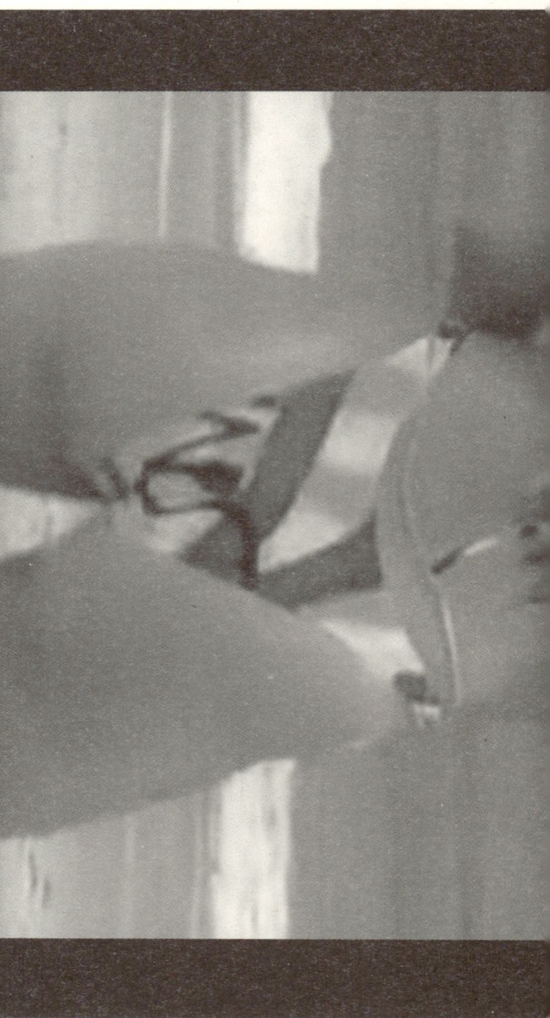

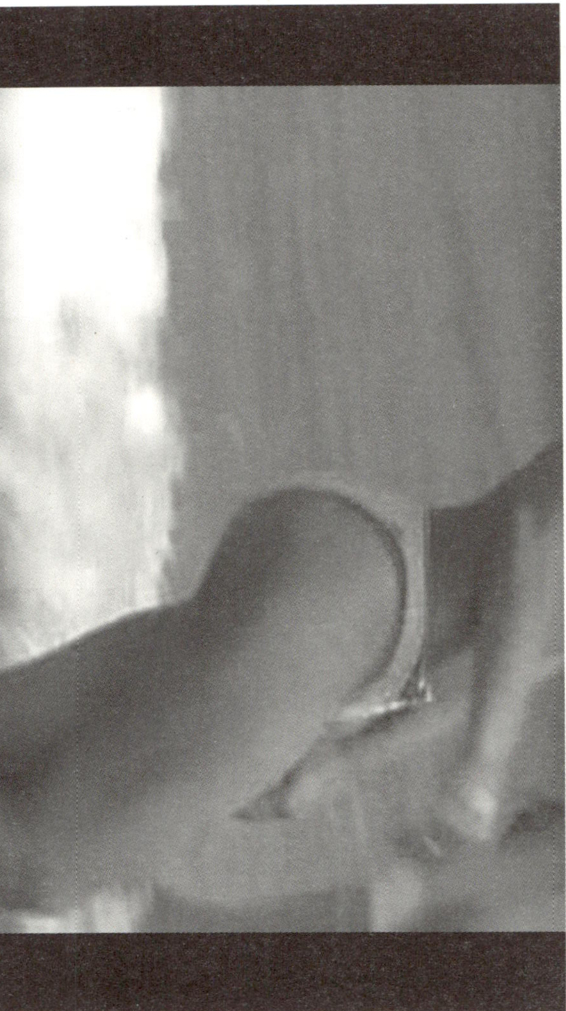

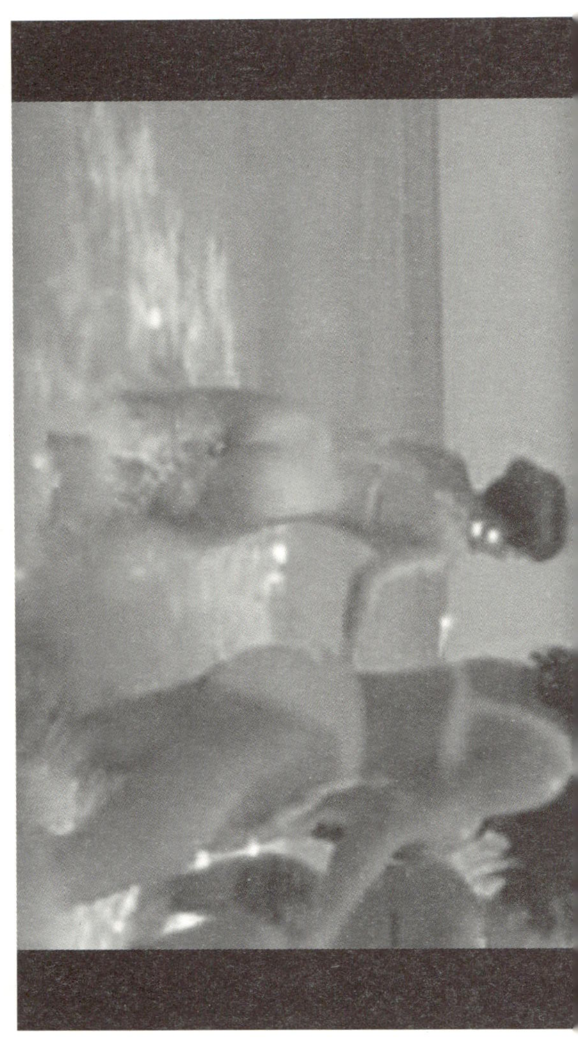



Rumpshaker, Wreckx-n-Effect, 1992

Do the Jubilee All, Dj Jubile, 1993

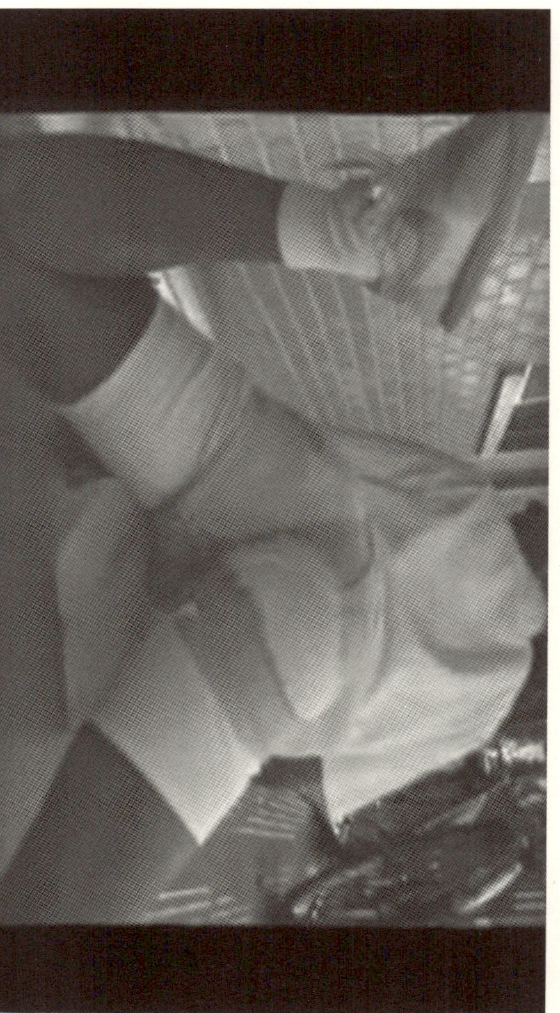

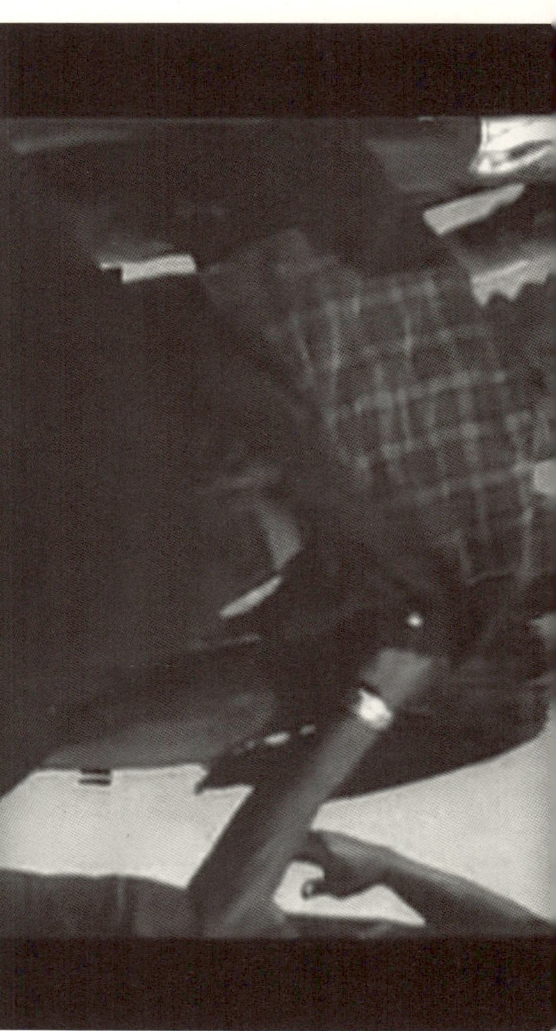

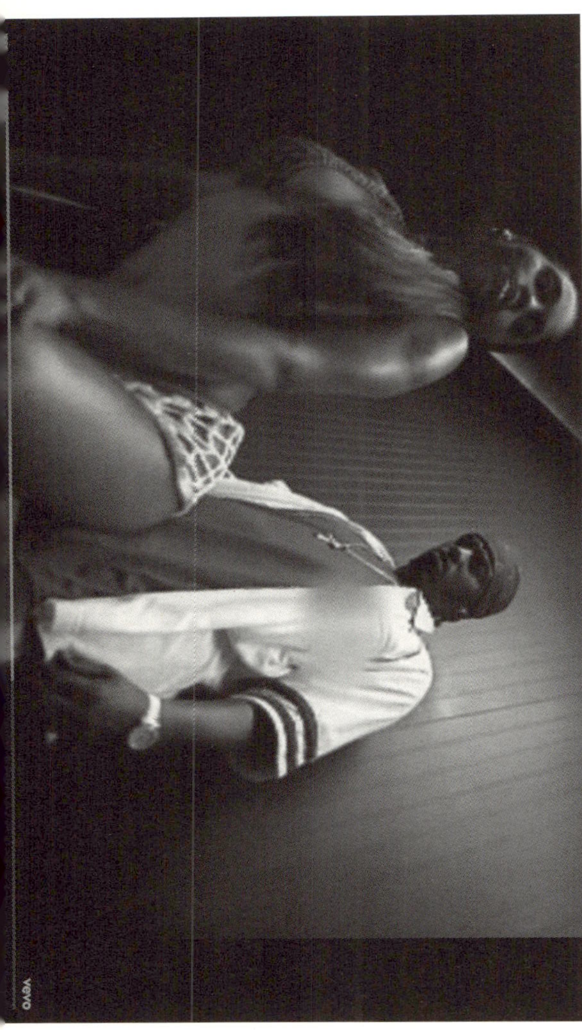


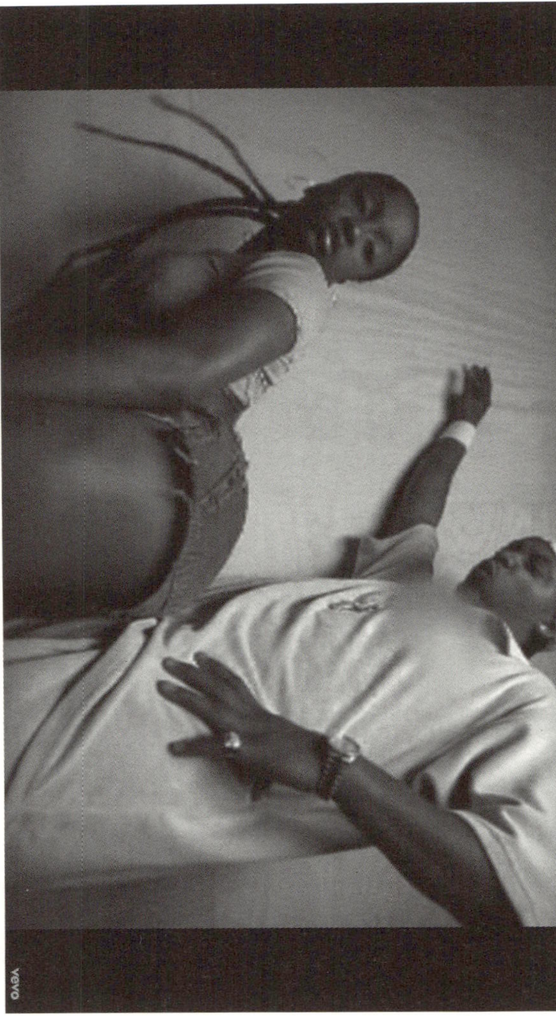


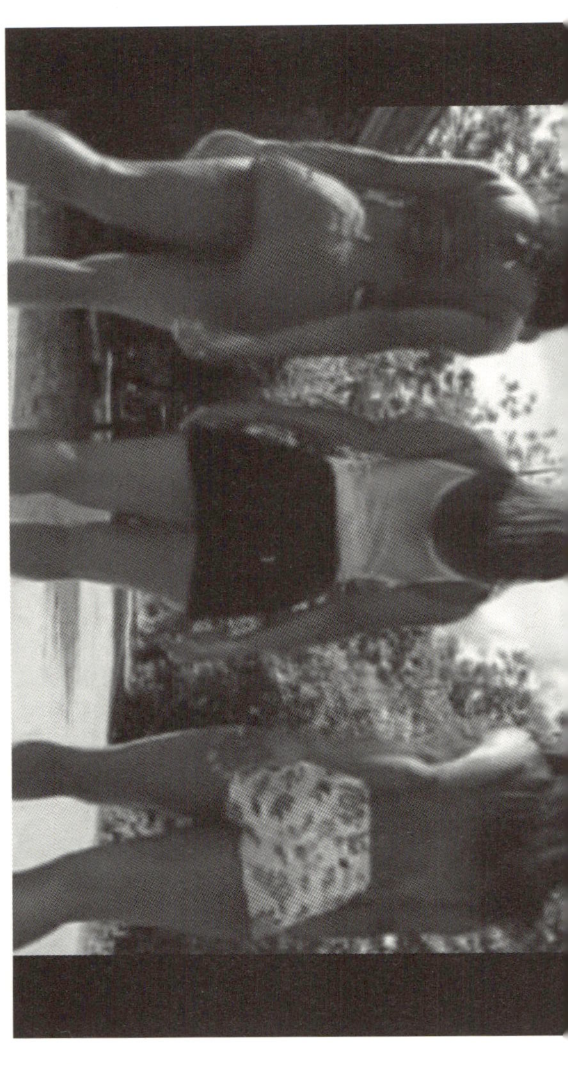

Shake Yaa Ass, Mystikal, 2000

Shake Yaa Ass, Mystikal, 2000

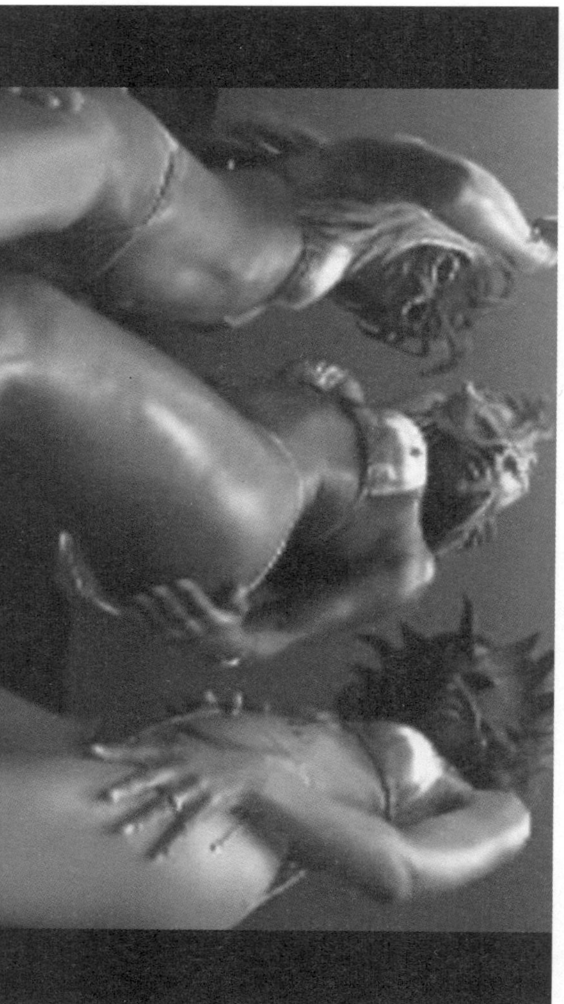

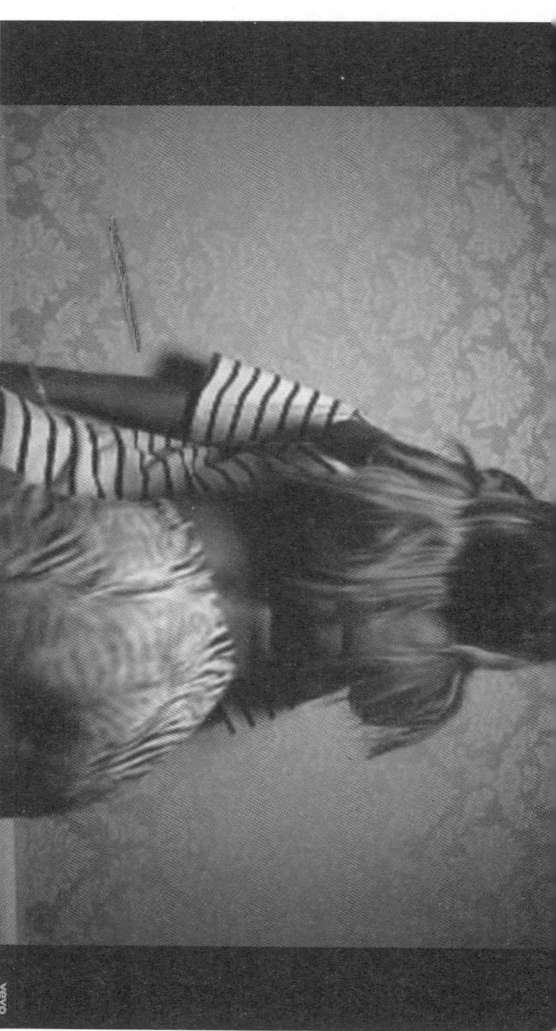

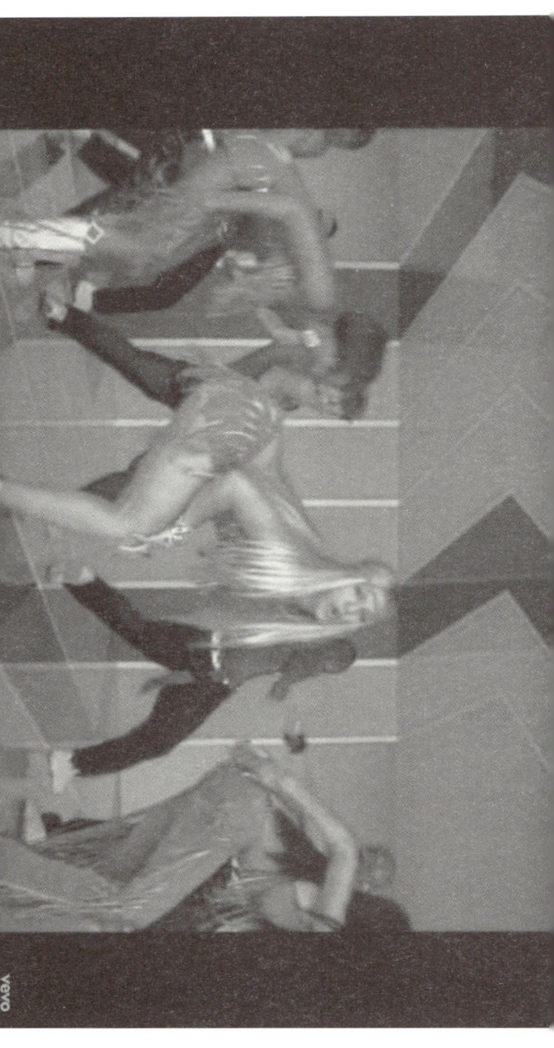


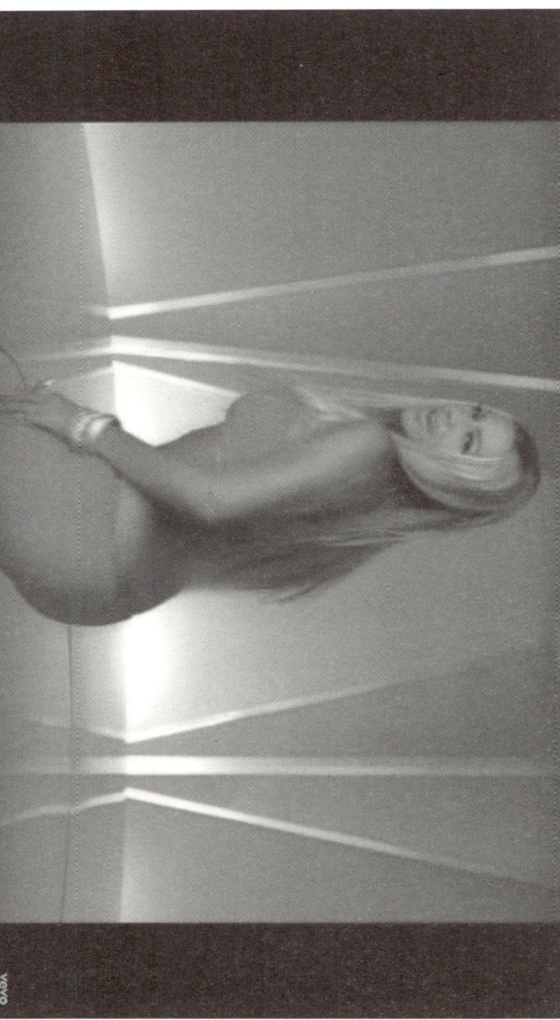


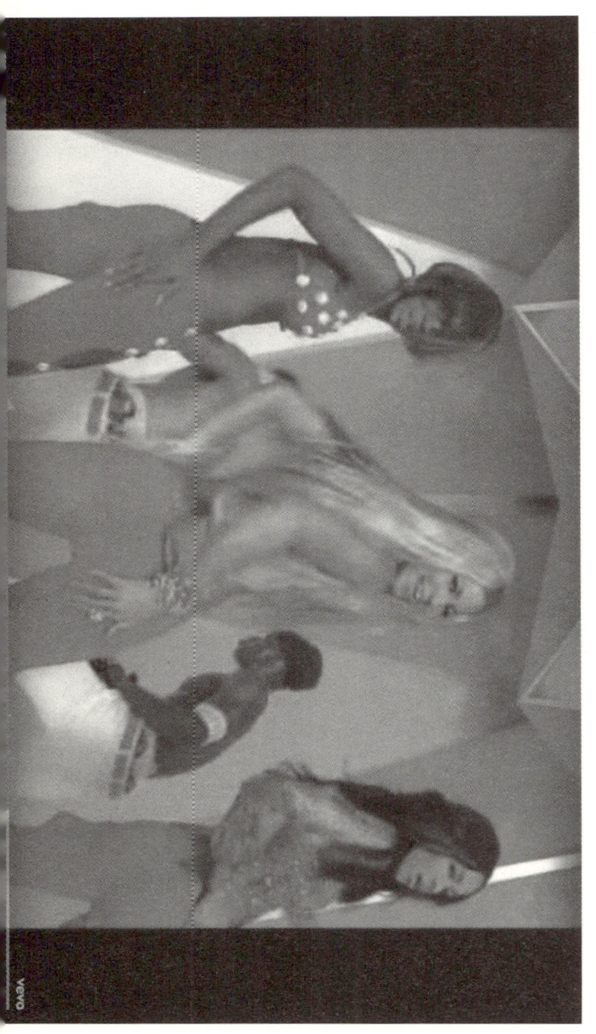


Bootylicious, Destiny's Child, 2001

Ass Like That, Eminem, 2004

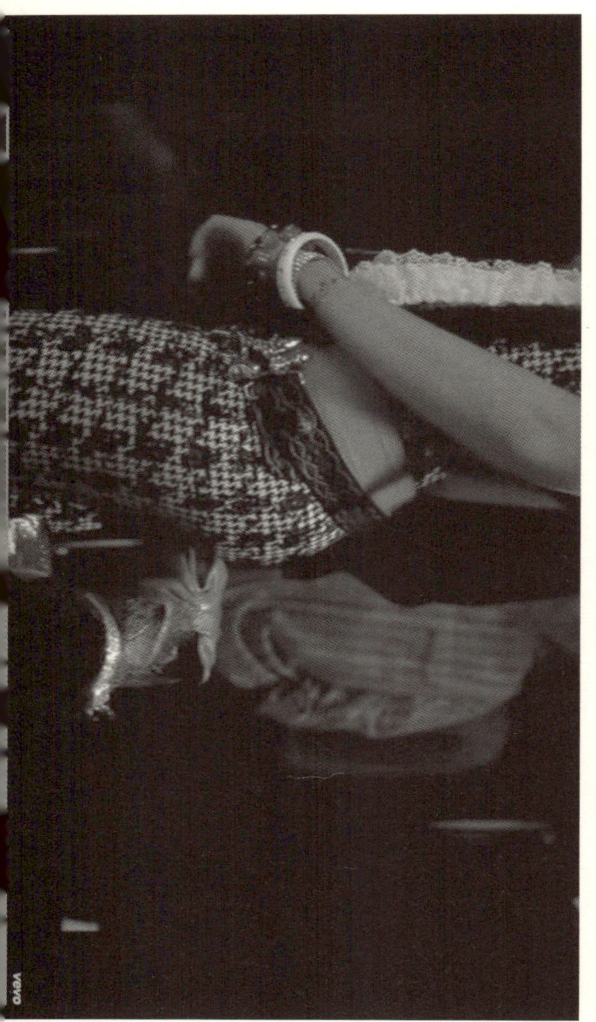

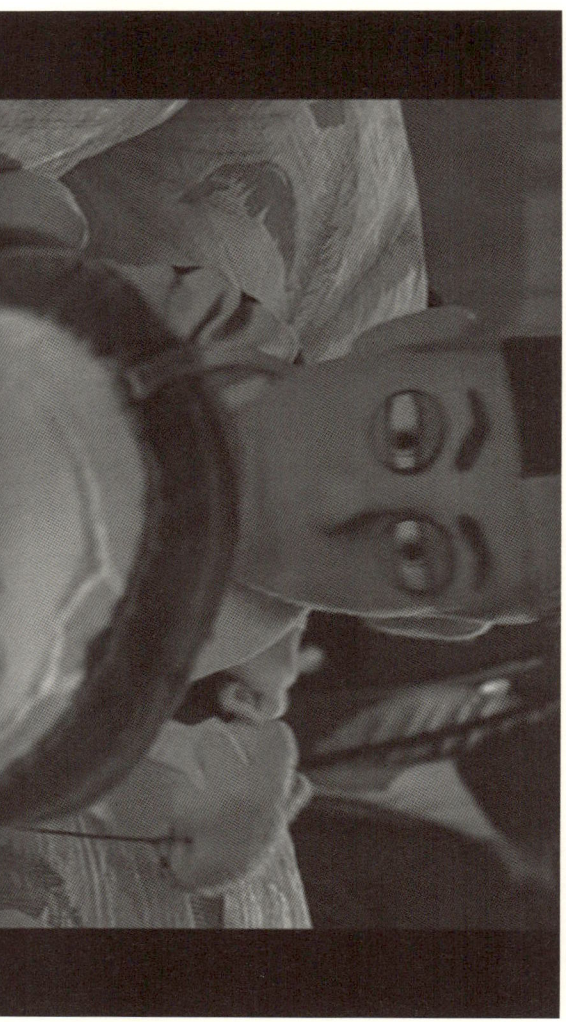

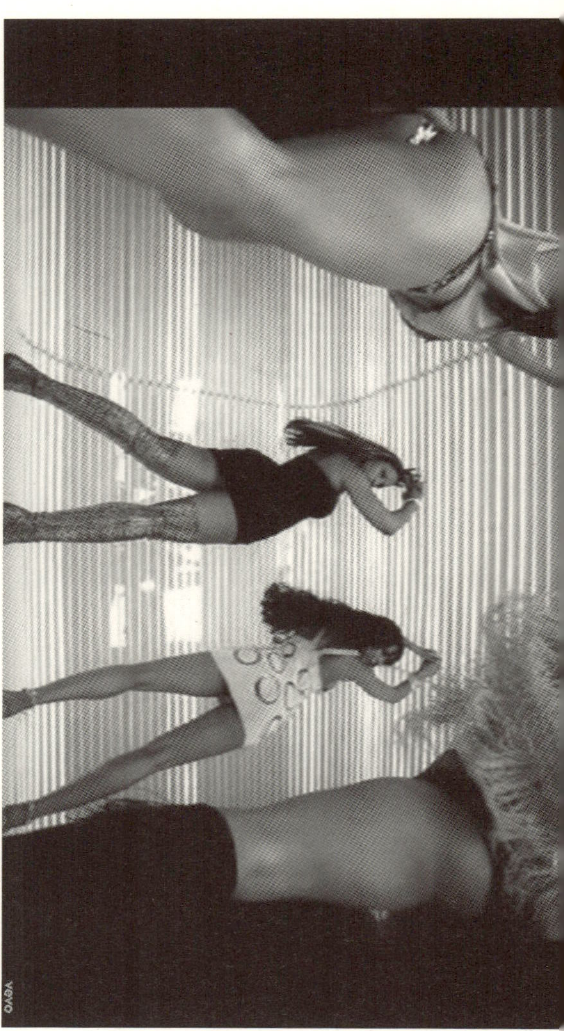

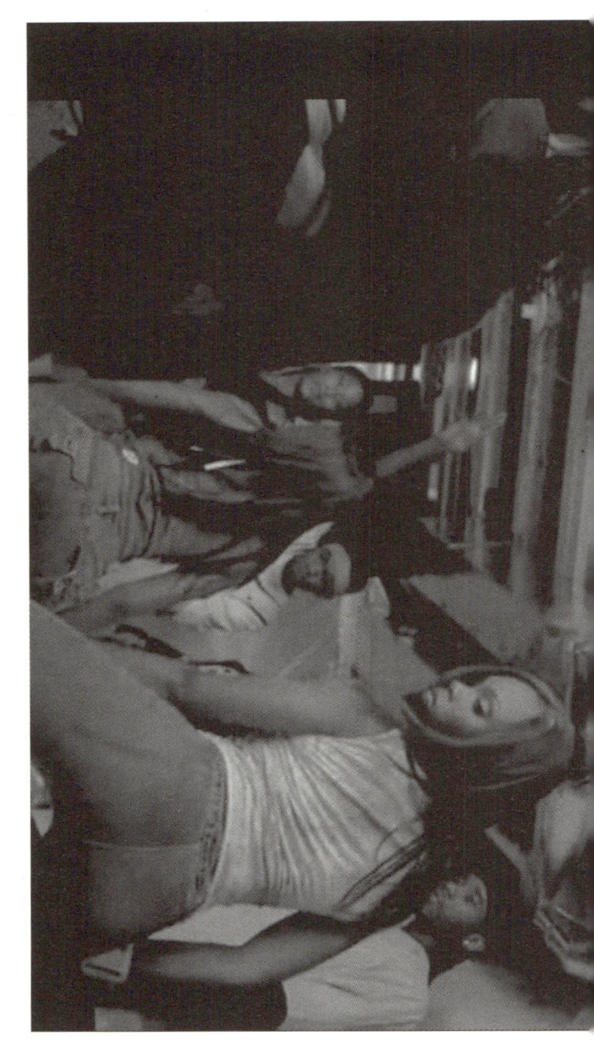



Get Busy, Sean Paul, 2004

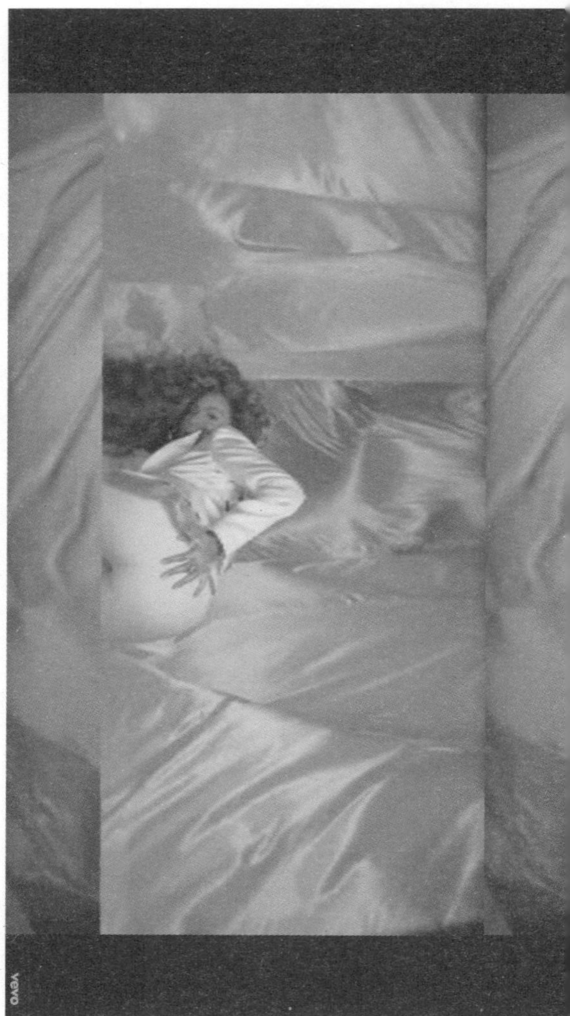


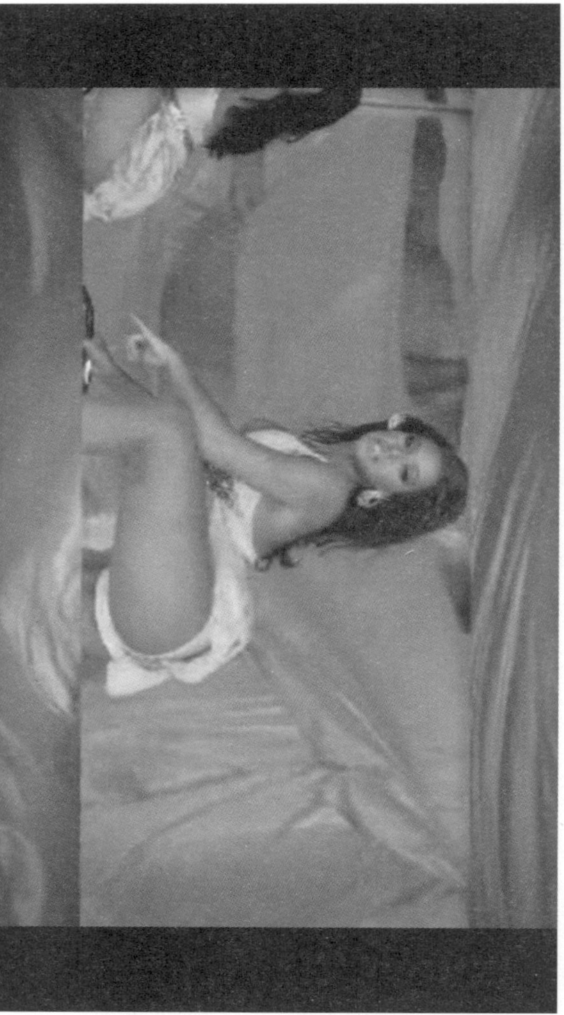


Check On It, Beyoncé, Bun B, Slim Thug 2005

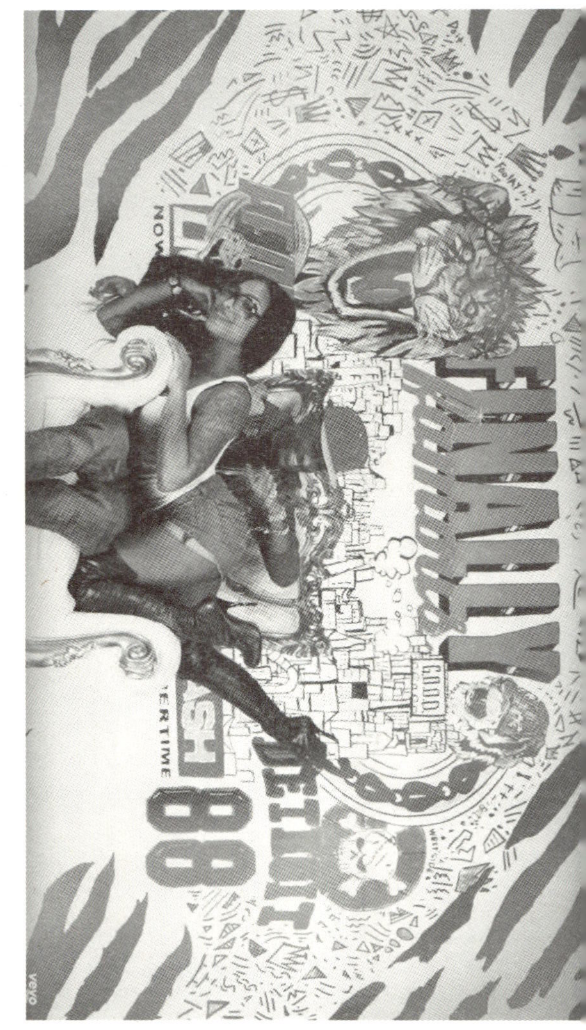


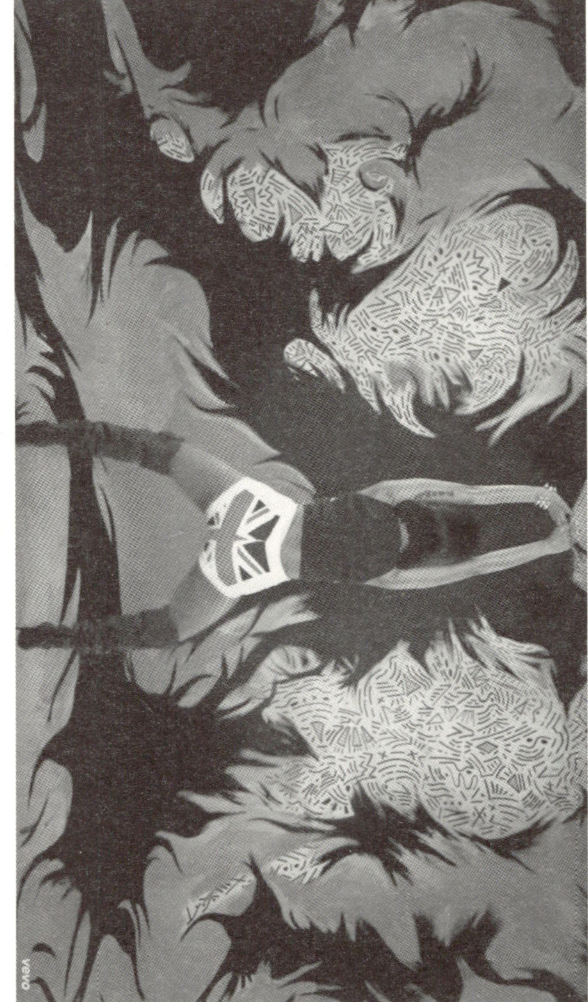


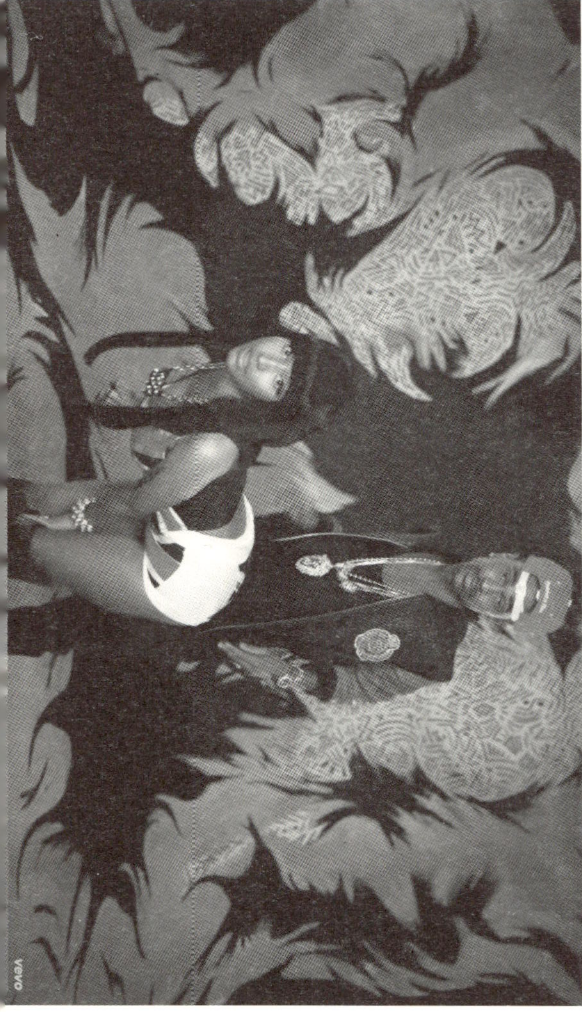


Dance A$$, Big Sean, Nicki Minaj, 2011

Dance A$$, Big Sean, Nicki Minaj, 2011

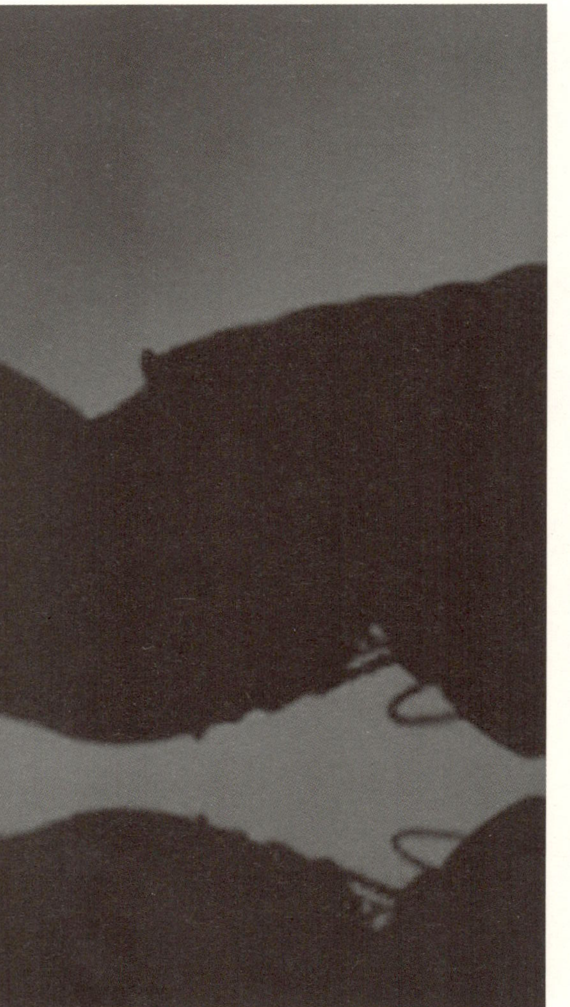

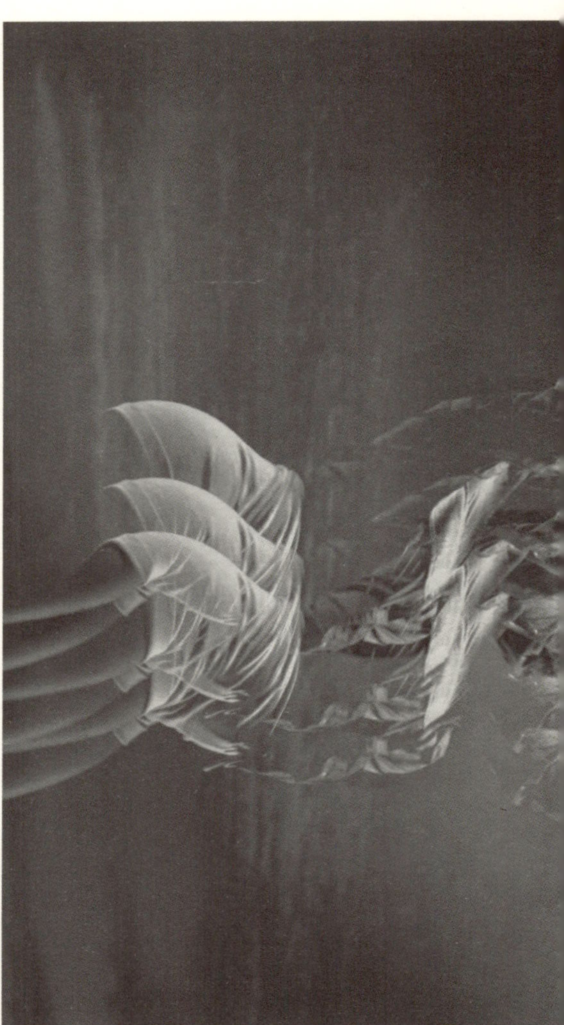

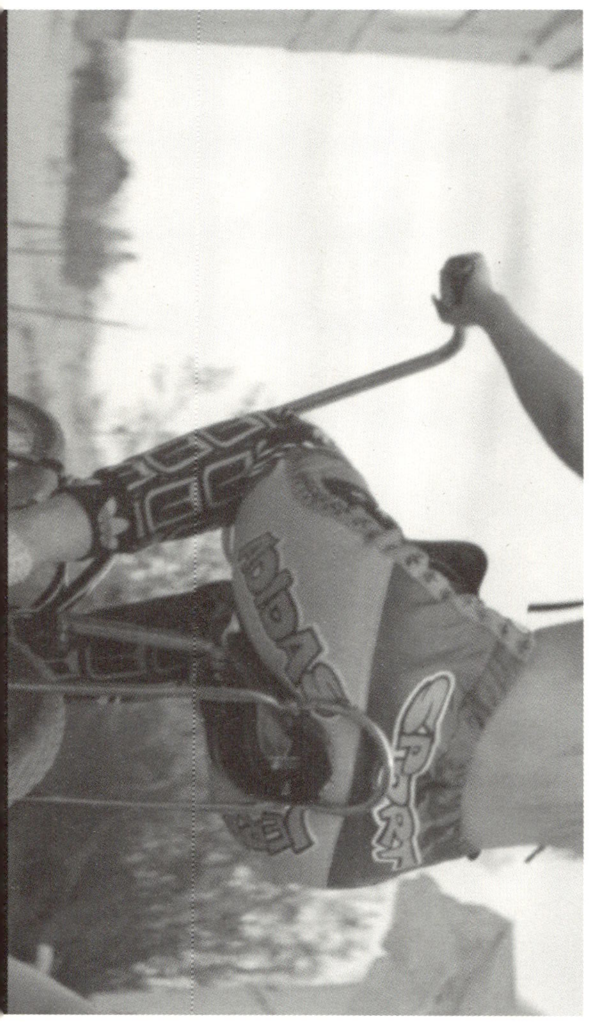

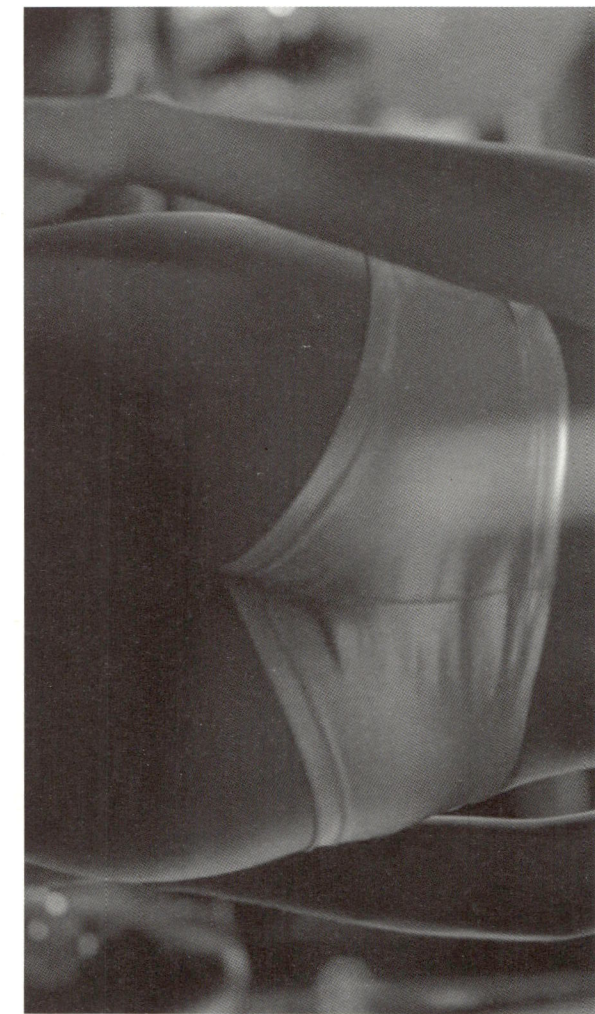

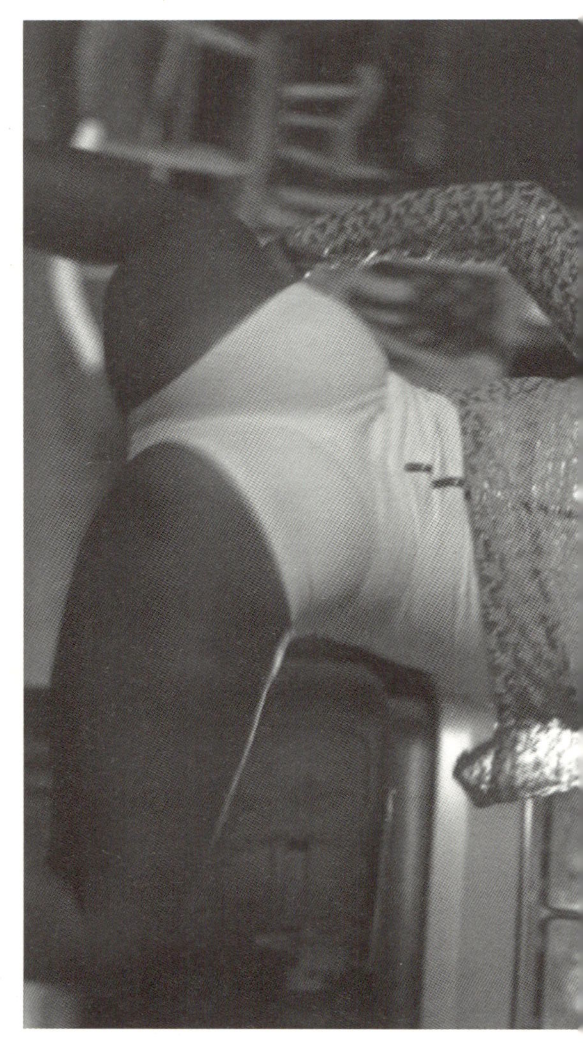

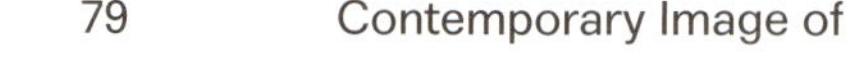



Work, Iggy Azalea, 2013

Work, Iggy Azalea, 2013

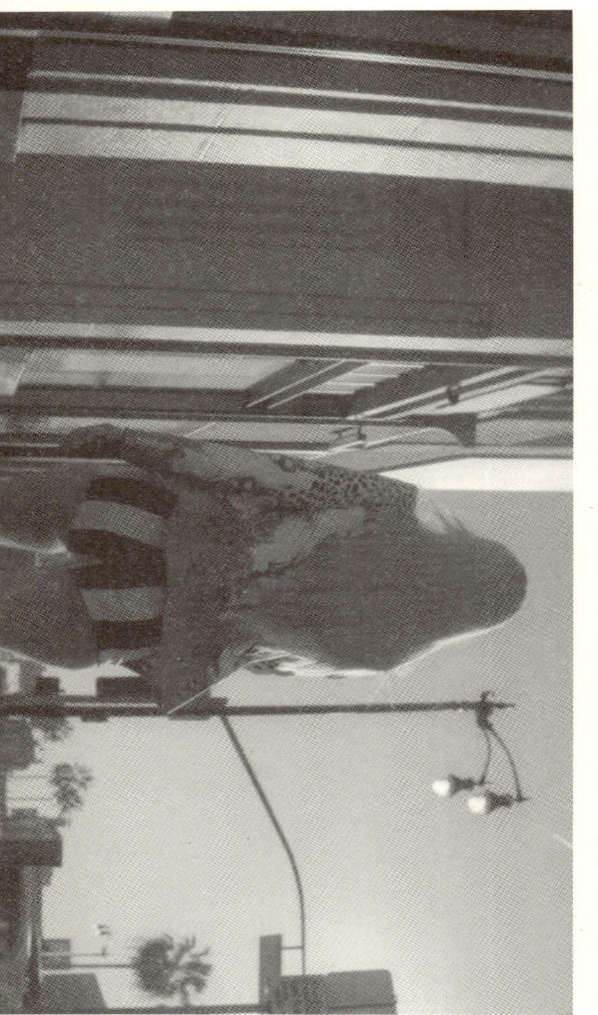

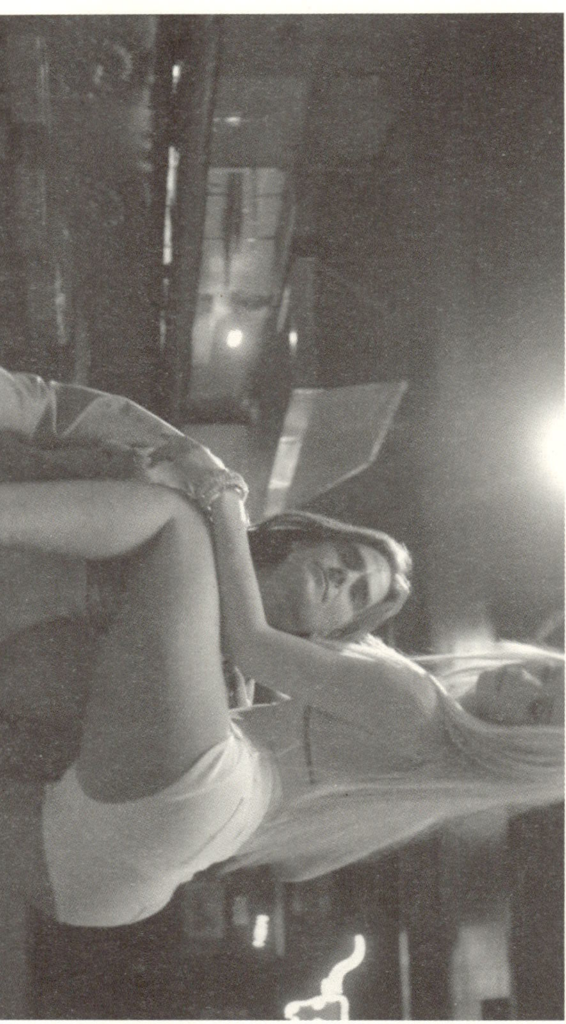

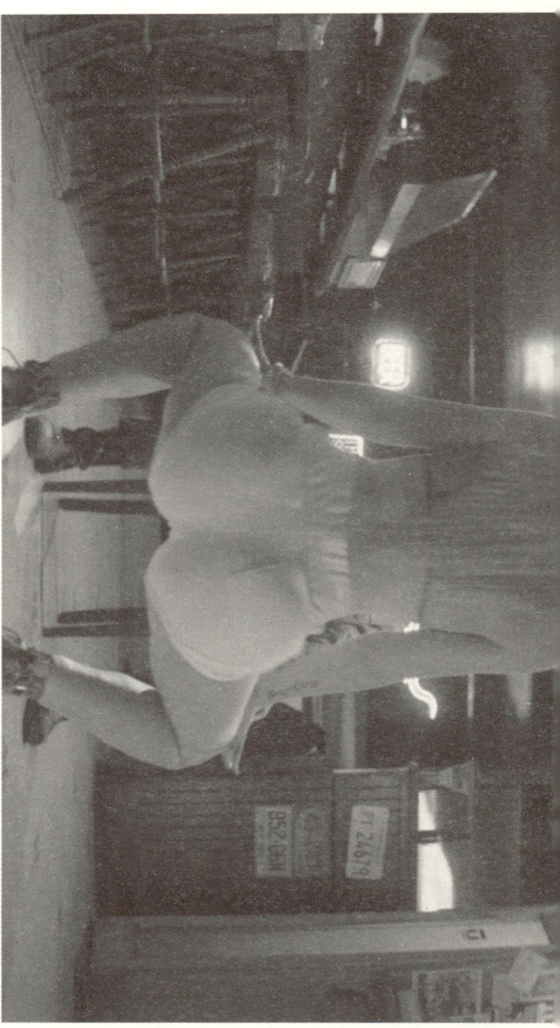

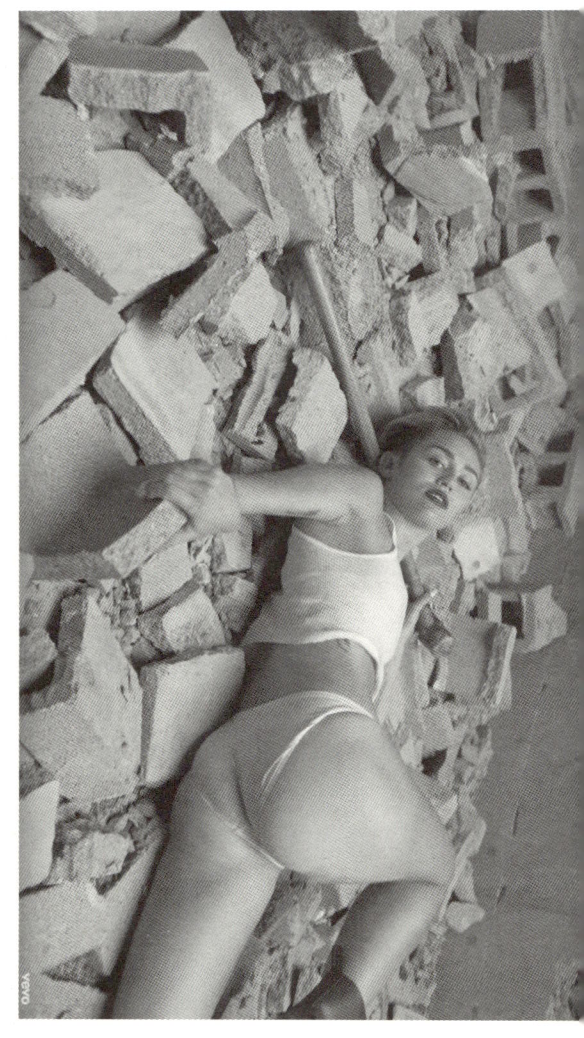


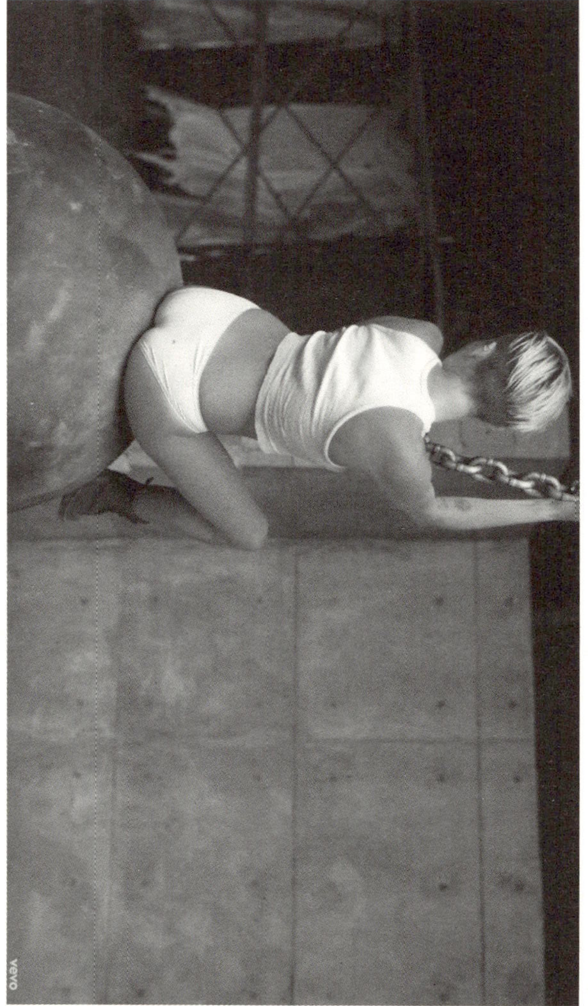


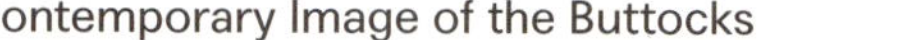
Wrecking Ball, Miley Cyrus, 2013

Can’t Remember to Forget You, Shakira, Rihanna, 2013

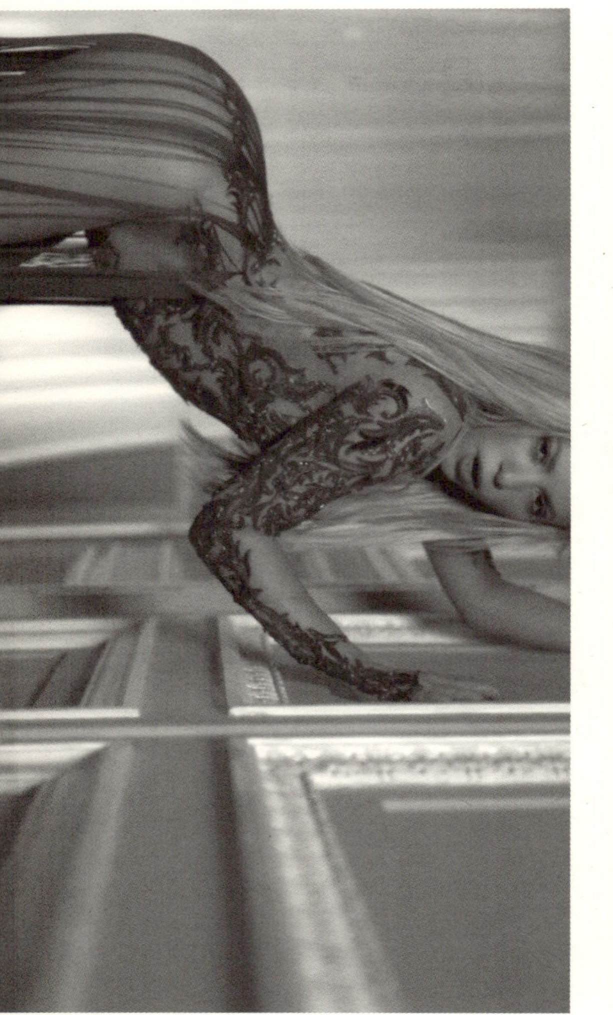

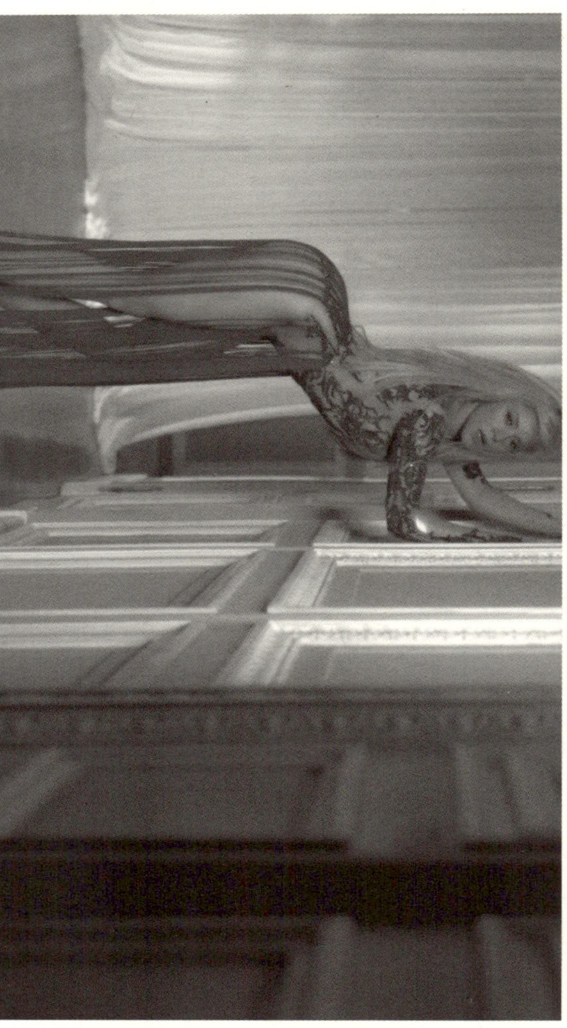

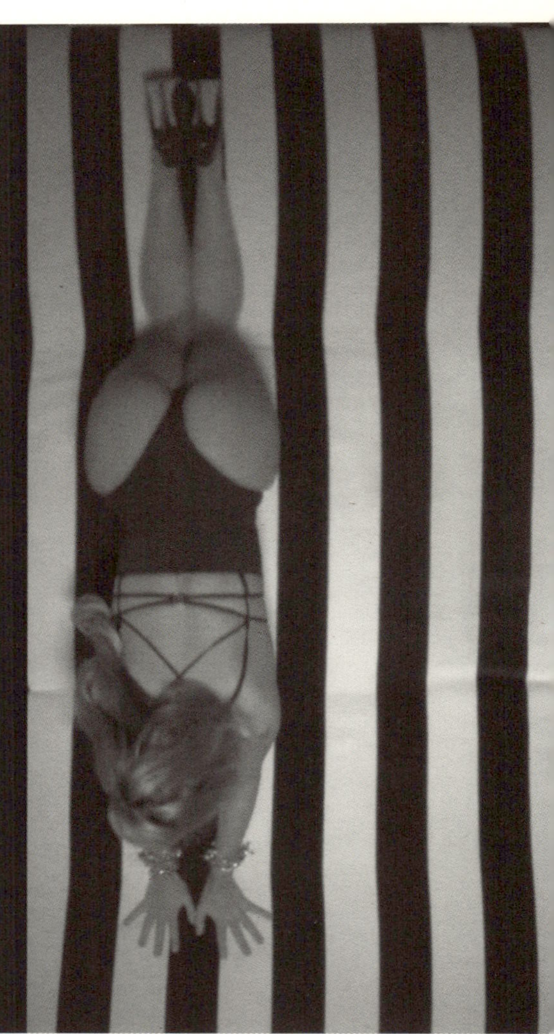

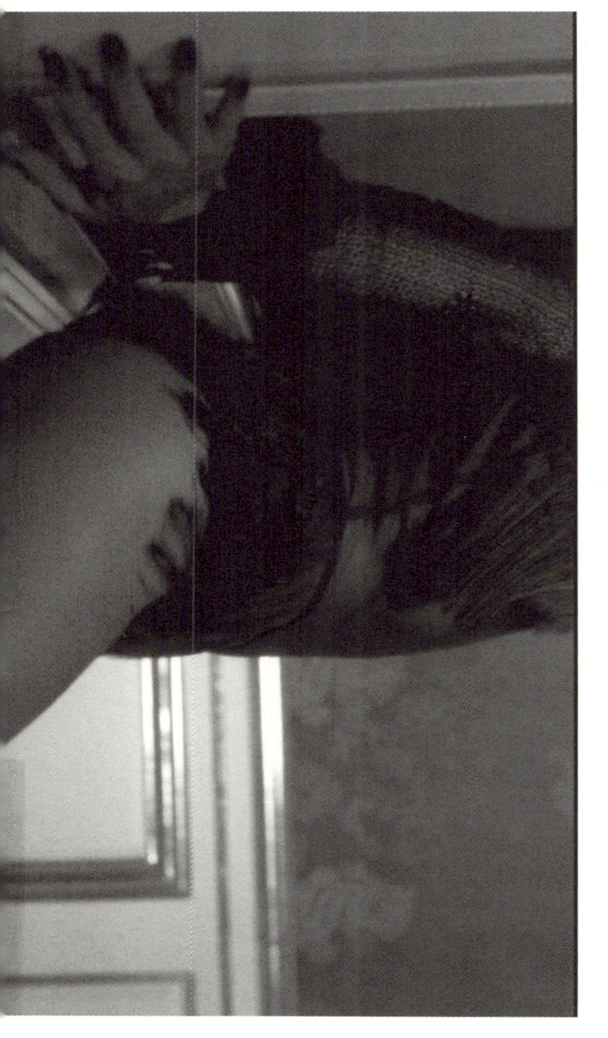

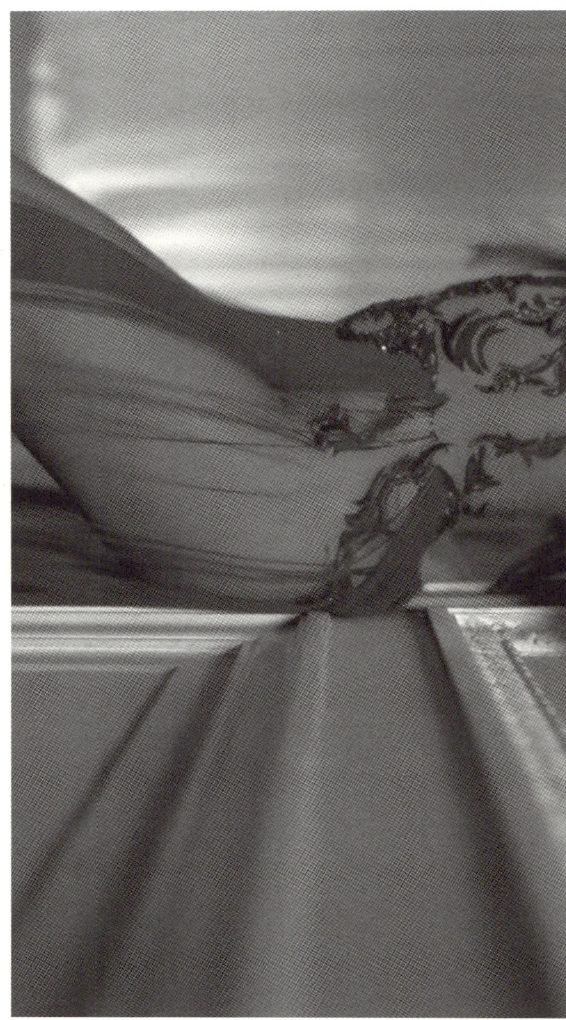

Can’t Remember to Forget You, Shakira, Rihanna, 2013

Can’t Remember to Forget You, Shakira, Rihanna, 2013

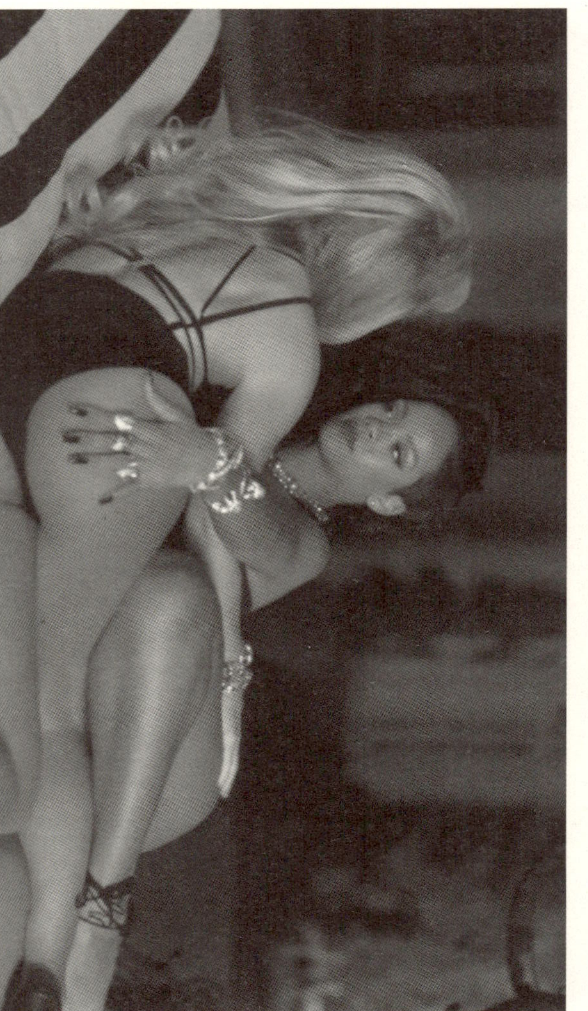

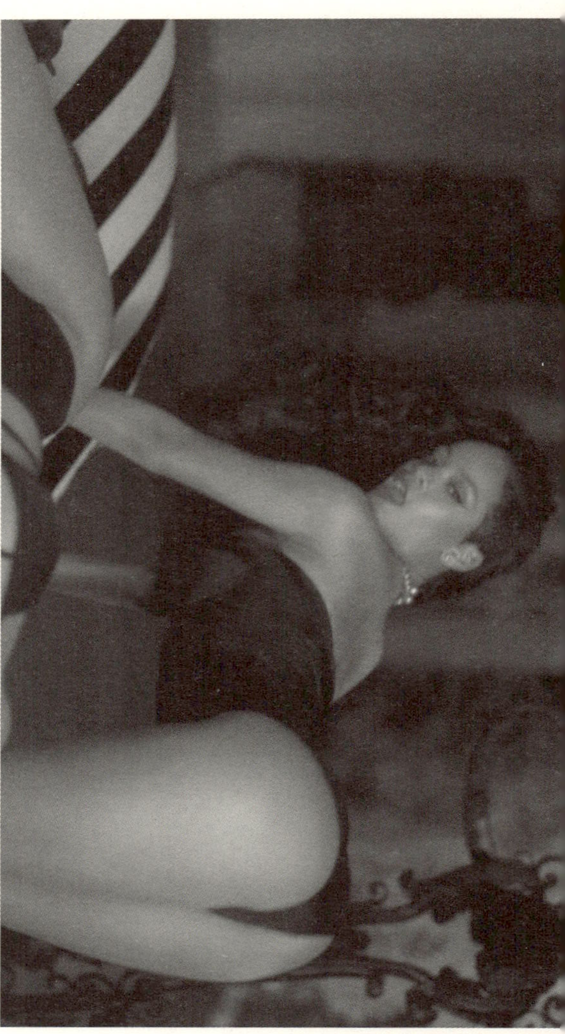

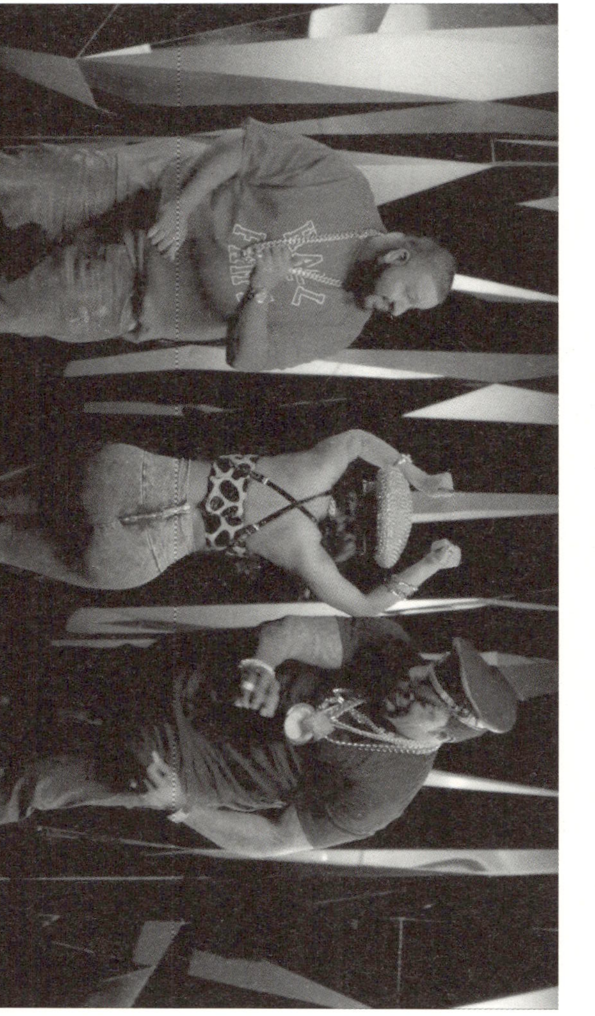

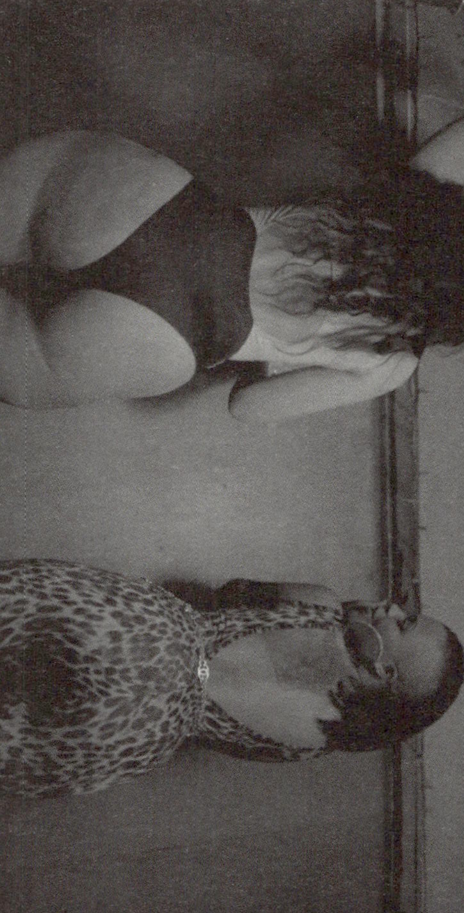

Twerk it, Busta Rhymes, Nicki Minaj, 2013

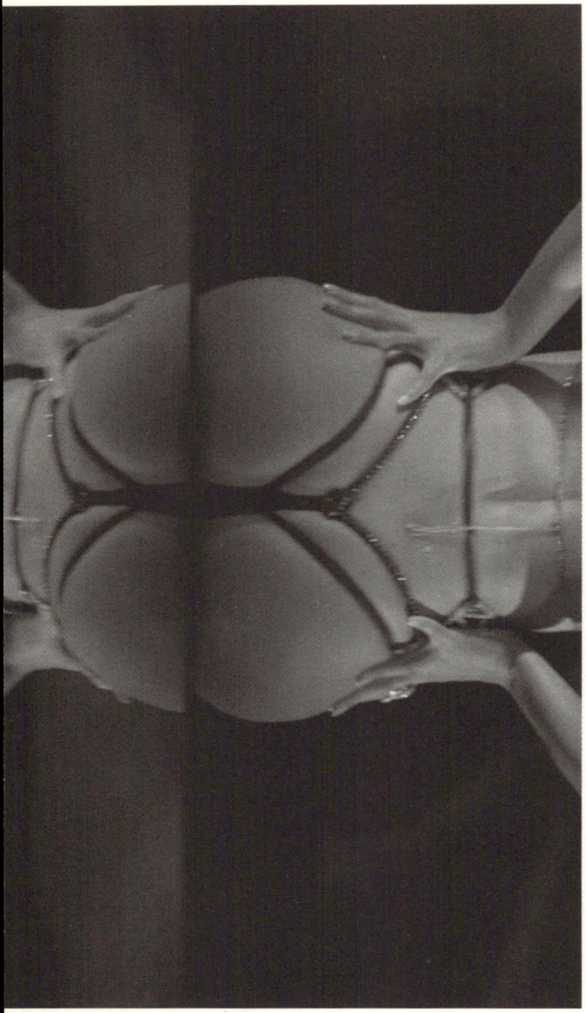

Partition, Beyoncé, 2013

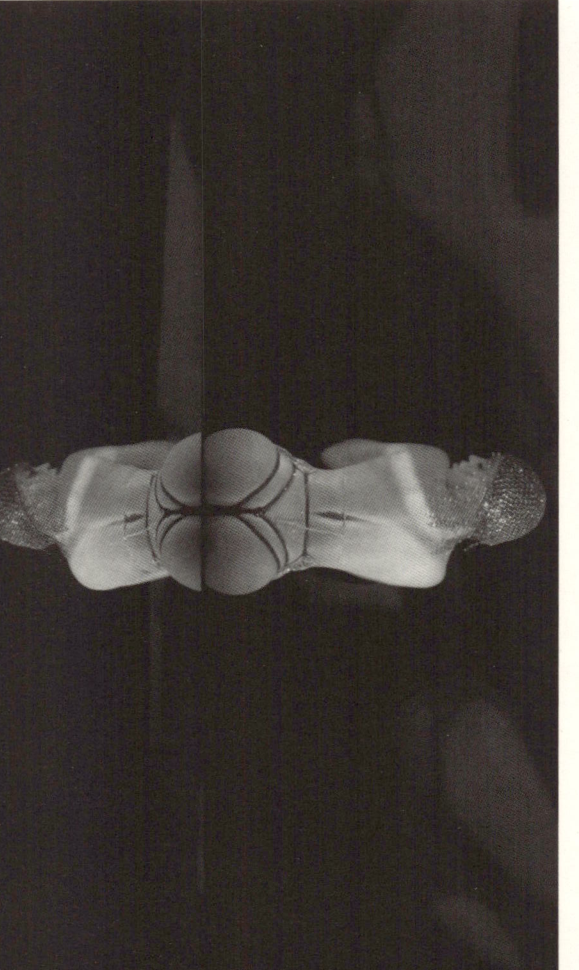

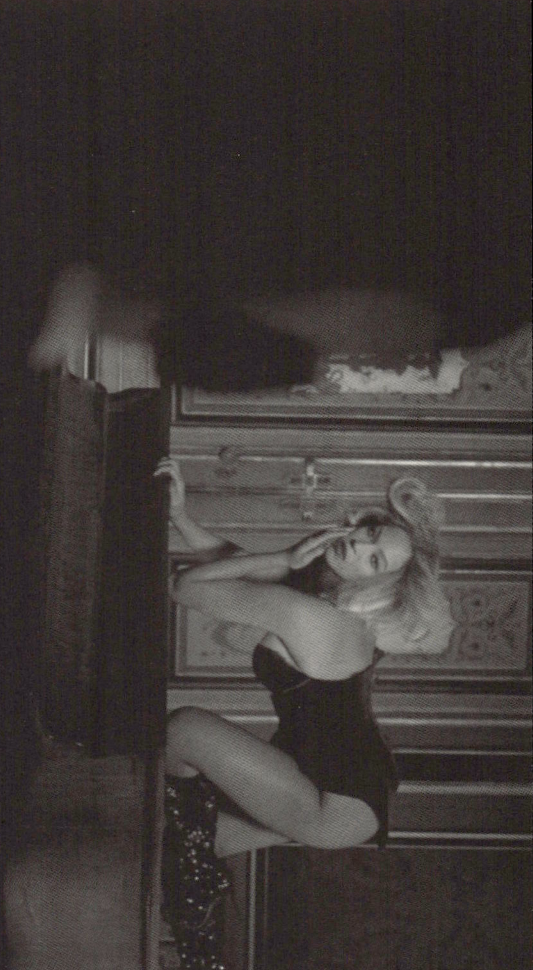

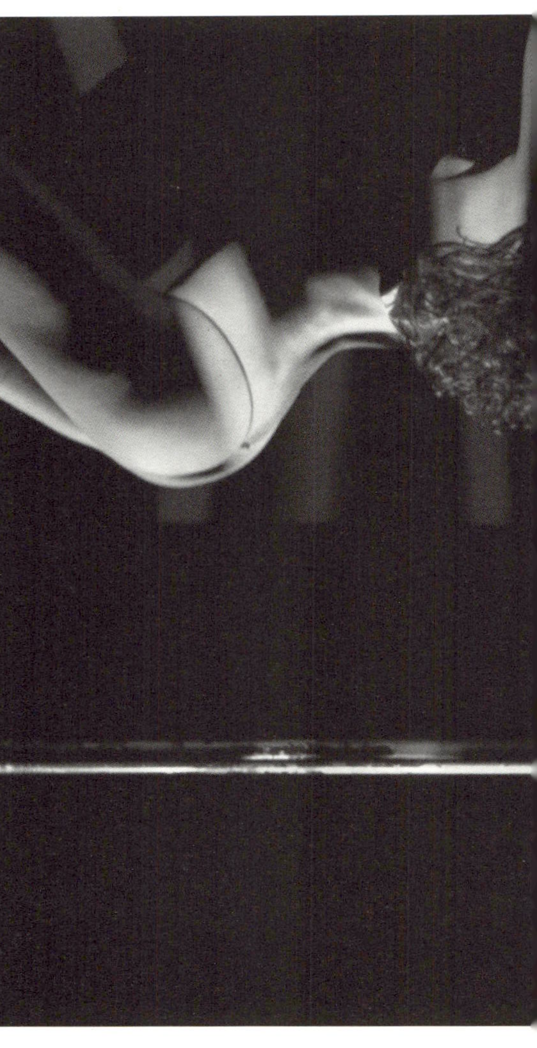

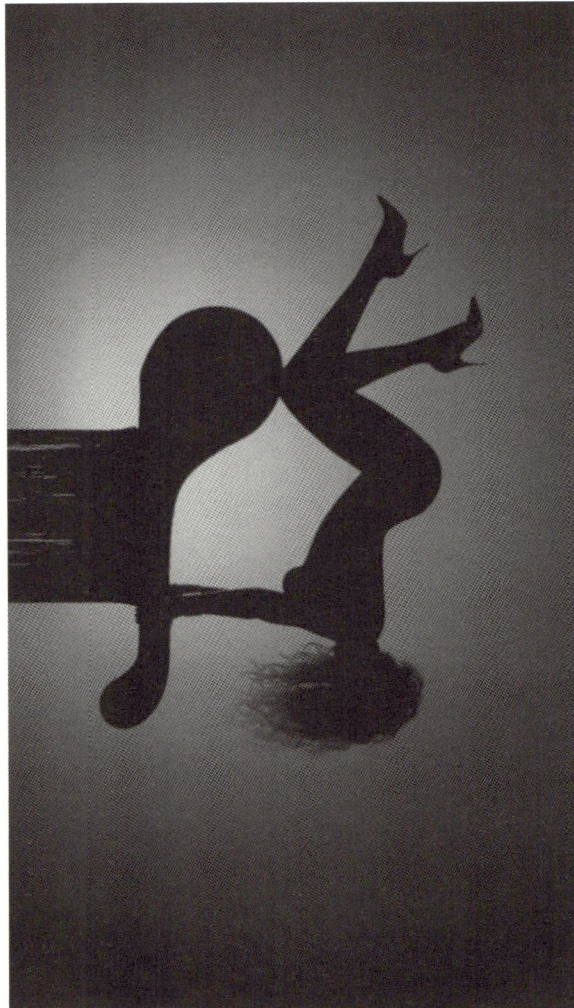

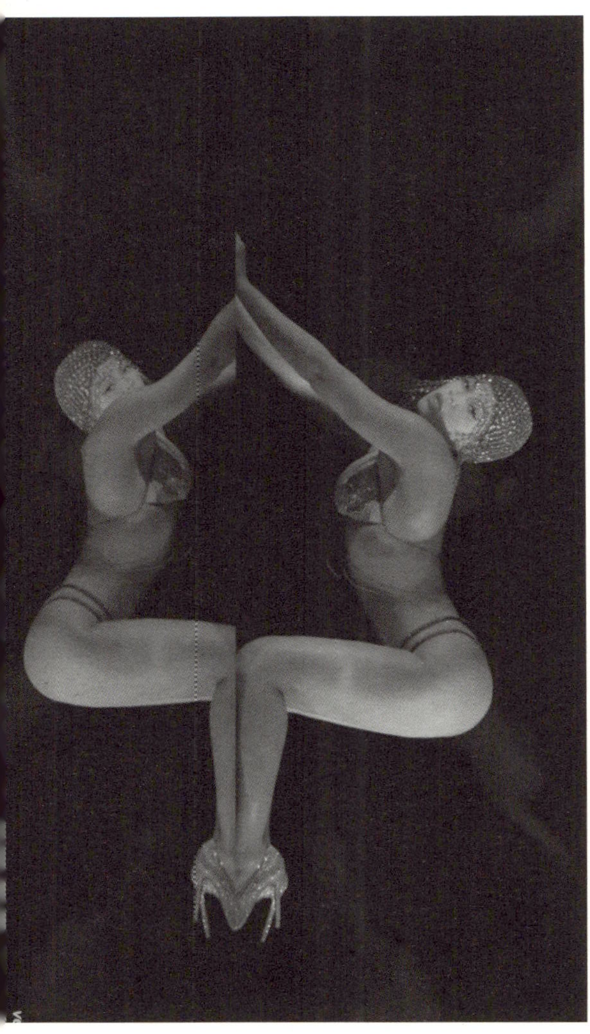



Partition, Beyoncé, 2013

Rocket, Beyoncé, 2013

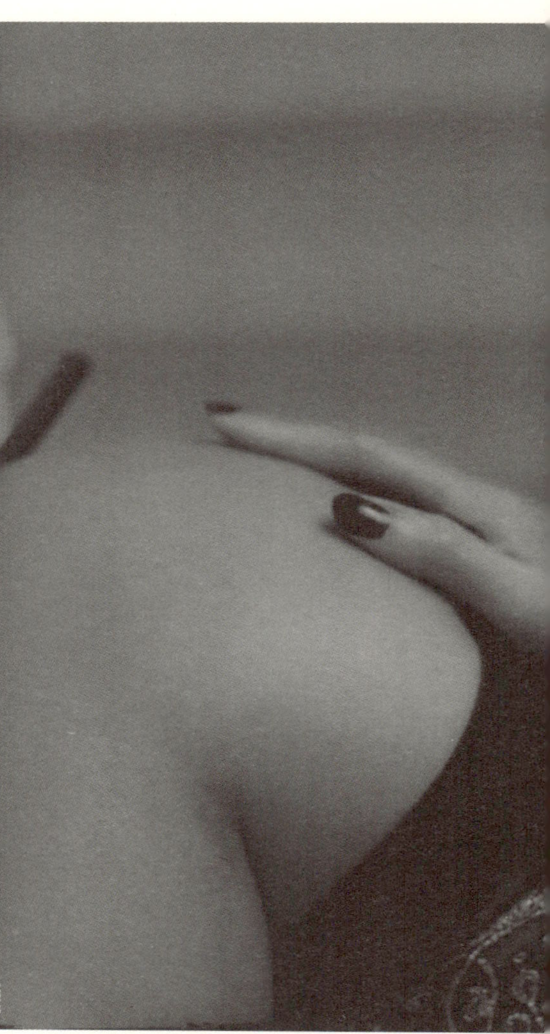


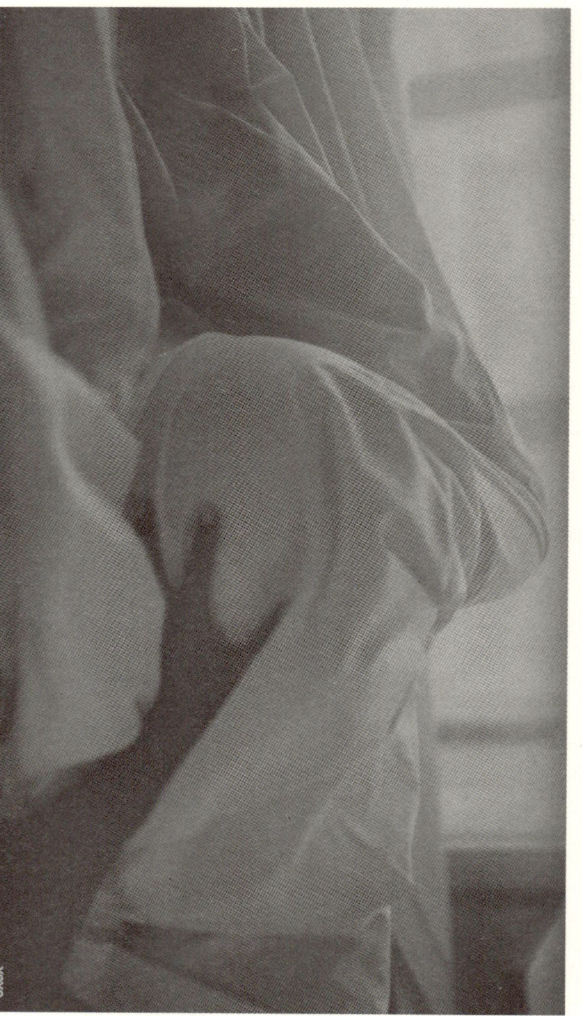


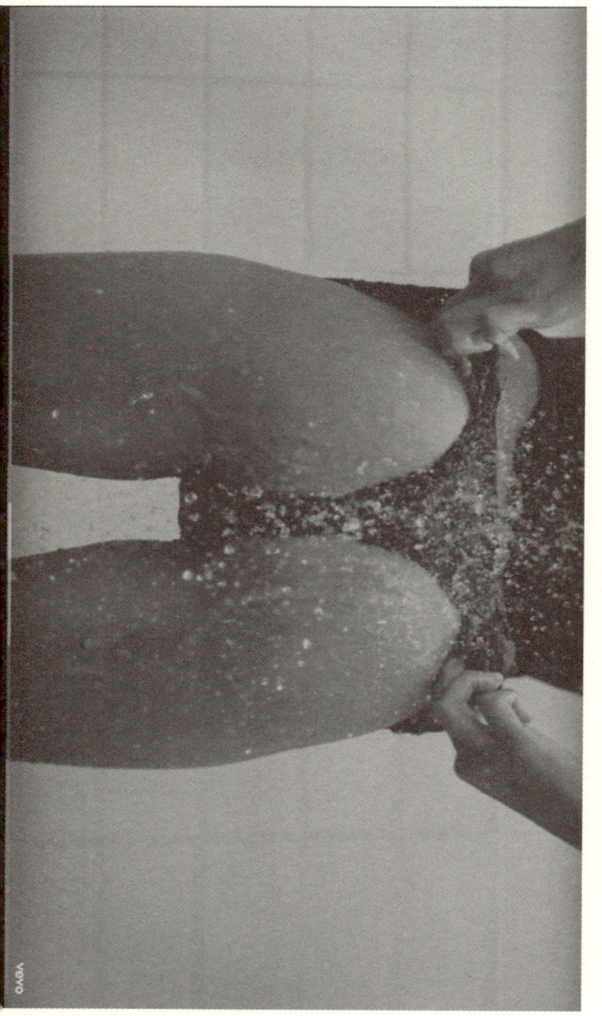

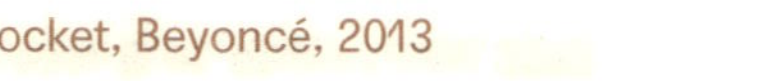

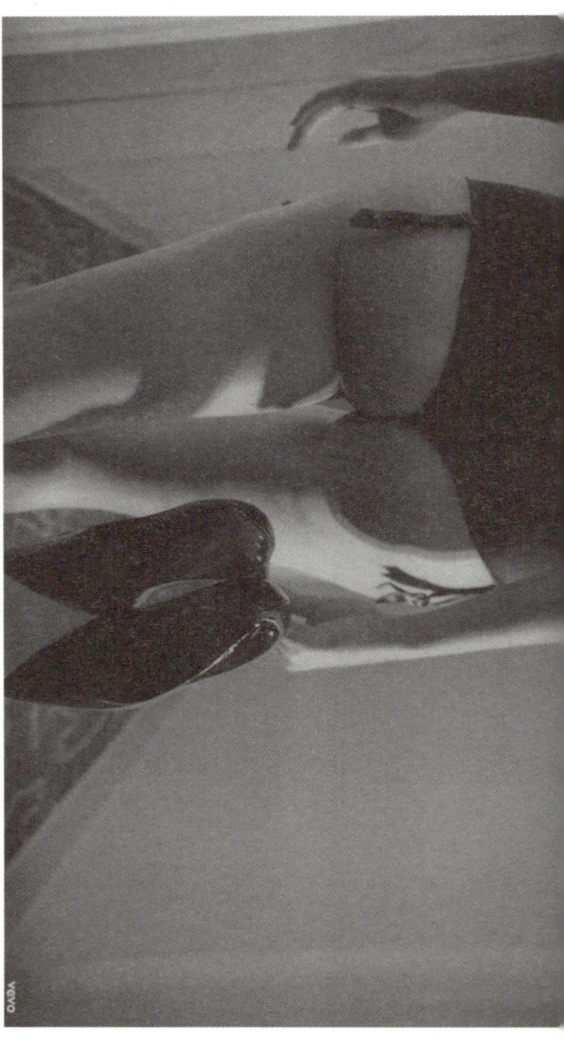


Rocket, Beyoncé, 2013

Bubble Butt, Major Lazer, 2013

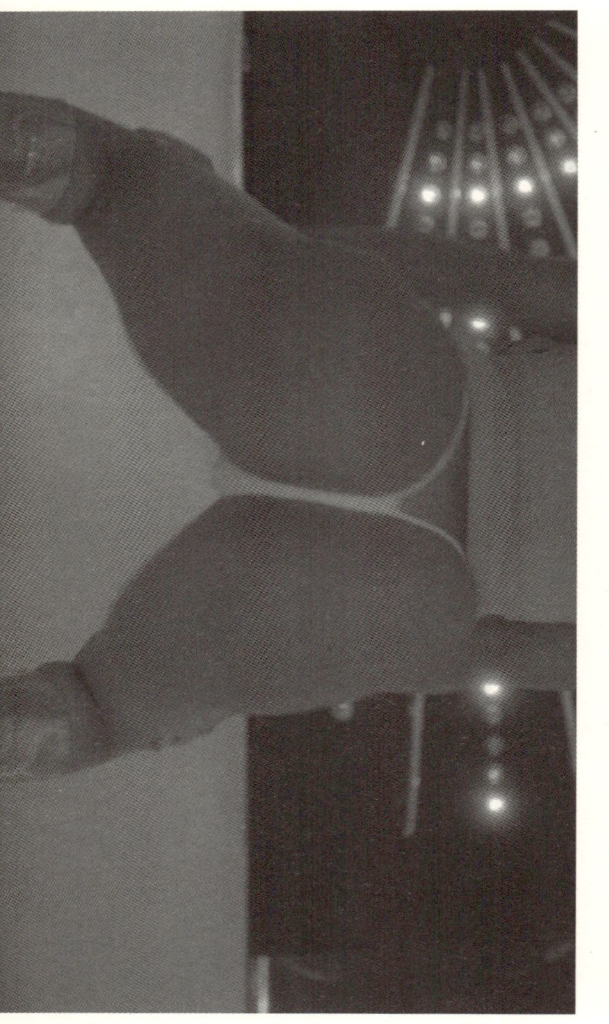

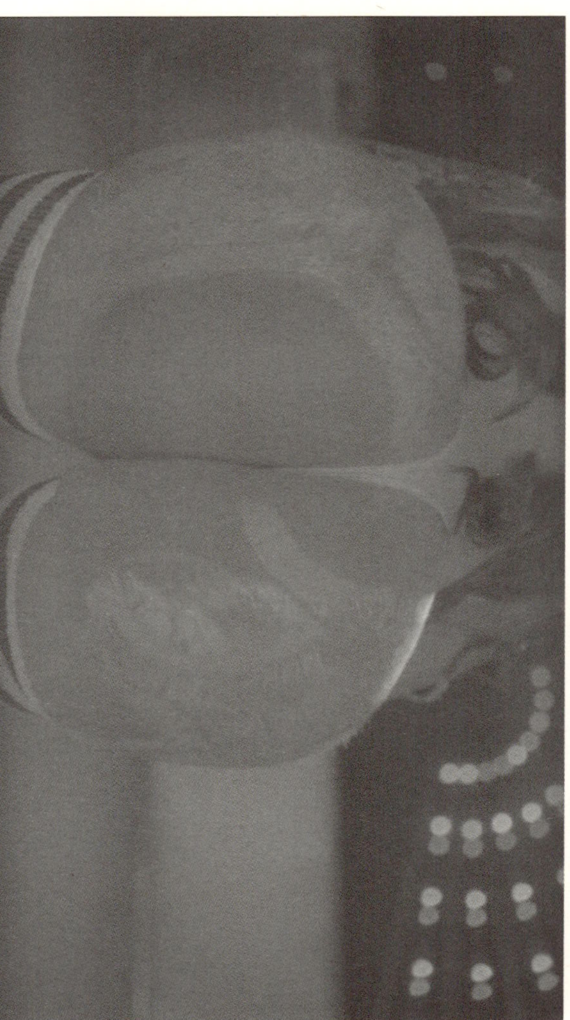

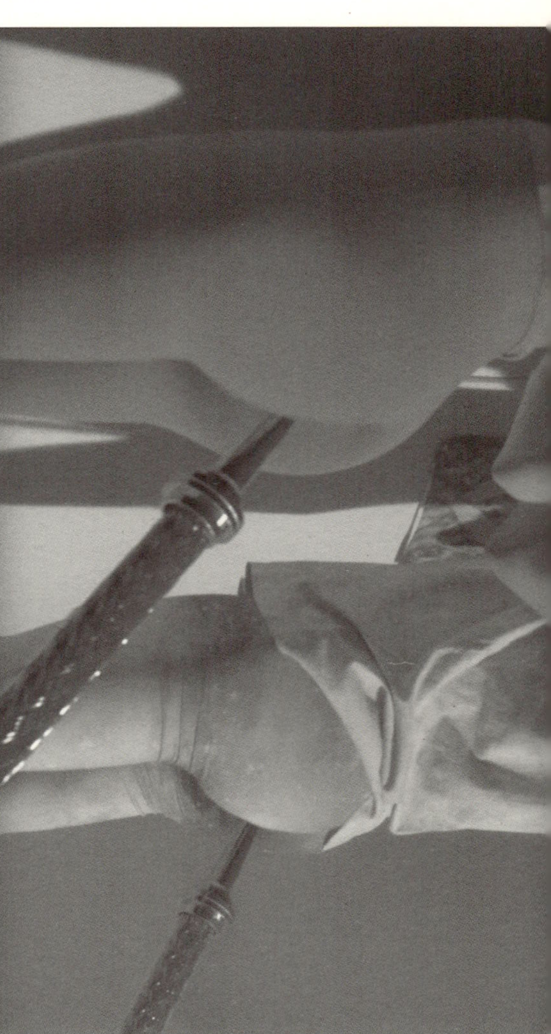

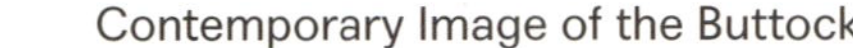

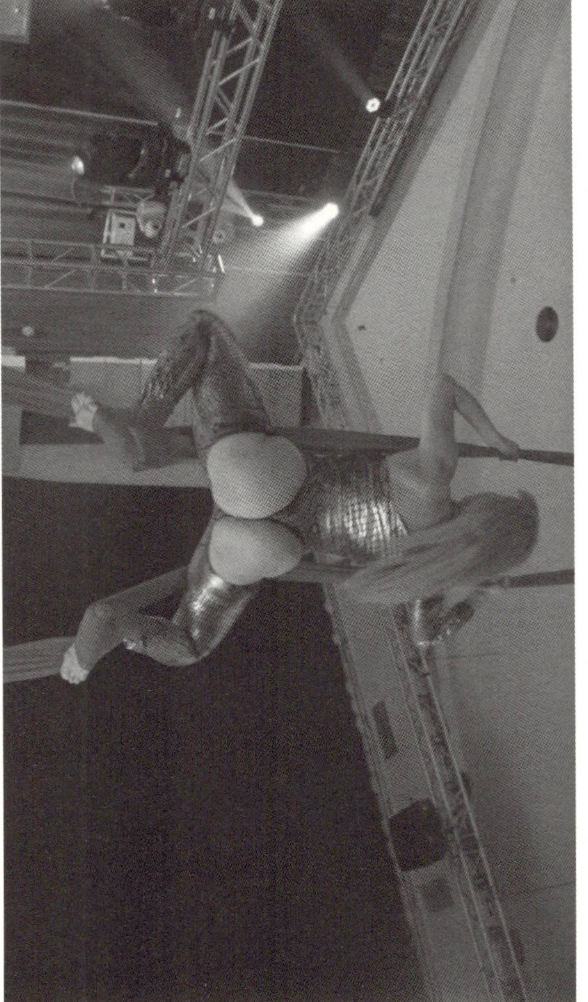

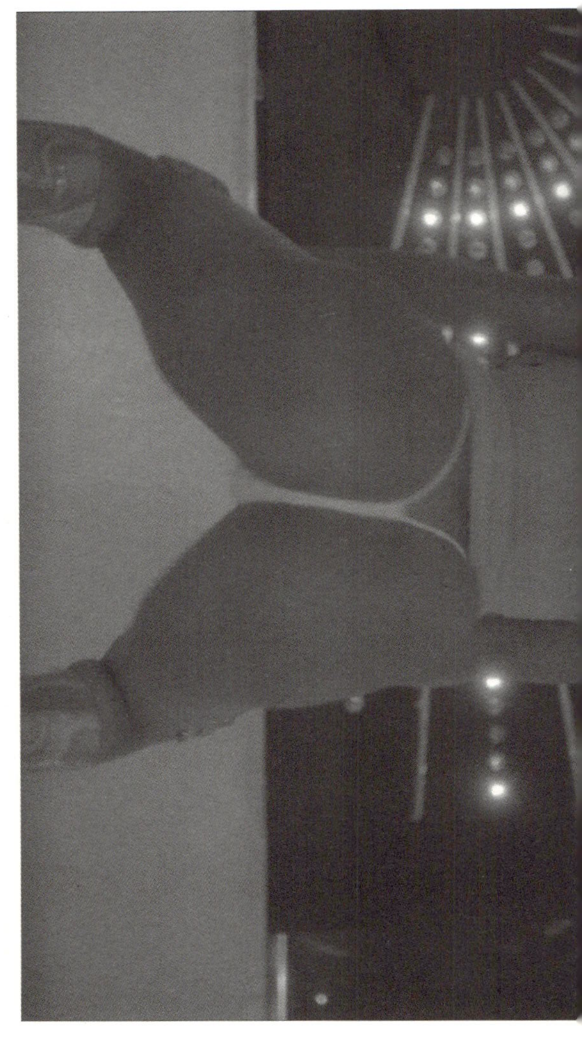



Bubble Butt, Major Lazer, 2013

Rella, Odd Future, 2013

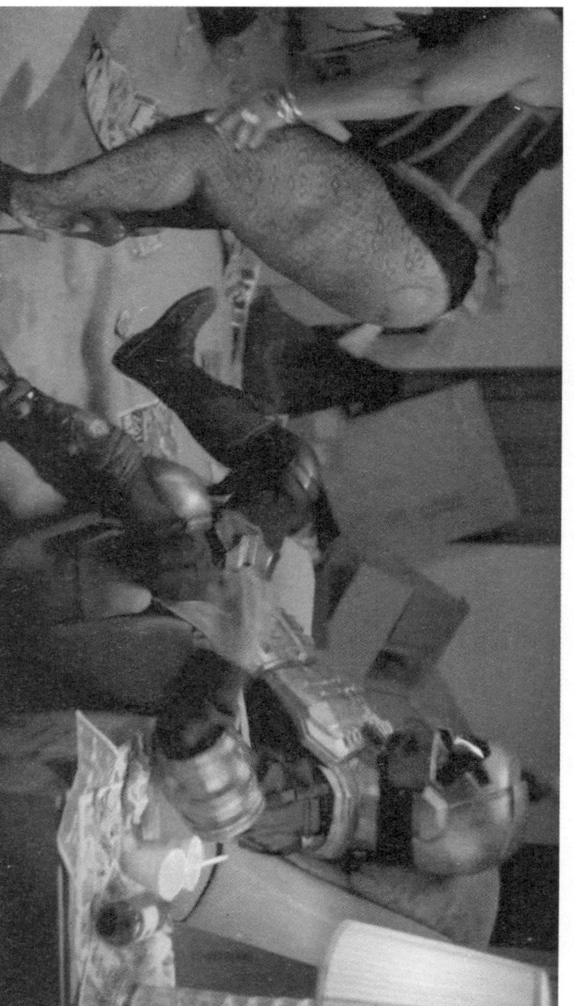

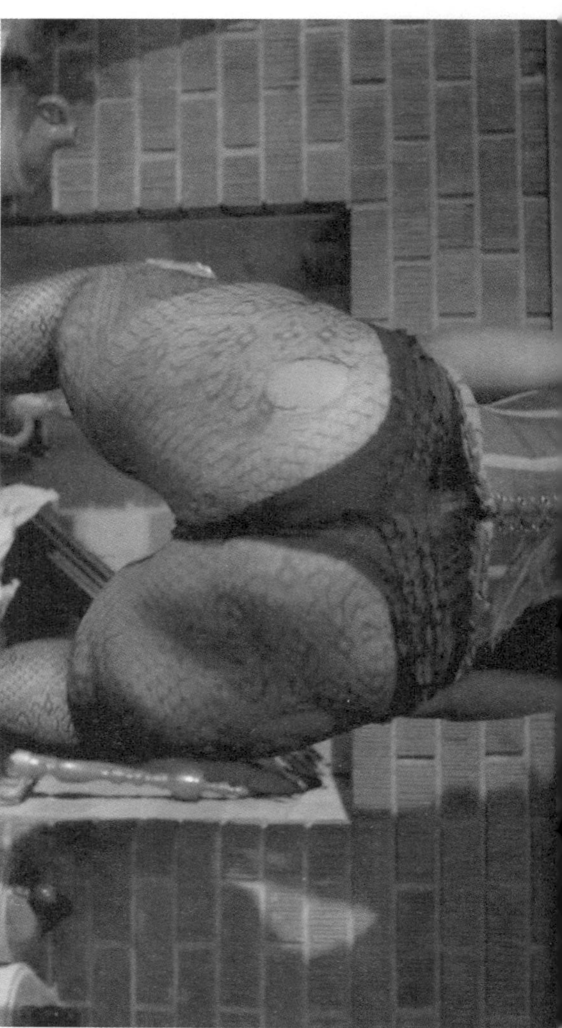

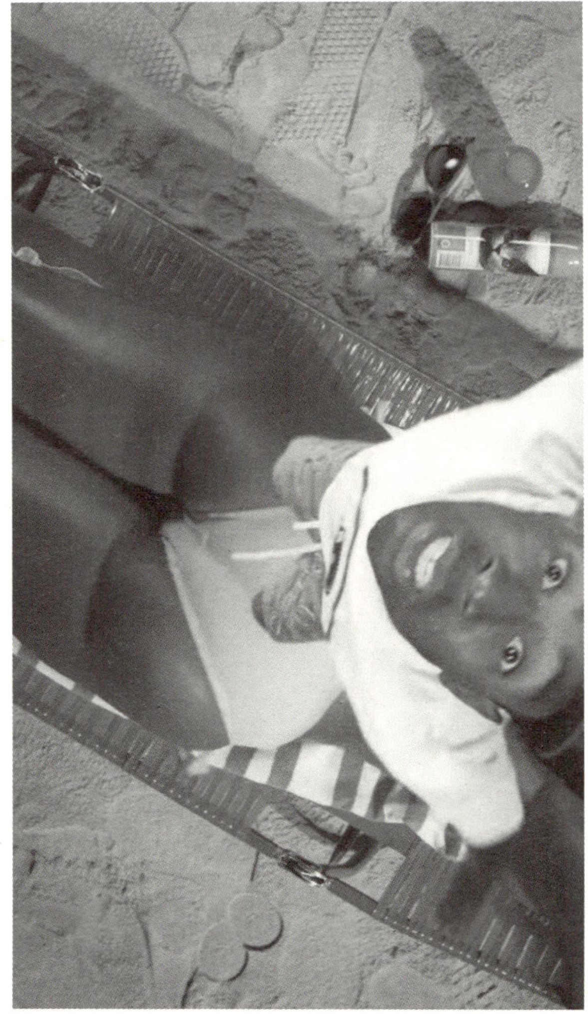

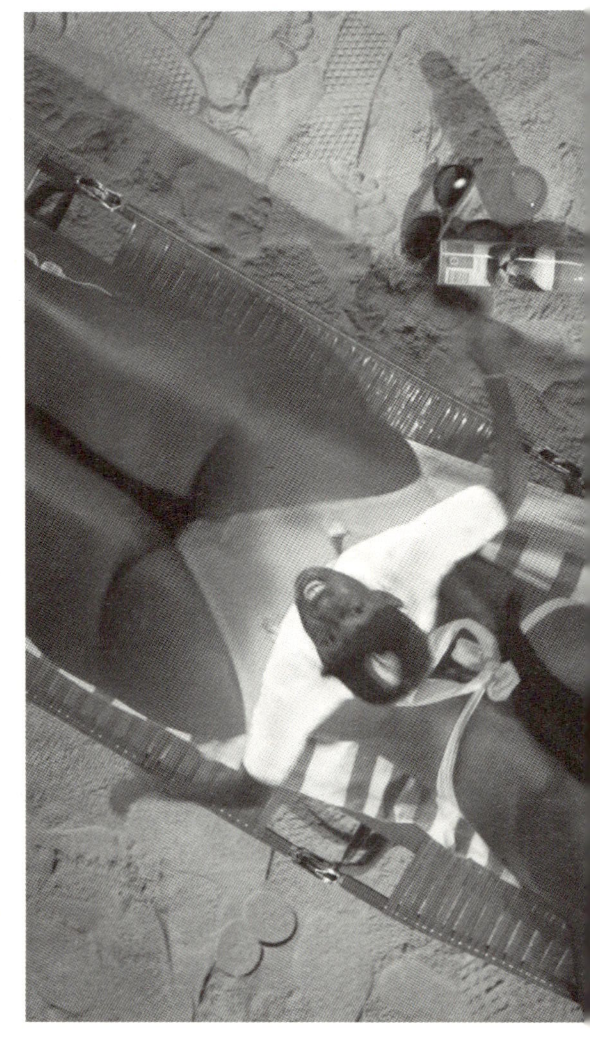



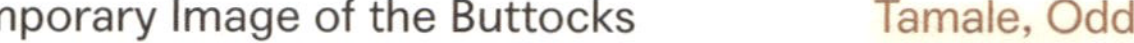
Tamale, Odd Future, 2013

Anaconda, Nicki Minaj, 2014

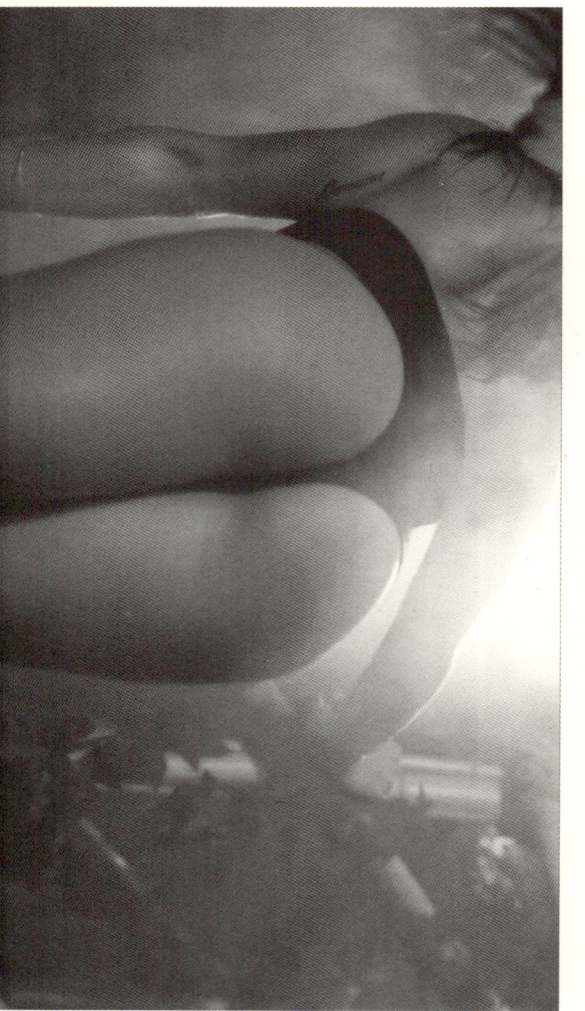

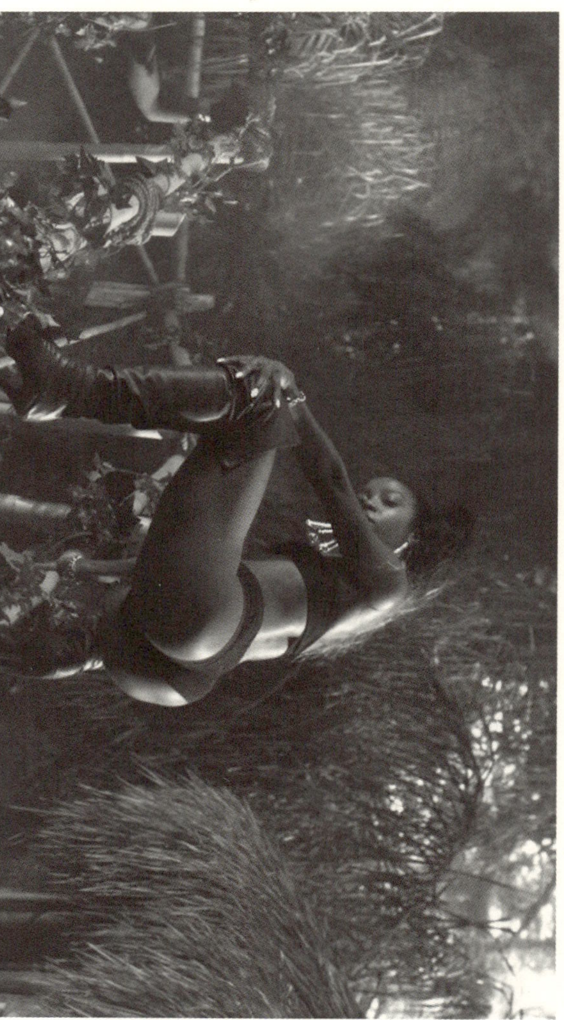

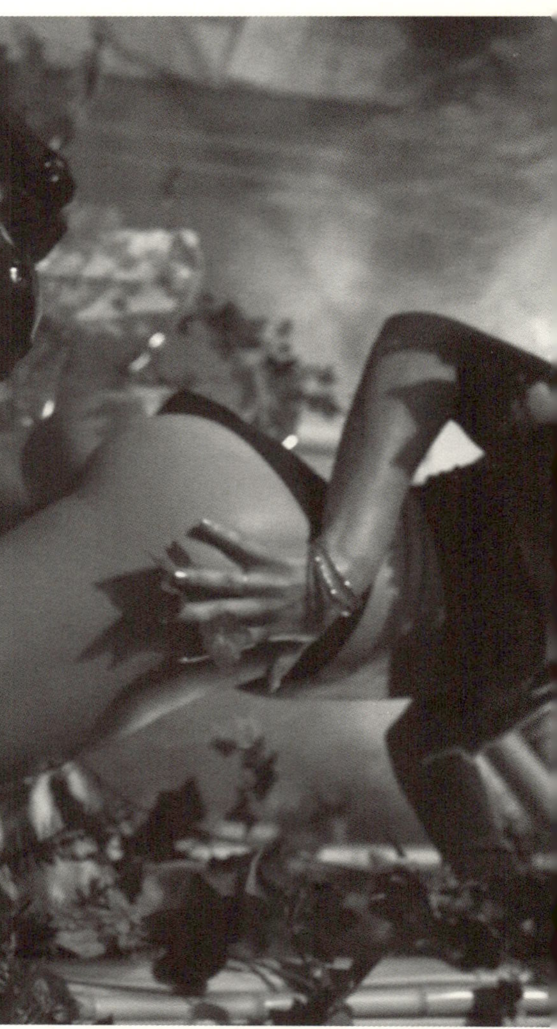

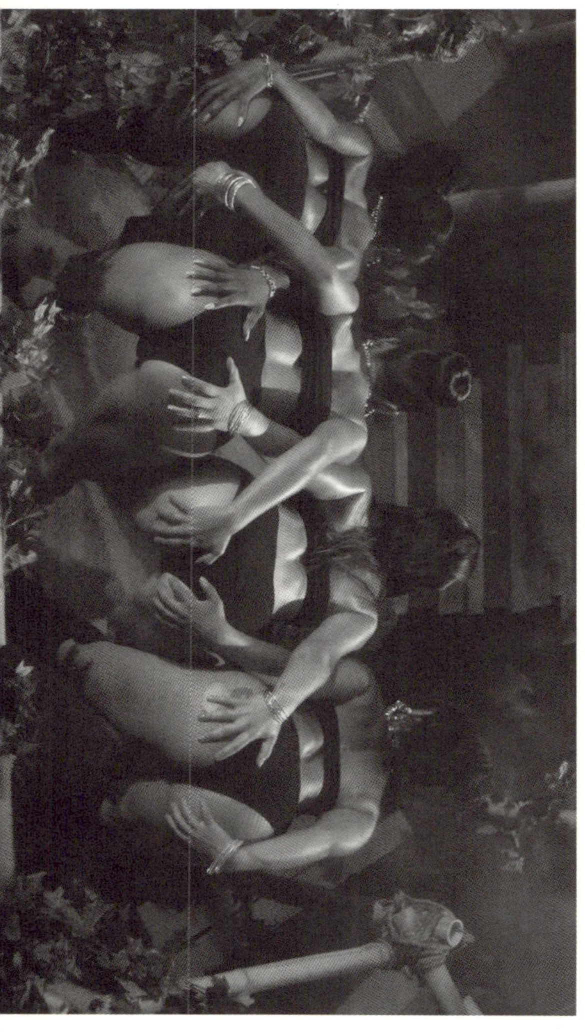

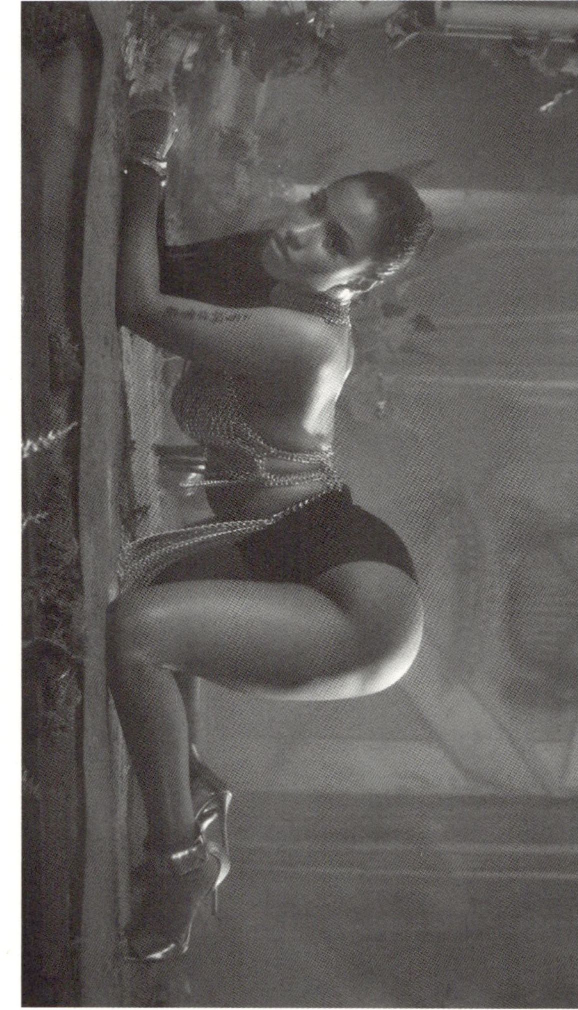

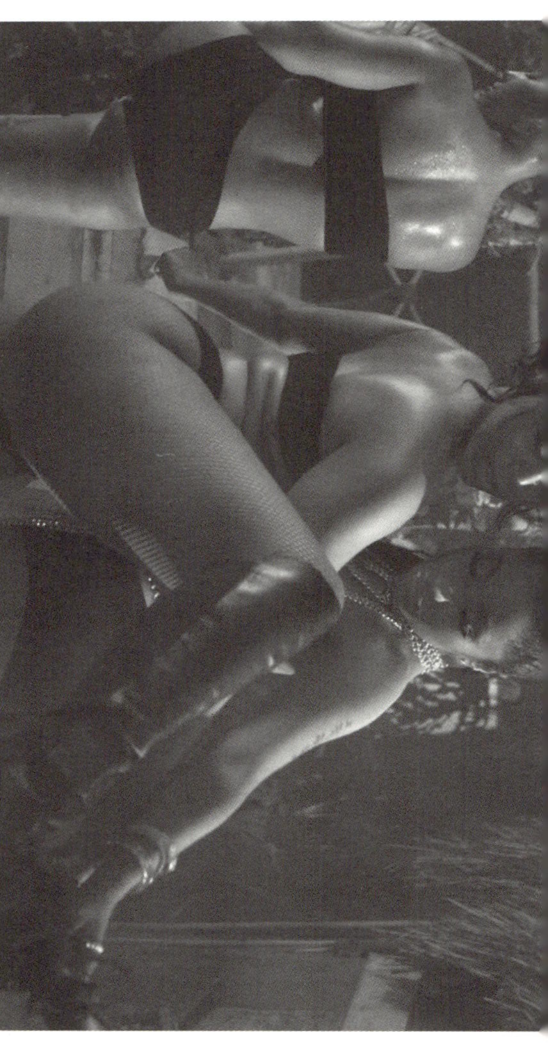

Anaconda, Nicki Minaj, 2014

Anaconda, Nicki Minaj, 2014

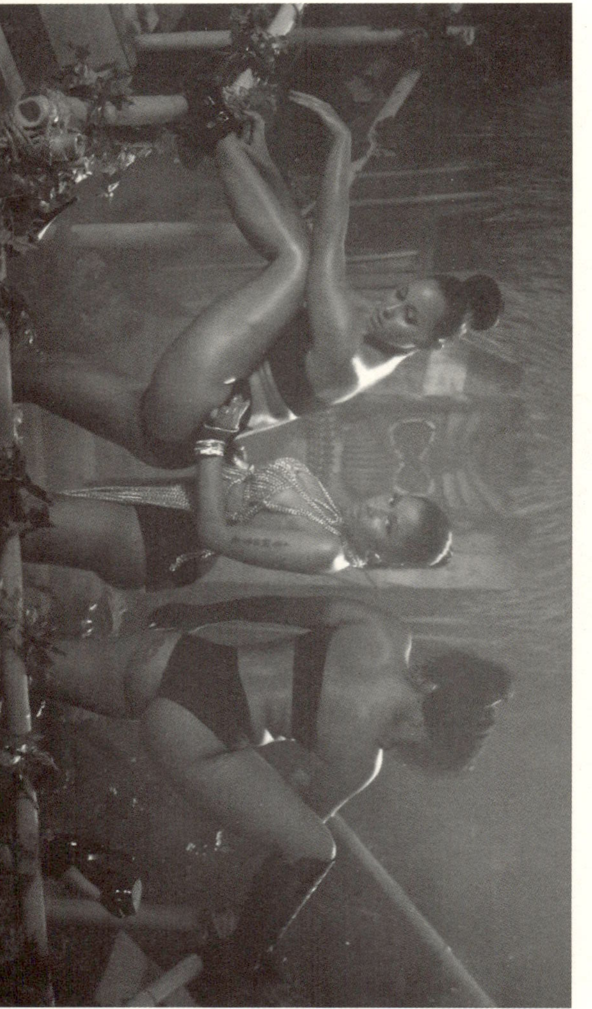

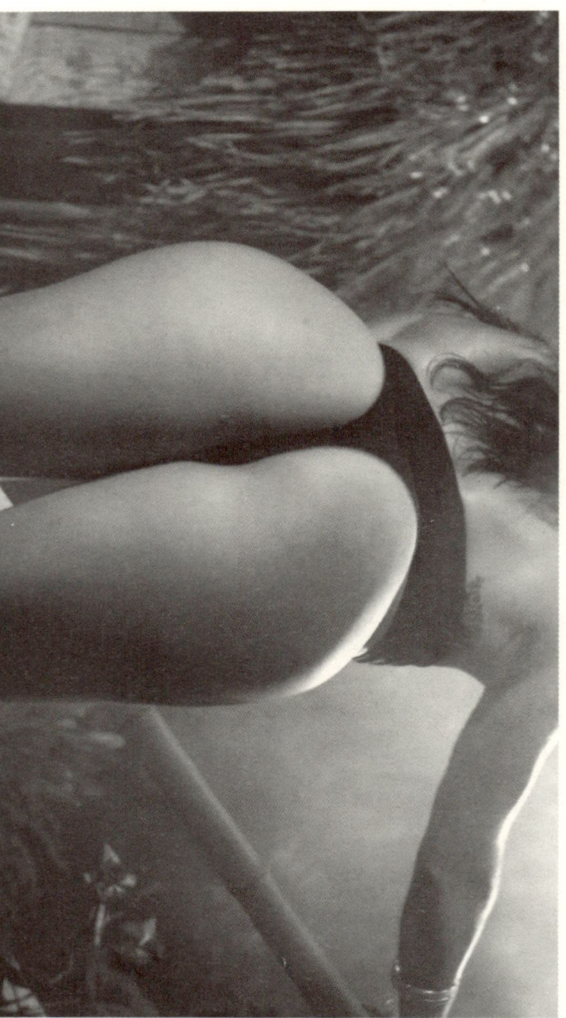

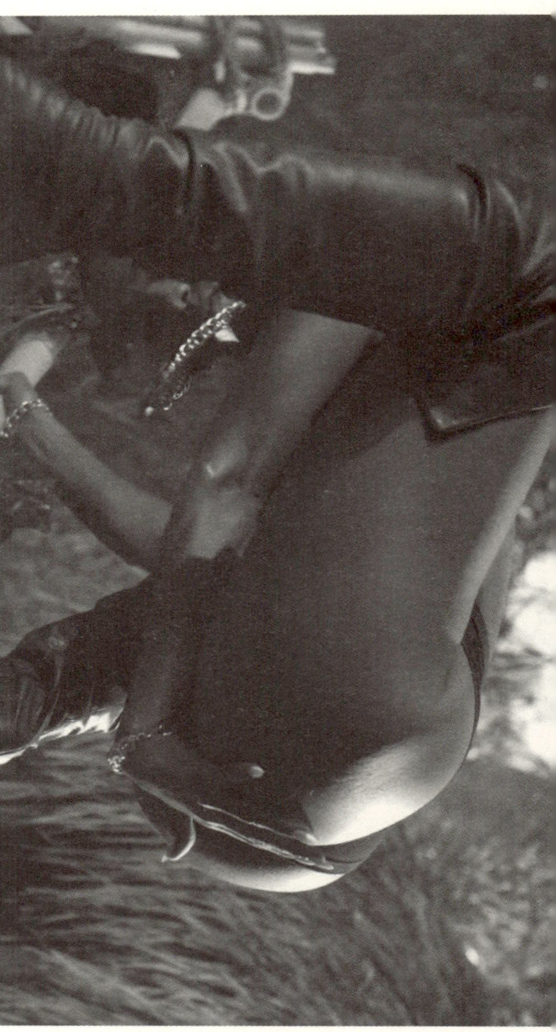

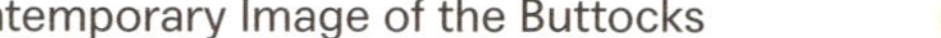

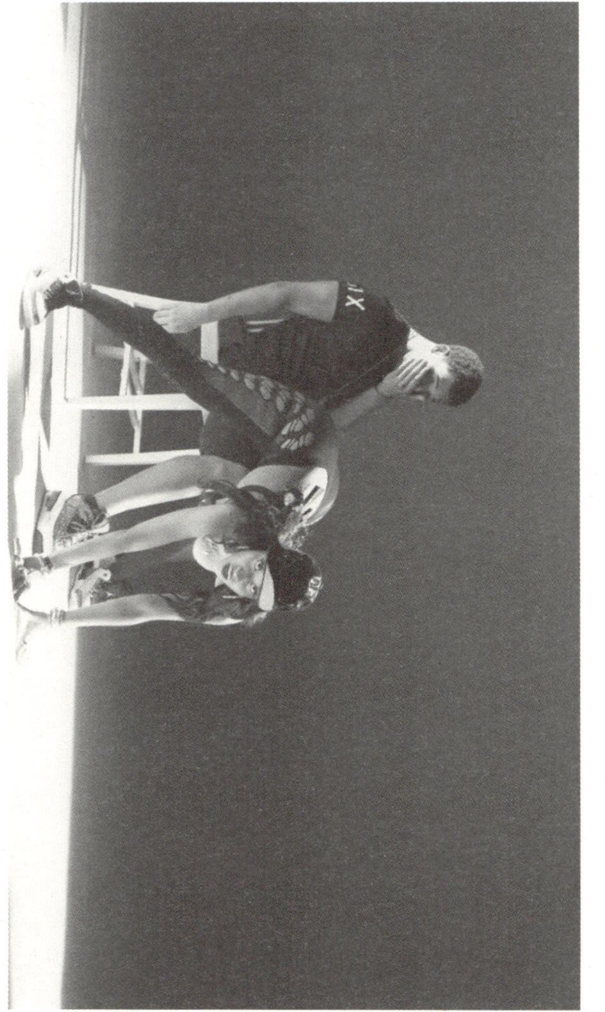


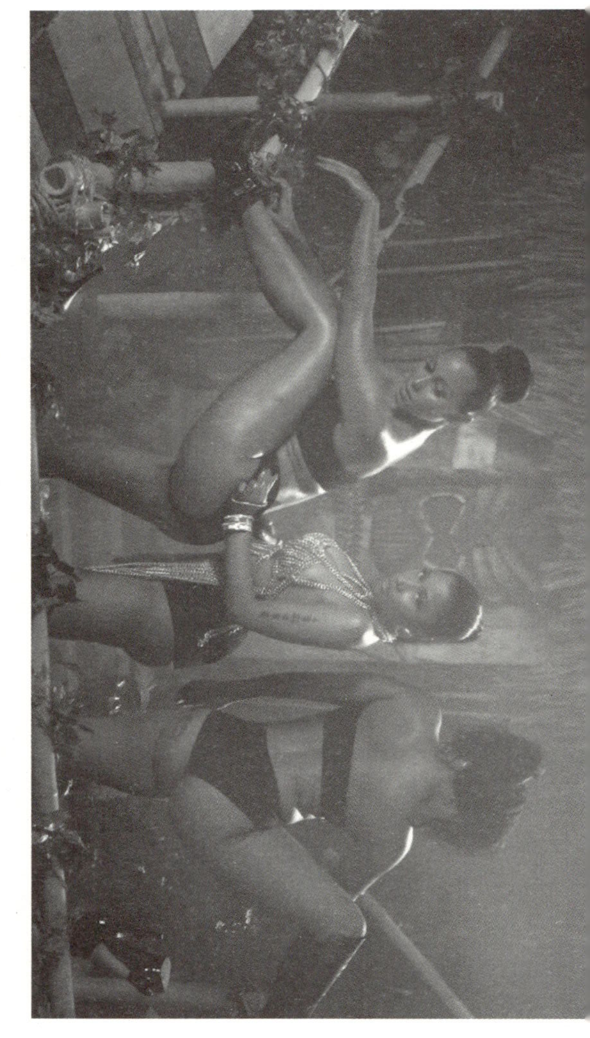



Anaconda, Nicki Minaj, 2014

Booty, Jennifer Lopez Iggy Azalea, 2014

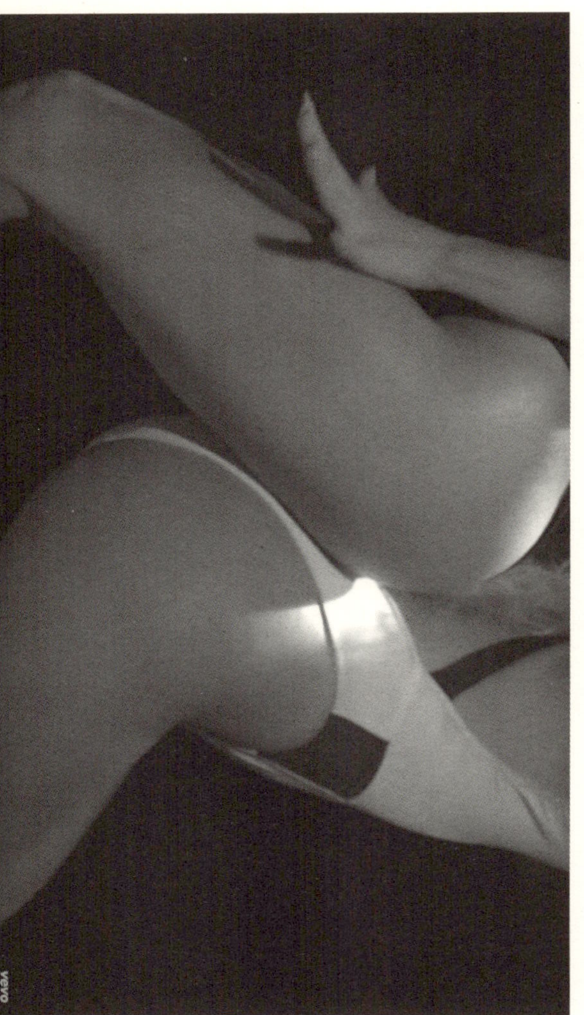


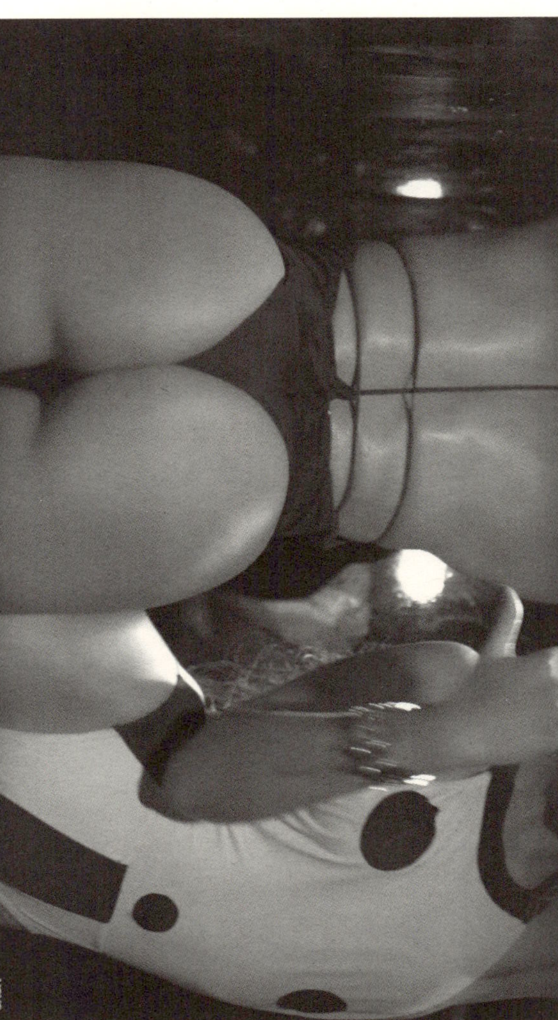


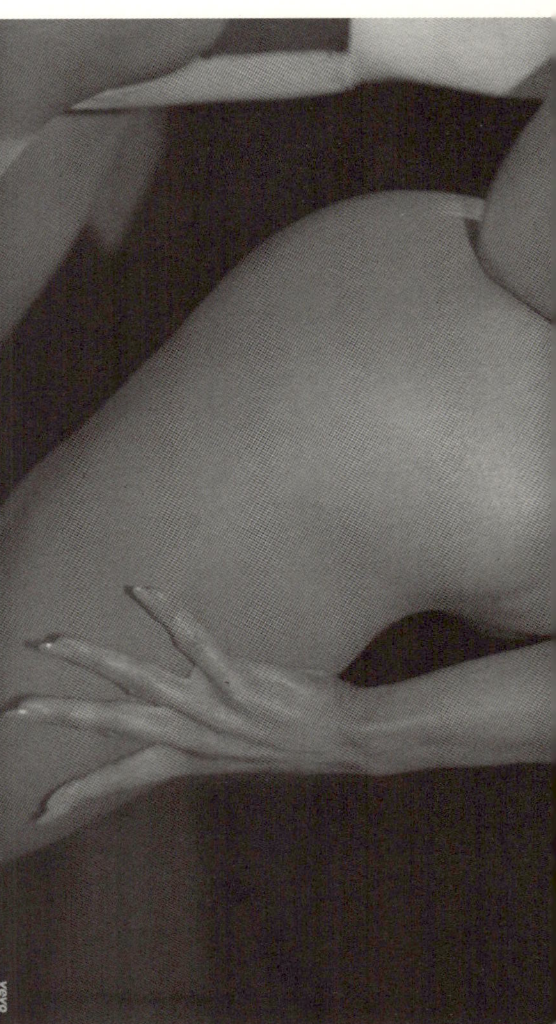

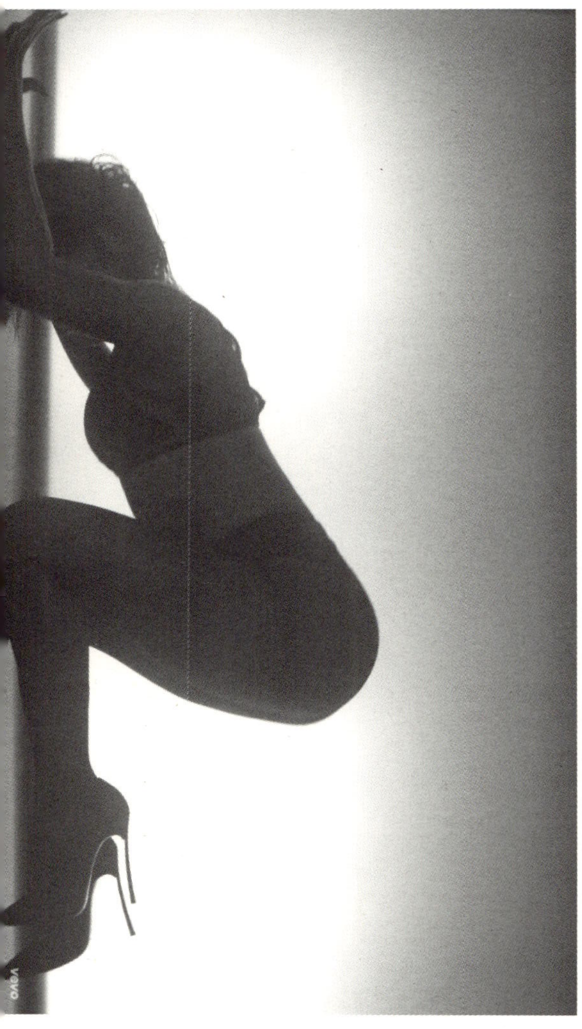


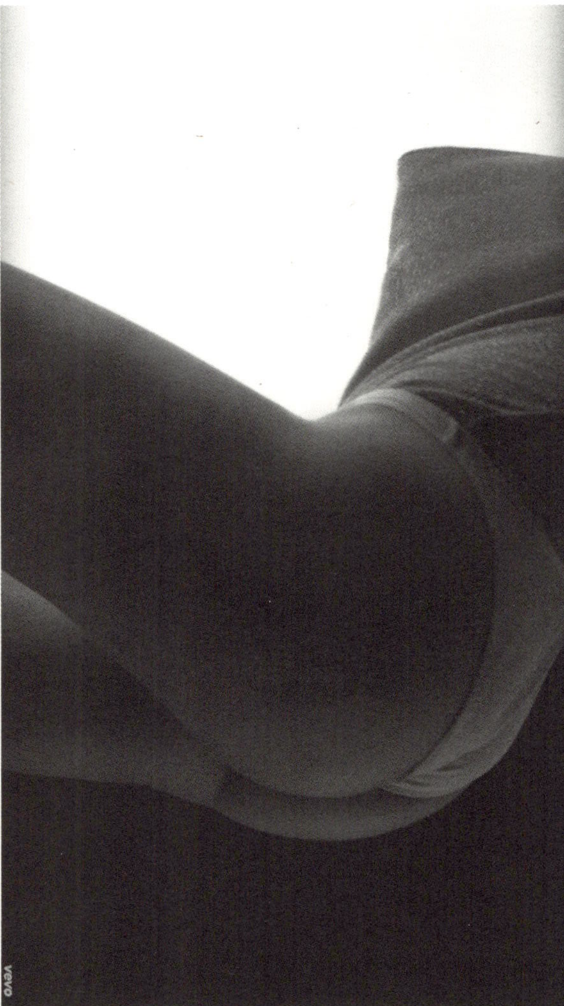




Booty, Jennifer Lopez Iggy Azalea, 2014

Booty, Jennifer Lopez Iggy Azalea, 2014

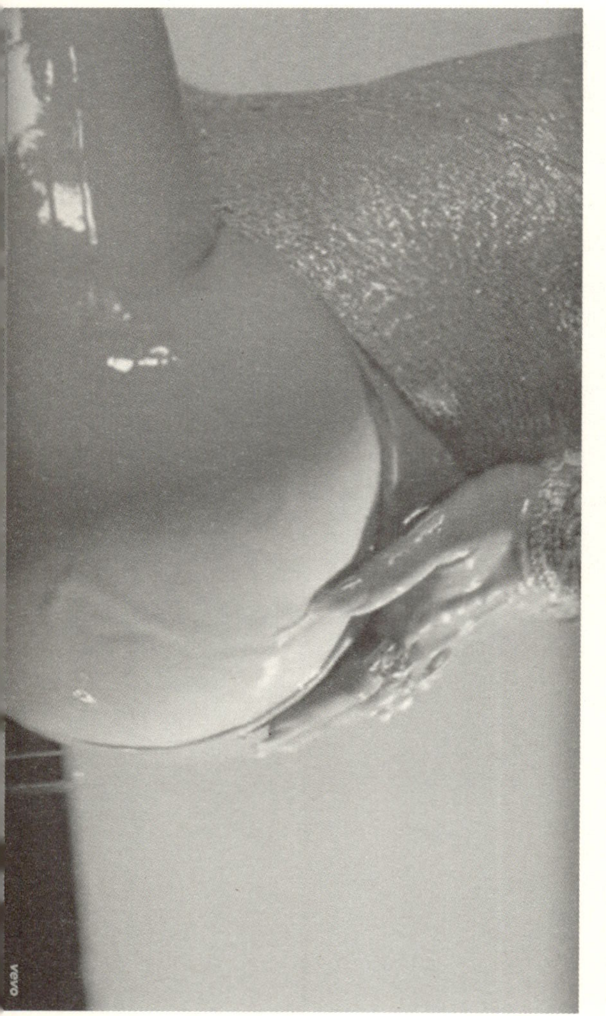

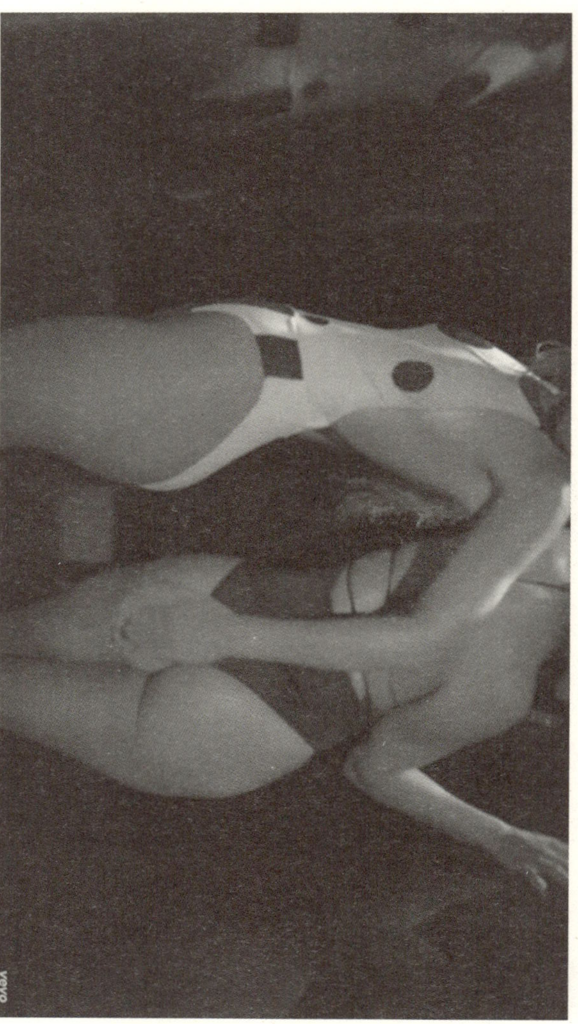

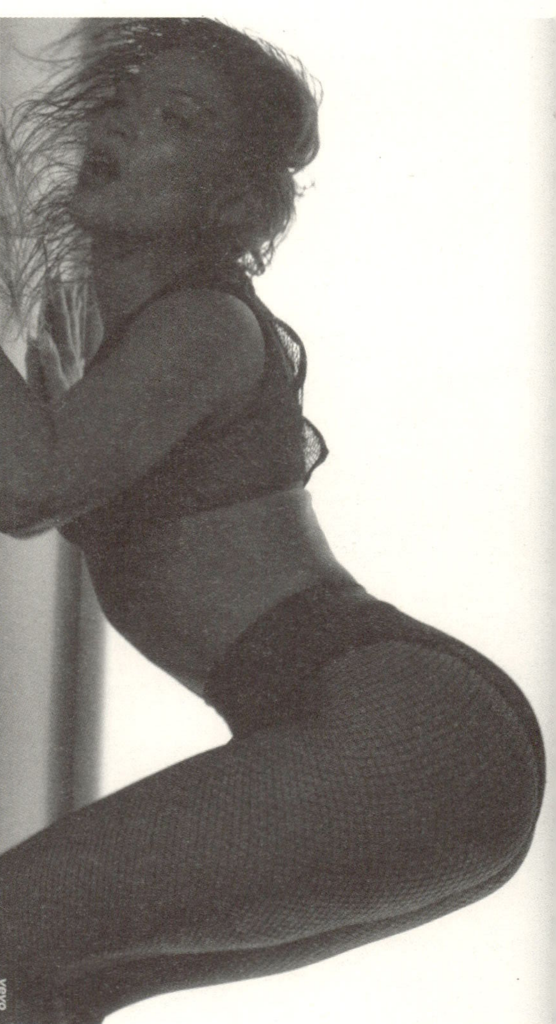

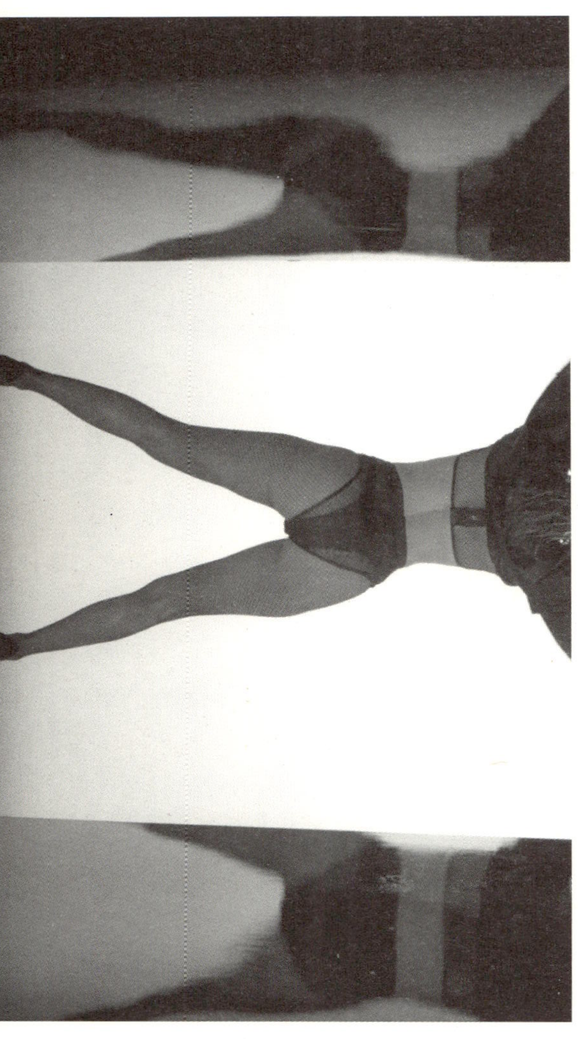

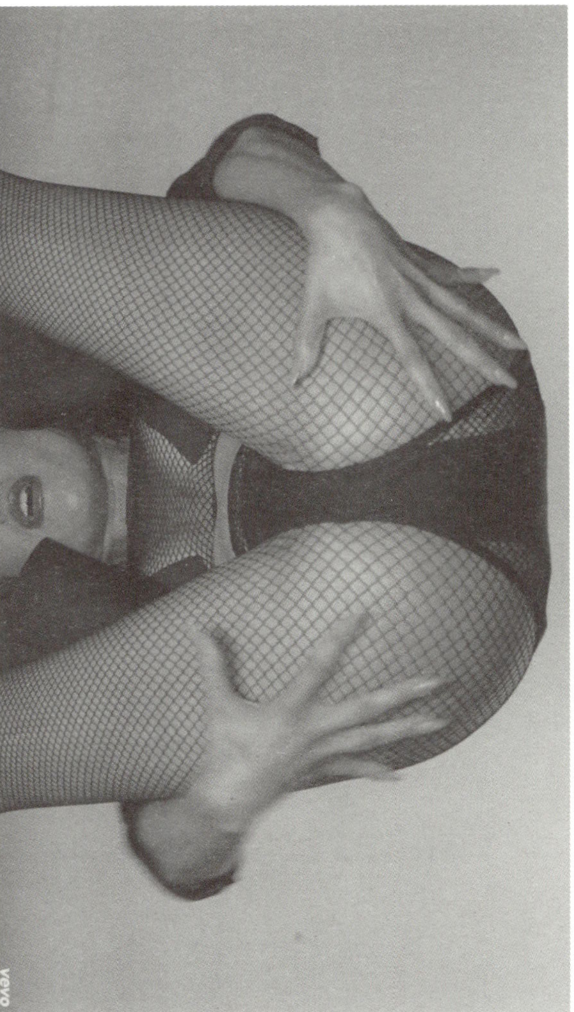

Booty, Jennifer Lopez Iggy Azalea, 2014

Milk, Milk, Lemonade, Amy Schumer, 2015

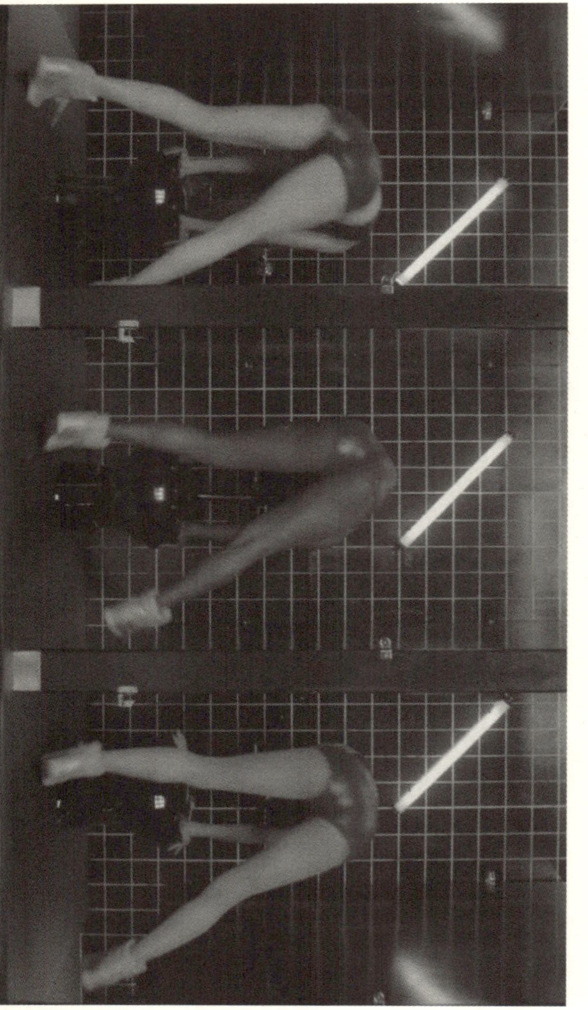

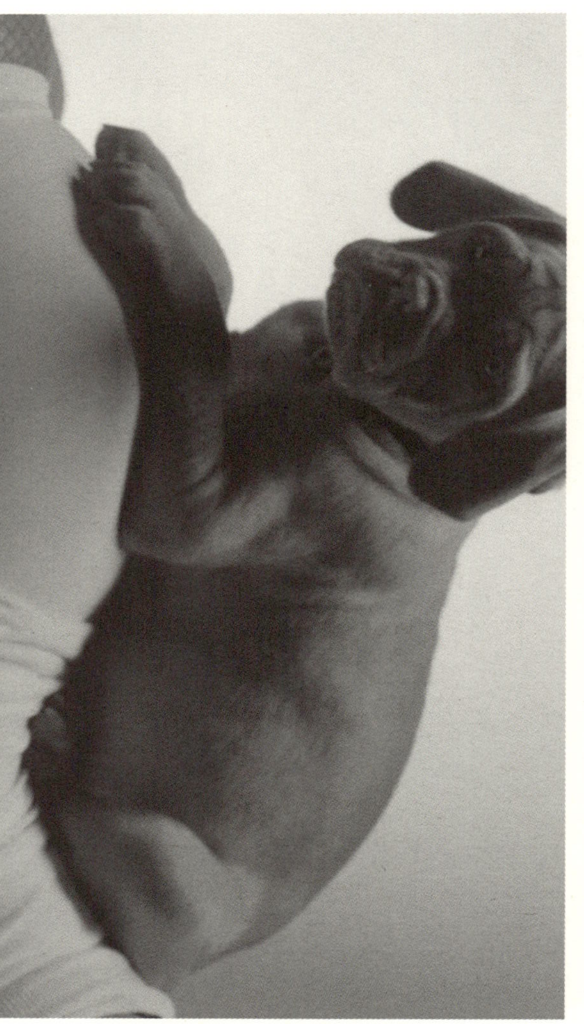

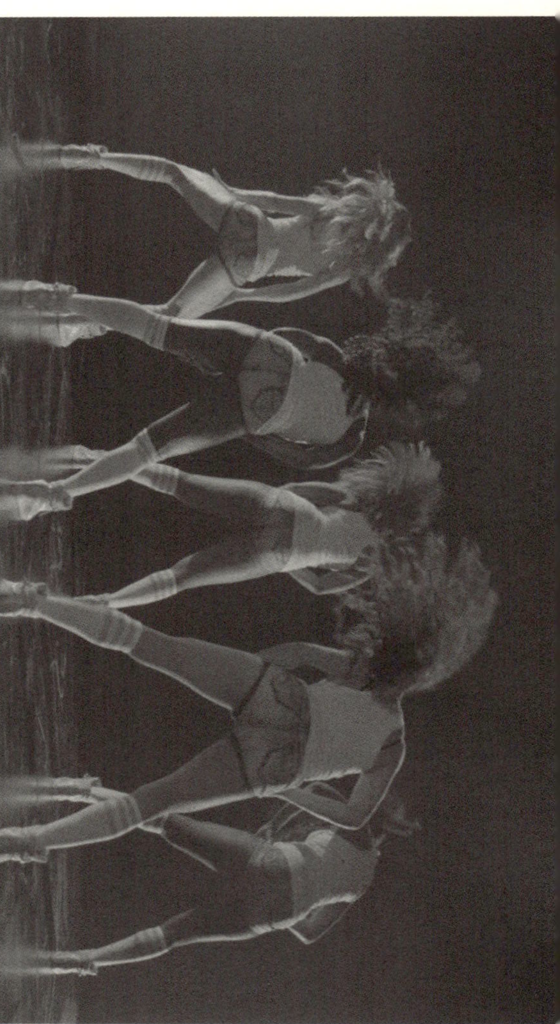

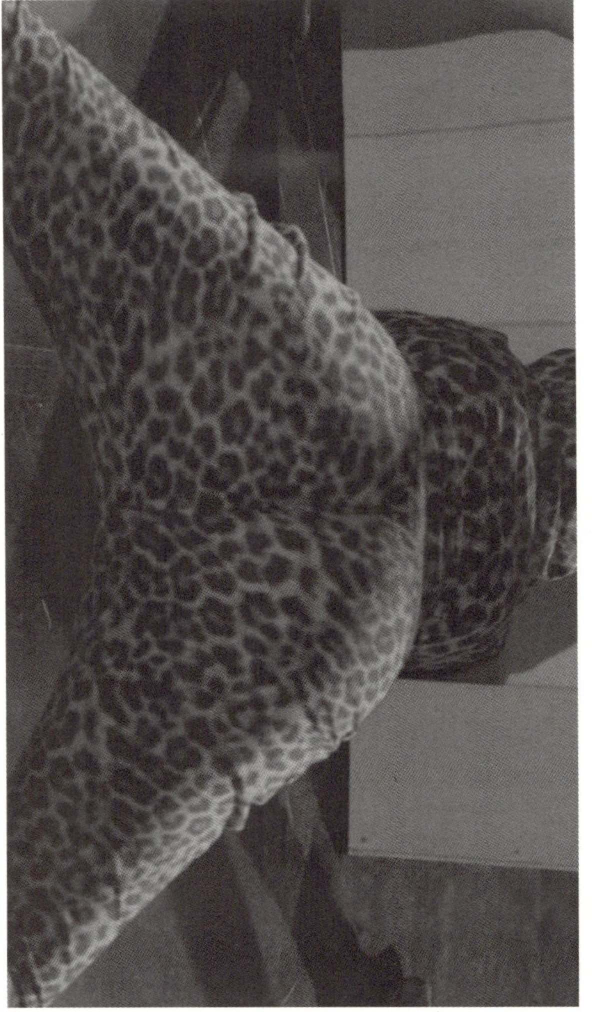

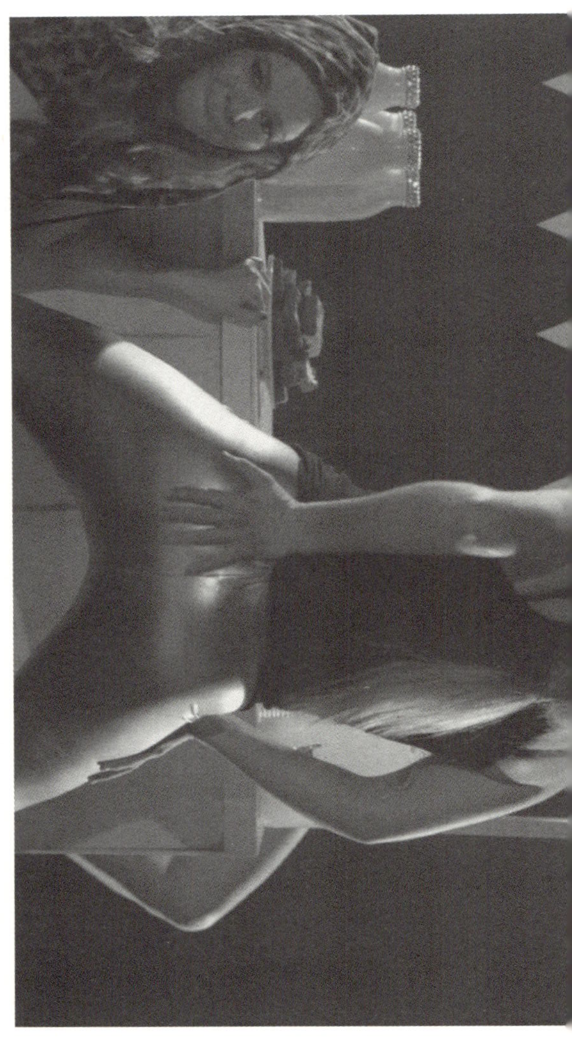

Milk, Milk, Lemonade, Amy Schumer, 2015

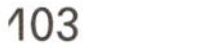

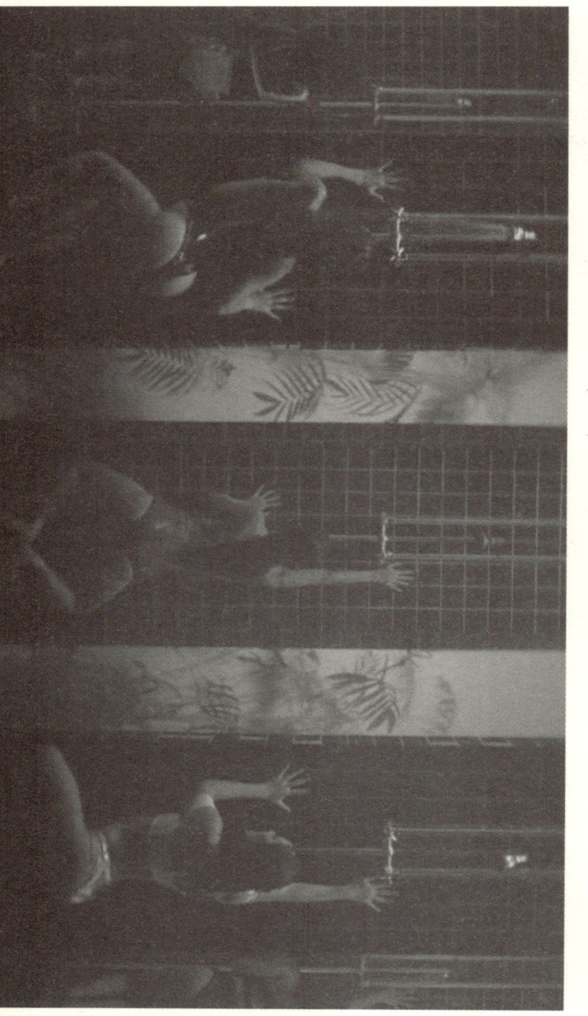

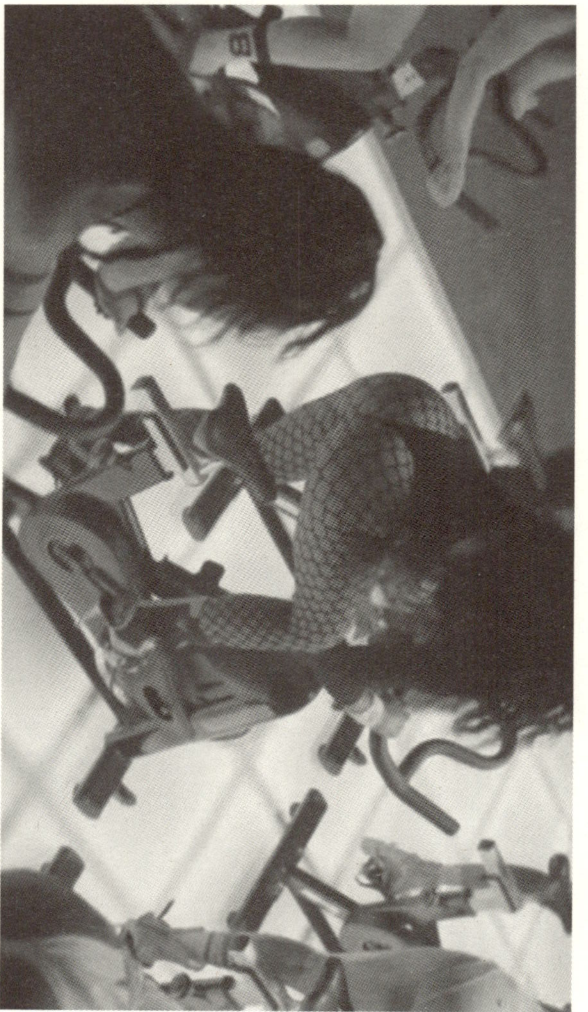

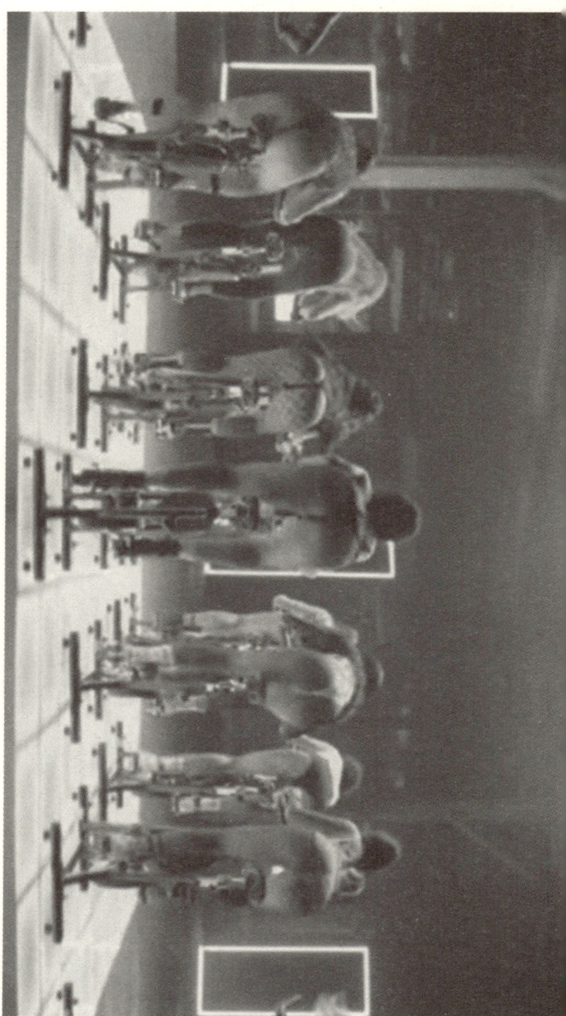

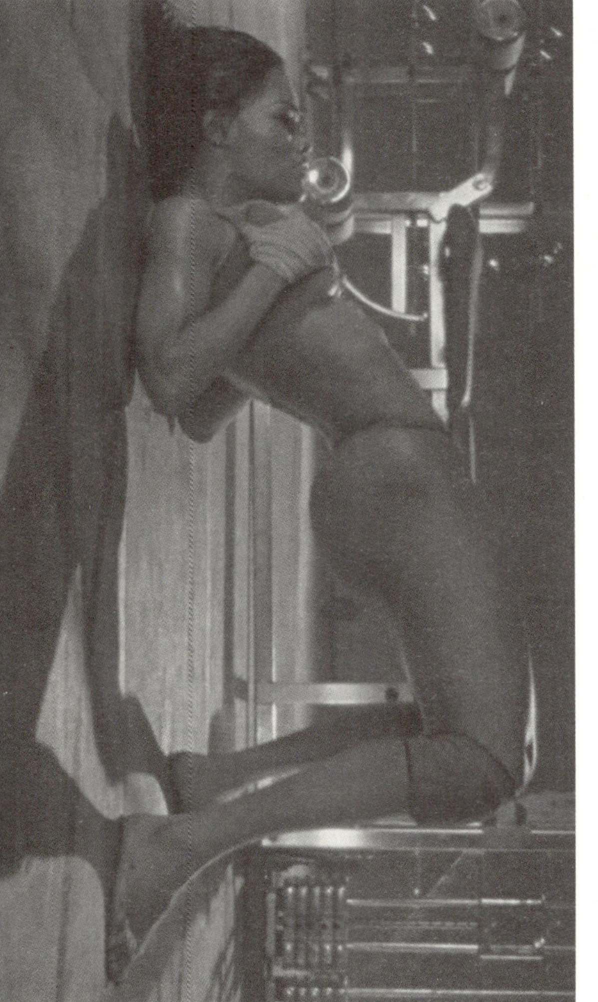
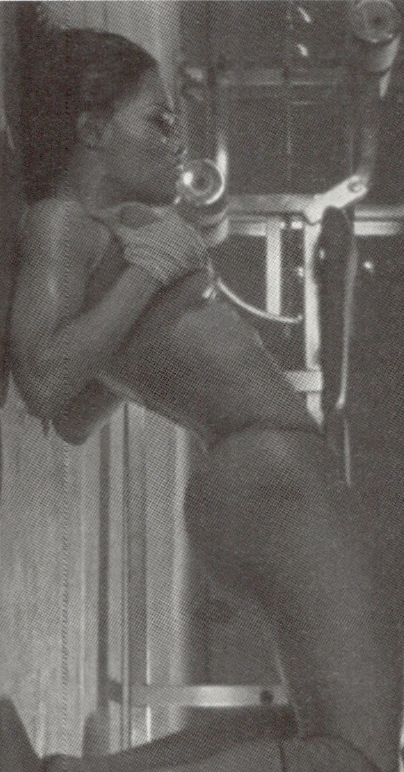
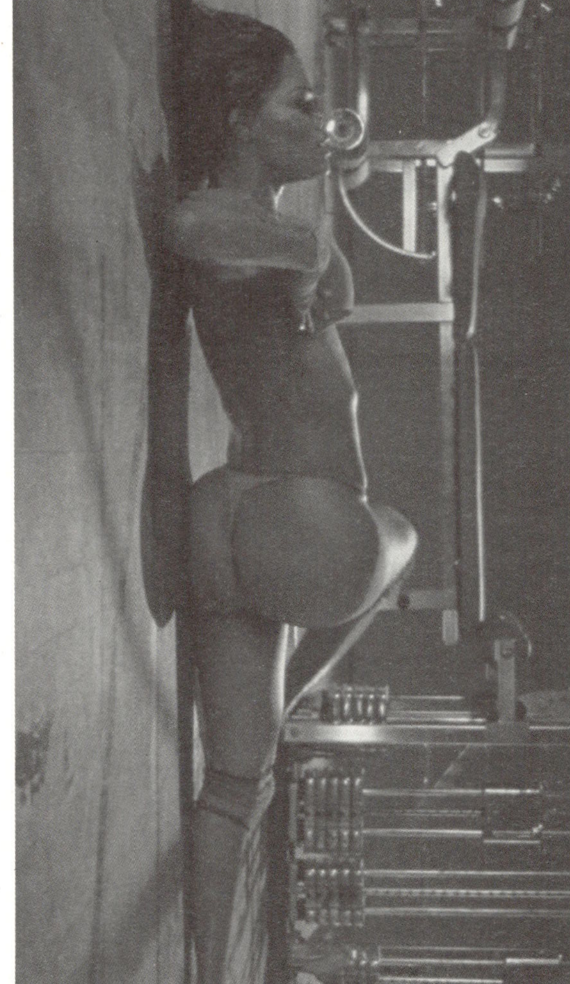
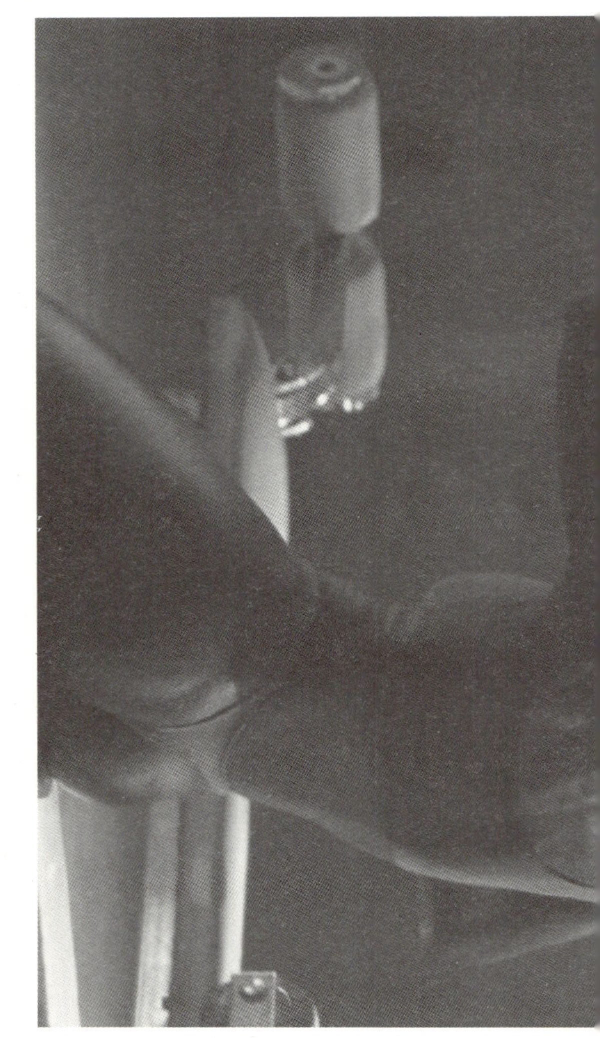

Fade, Kanye West, 2016

Fade, Kanye West, 2016

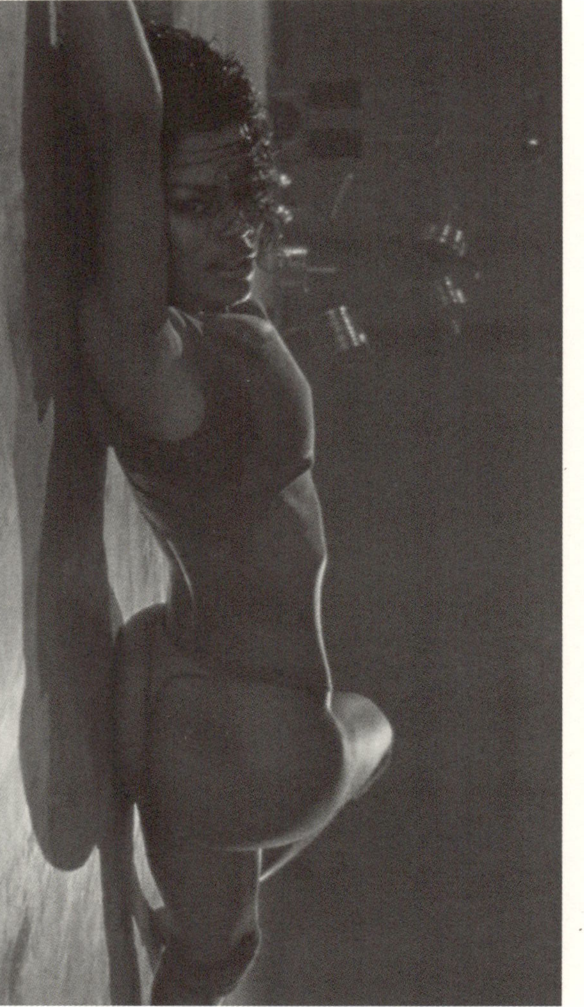

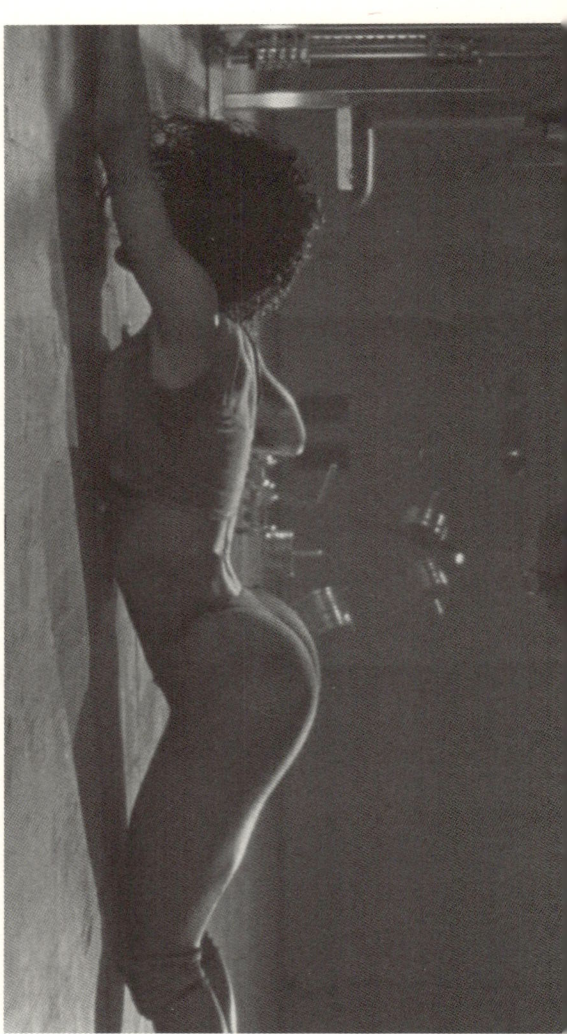

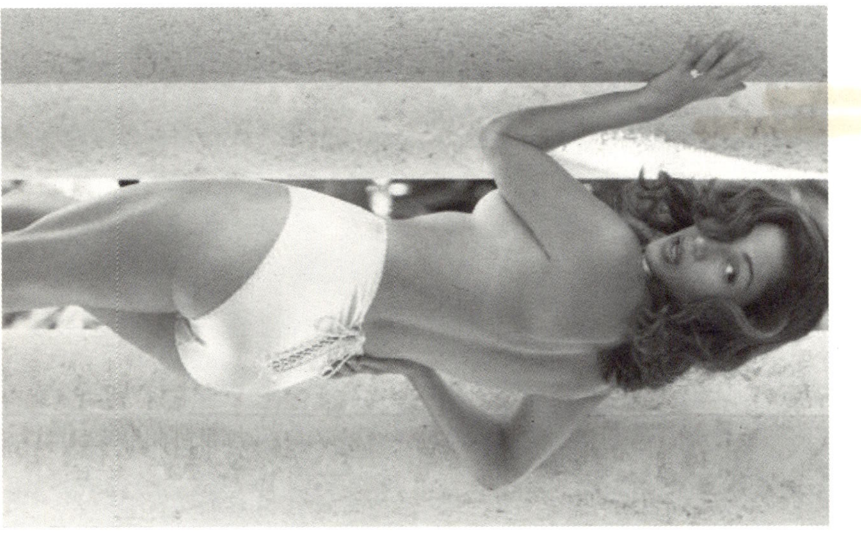

Jennifer Lopez, 1997

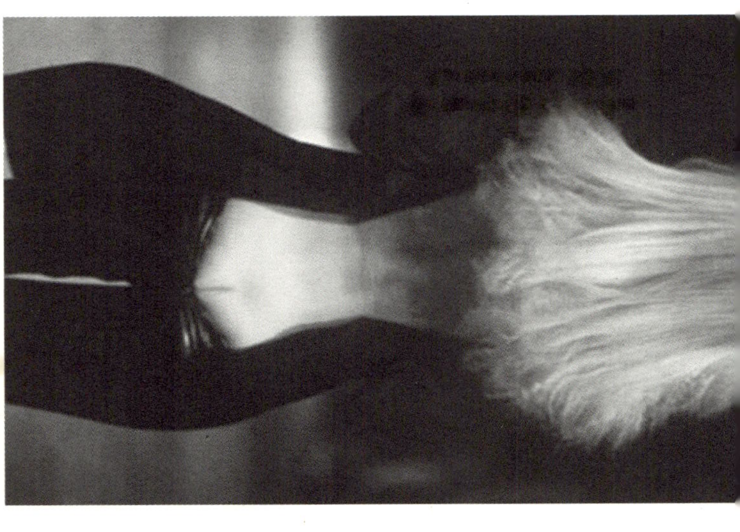

Bumster, Alexander McQueen, 1996

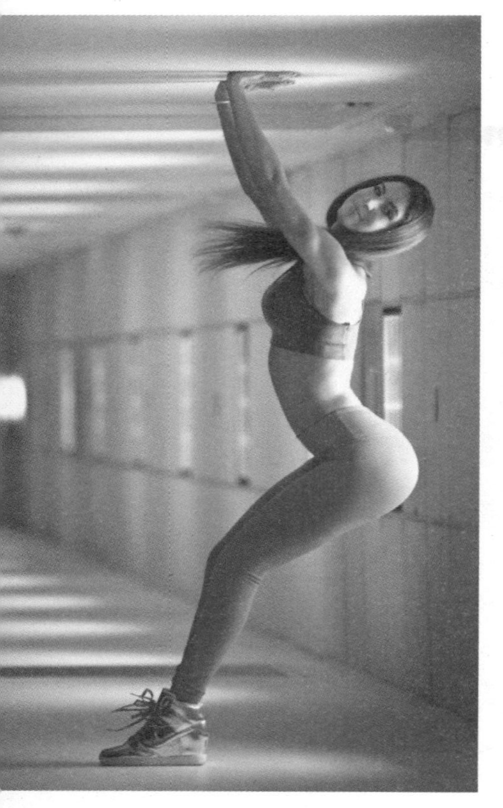

Jen Selter, Instagram, 2011

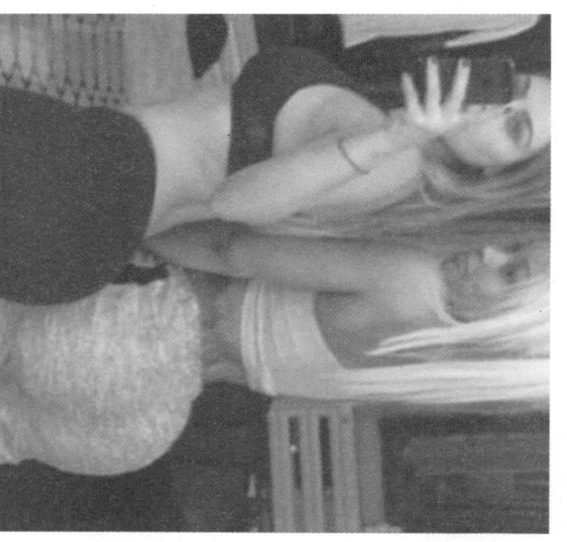

Kim Kardashian, Black China, Instagram, 2010

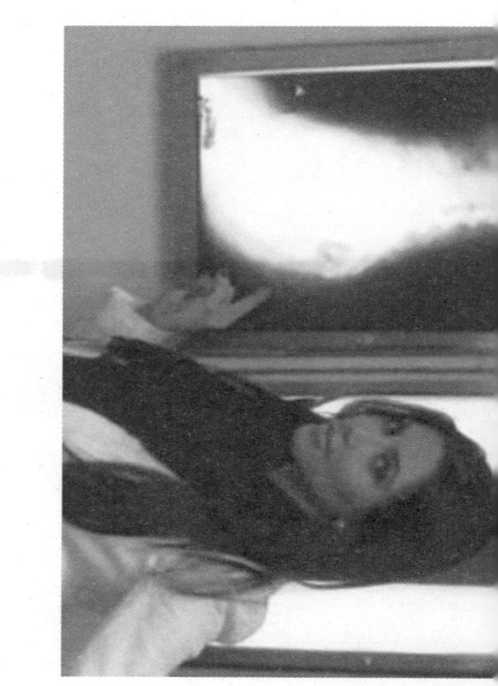

Keeping Up With The Kardashians, 2008

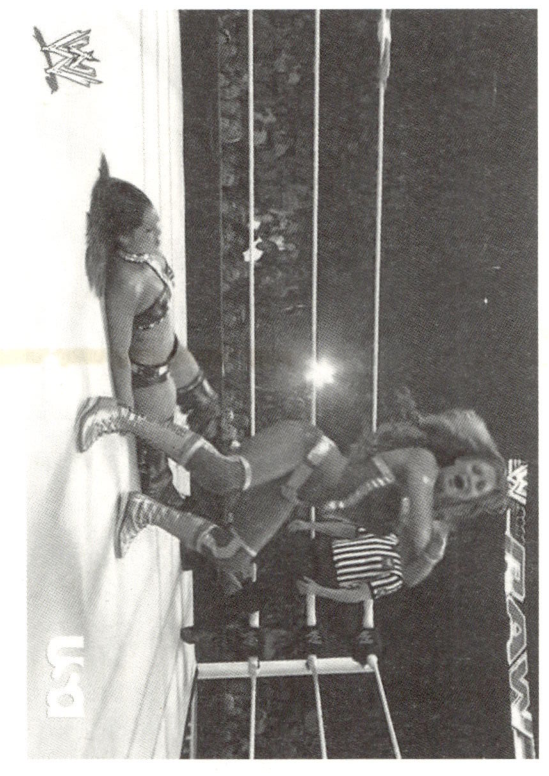


Eve Torres, Smackdown, 2016

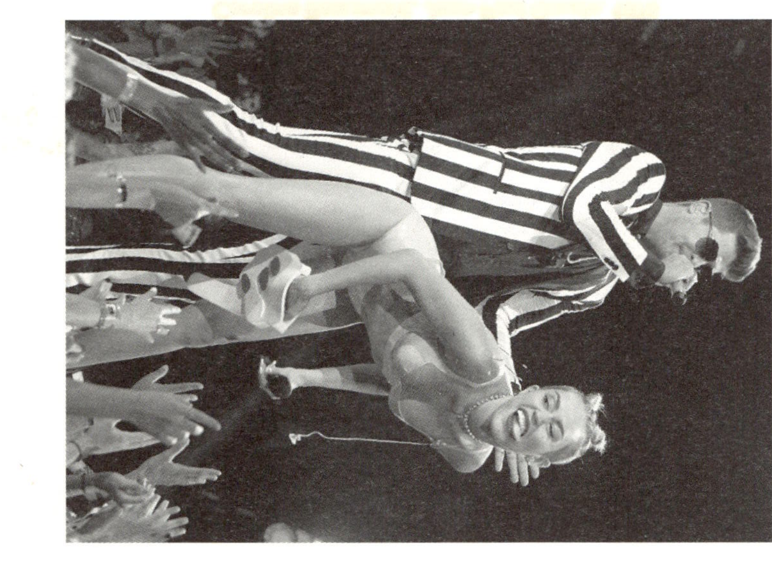

Miley Cyrus, Robin Thicke VMA, 2013

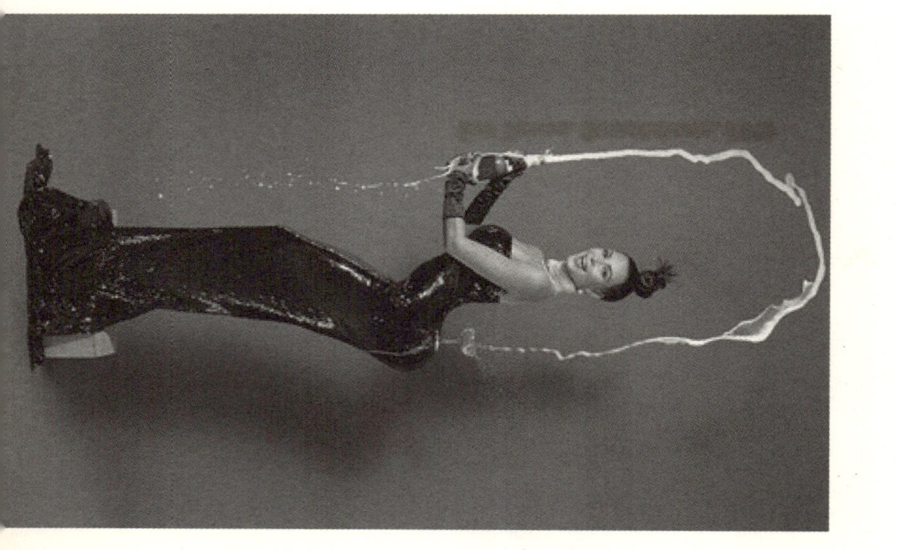

Kim Kardashian, Jean-Paul Goude, 2014

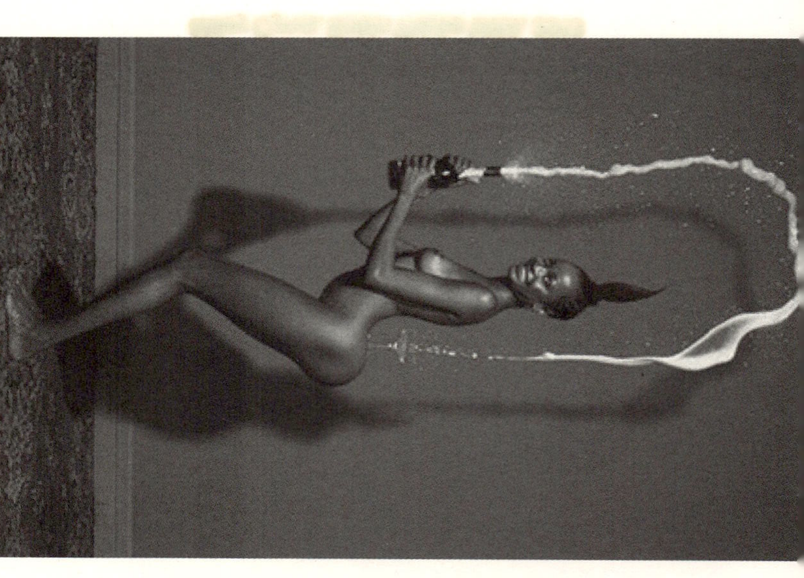

Carolina Beaumont, Jean-Paul Goude, 1976

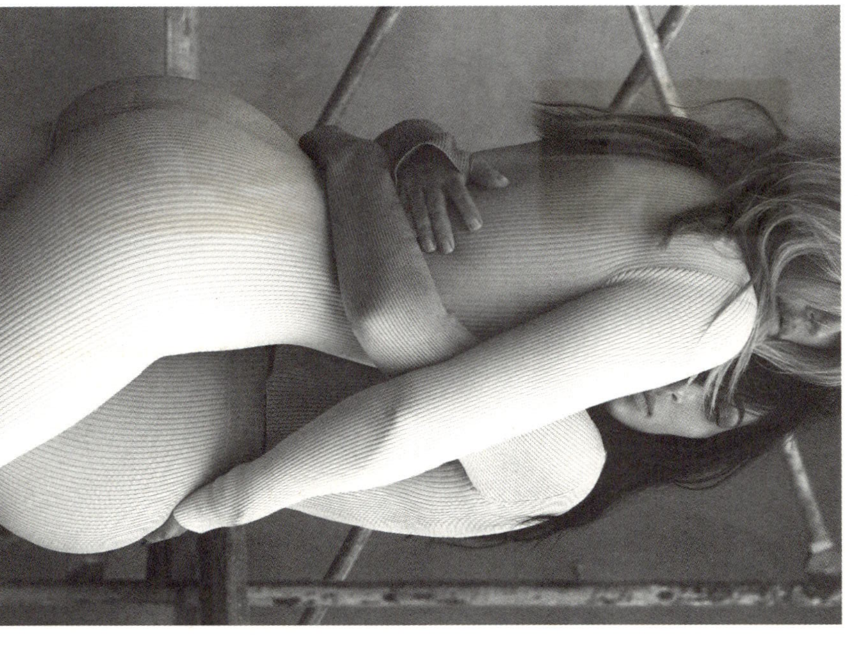

Kim and Khlóe Kardashian wearing Yeezy, for 032c

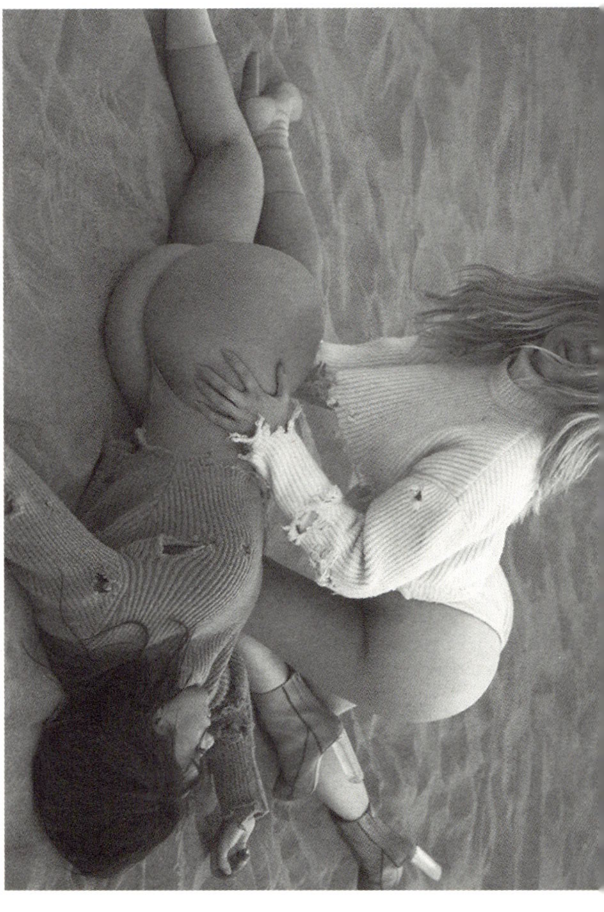

Kim and Khlóe Kardashian wearing Yeezy, for 032c

“We’re officially in the era of the big booty”, was the title of Vogue’s probably most discussed article, published online by Patricia Garcia on the 9th September 2014. The article mentions different events and personas that are responsible for the increasing visibility of buttocks.
She argues that the measurability of the sex appeal of today’s most popular female celebrities is linked to the prominence of their behind. Different fashion statements were made around the breasts, making the nipples acceptable and part of the runway, while the butt remained something “one tried to tame in countless exercise classes”, and something that was traditionally shunned.

In 1996 Alexander McQueen brought the *Bumster* (fig. 1) to the runway, these were pants that had extremely low waists and showed the buttocks like cleavage – inciting a horrified reaction from an unprepared audience. The same happened when actress Rose McGowan attended the 1998 Video Music Awards presenting herself in a transparent dress that showed her entire uncovered back. Many bloggers responded to Patricia Garcia’s article by accusing her of being racist and having a purely “white perspective” on the topic. Nevertheless Patricia Garcia names Jennifer Lopez (fig. 2) responsible for spreading the movement. She was the first in the pop-music scene, that in the late 90s became famous and had this voluminous back part.
For many years she stood out for this feature as other sex symbols of the time like Kate Moss and Britney Spears where famous for slimmer body types. While on the other hand celebrities like Pamela Anderson were artificially enlarging their breasts. Lopez’s behind was unique at that time. “Miss Lopez’s rounded posterior is credited with

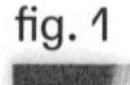

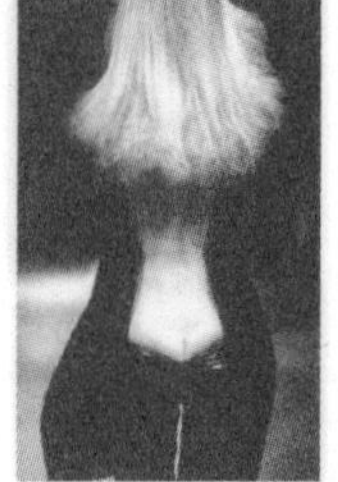

fig. 2

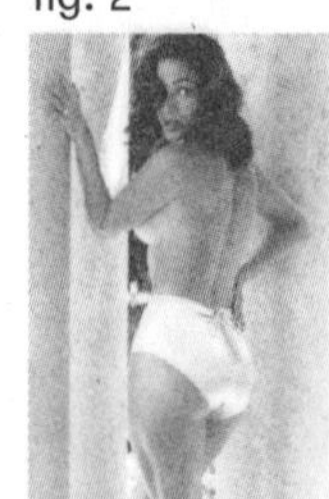

making curvy bottoms trendy again and is said by American plastic surgeons to have created a demand for silicone buttock implants".[1] Jennifer Lopez was able to do so because she represented Latin beauty in general. Cháves Silverman, U.S. Latina writer, explained that "Latin beauty is performed in harmony with prevailing commercial, political and cultural repertoires; these are used to justify hierarchies of race, ethnicity and gender. Binding Latina femininity to bodily excess, sexuality, or indulgence and imbuing Latinidad with a fixed set of traits, values and images." The buttocks in fact, are functioning as a commodity that then fetishise objects by creating an economic desire around them. A desire in which the butt and therefore the body become a material good. Something that women want and can in fact then can buy through a plastic surgery procedure. In *From Bananas to Buttocks,* Myra Mendable speaks about bodies being turned into a market by the social system. They sell goods and ethical values, for example Latinas stand for family values and their image represents the cultural values of South America. She also describes how Latina bodies help sell America's multicultural image: "Ethnic beauty is incorporated – turned into a spectacle of inclusion and participation."[2] This is extremely relevant since the dominant minority in the United States is in fact Latin and not Afro-American, as many might assume. Jennifer Lopez's position as a curvy Latina in the pop-and-music culture generated a debate: As Mary Beltrám argues "To declare beautiful and unashamedly display her well-endowed posterior...could be viewed as nothing less than positive – a revolutionary act with respect to Anglo beauty ideals"[3]. Latinas and their curves have become a symbol of ethnic pride.

1. M. Mendible, From Bananas to Buttocks: The Latina Body in Popular Film and Culture, Austin, University of Texas Press, 2007, p. 1

2. M. Mendible, From Bananas to Buttocks: The Latina Body in Popular Film and Culture, Austin, University of Texas Press, 2007, p. 13

3. M. Mendible, From Bananas to Buttocks: The Latina Body in Popular Film and Culture, Austin, University of Texas Press, 2007, p. 2

As the writer Maria Figueroa puts it, Jennifer Lopez "reclaims and redefines Latina body from its 'fat', 'undesirable', and 'marginal' status, thus rescuing this body and transforming it into a body 'that matters'."[4] It can be said that Lopez has singlehandedly ushered in the butt focus that is now such a part of contemporary U.S. popular culture, and therefore has intervened in the coeds of beauty and modern femininity.
Her butt represents an ethnic difference and even though she positioned herself in a Latin cultural stereotype she was able to influence the whole of hip-hop. To have a more complete overview of the phenomenon it is best to look first at a more recent history of the music industry. The contemporary story of the buttocks is actually defined by the songs, lyrics and images that conquered first the music scene and then the entire world. Already in 1961 the track *Shake Your Moneymaker* by Elmore James became a blues classic. Even though no kind of provocative images were produced, the lyrics were a strong statement at that time. In the late 70s other songs emerged like Queen's *Fat Bottomed Girls* and KC and the Sunshine Band's *Shake Your Booty*. While their music videos were focusing exclusively on the bands themselves, they made statements like Queen's "Heap big woman you made a bad boy out of me".

4. M. Mendible, From Bananas to Buttocks: The Latina Body in Popular Film and Culture, Austin, University of Texas Press, 2007, p. 2

In 1989 *Da Butt* from E.U. (Experience Unlimited) came out as the official sound track for Spike Lee's movie *School Daze*. The music video and the movie were shot on the same set, a historically black college, an institution of higher education in the United States, established for the African American community. At the beginning of the clip Spike Lee himself is introducing the dance style that goes with his movie, he calls it 'Da Butt'.

As the name promises the butt is specifically framed and pointed out in many shots.
Several scenes show a classroom full of dancing students, who also shake their asses in the corridors and on tables. The movie as well the music video were touching upon issues of racism within the African-American community.
In a particular verse of the song it defends bigger shaped women:

**Walked in this place, surprised to see**
**A big girl gettin' busy, just rockin'**
**to the go-go beat**
**The way she shook her booty sho'**
**looked good to me**
**I said, 'Come here, big girl,**
**won't you rock my world?**
**Show that dance to me'**

Yet more provocative was the breakthrough song: *Baby got Back* written by American rapper "Sir Mix-a-Lot" in 1992. The song had the most explicit lyrics and imagery so far. In the music video the rapper is dancing on an enormous plastic landscape made out of buttock-mountains. African American women with big posteriors were shown from behind for most of the video. It's also interesting to note the visual references to Josephine Baker and her banana skirt.
One particularity is found at the beginning of the video where two white girls are looking at the woman who has started dancing in the clips – they look on and judge. This is what one is saying to the other:

**Oh, my, god. Becky,**
**loot at her butt. It is so big.**
**She looks like one of**
**those rap guys' girlfriends.**

**But, you know,**
**who understands those rap guys?**
**They only talk to her, because, she looks like**
**a total prostitute, 'kay?**
**I mean, her butt, is just so big.**
**I can't believe it's just so round, it's like,**
**out there, I mean–gross. Look!**
**She's just so...black!**
**I'm tired of magazines**
**Saying' flat butts are the thing**
**Take the average black an**
**and ask him that...**

**I like 'em round, and big**
**And when I'm throwing' a gig**
**I just can't help myself, I'm actin' like**
**an animal...**
**I ain't talkin' bout Playboy**
**'Cause silicone parts are made for toys**
**I want 'em real thick and juicy**
**So find that juicy double...**

**So I'm looking' at rock videos**
**Knock–needed bios walkin' like hoes**
**I'll keep my women like Flo Jo...**

**My anaconda don't want non**
**Unless you've got buns, hun**
**You can side bends or sit–ups,**
**But please don't lose that butt...**

The song is clearly rejecting the stereotypical image of the white skinny woman that was celebrated on every magazine cover, in every movie and in most ad campaigns. It claimed space for the Afro-American beauty. The song was an enormous success and in 1992 it sold 2,392,000 copies. In the same year the song *Rumpshake* from Wreckx-n-Effect triumphed with the glorification of the booty, it celebrated the female behind with a video on the beach that included colourful bikinis. It took quite a few years for the music industry to come up with something comparable when finally in 2000 Mystikal released their first single *Shake Yaa Ass*. The clear statement of the chorus makes this song another hymn for the Afro-American posterior:

**Attention all y'all players and pimps**
**Right now in the place to be**
**(shake ya ass)**
**I thought I told y'all niggas before**
**Y'all naggers can't fuck with me**
**(watch yourself)**
**Now this ain't for no small booties**
**No sir cause that won't pass**
**(show me watcha workin with)**
**But if you fell you got the biggest one**
**Them momma come shake ya ass**

In 1993, DJ Jubile invented twerking. In the song *Do the Jubilee All*, he introduced the word in the lyrics as well as the movements in his music video. In the clip there is no objectification of the dancers. For moment he is twerking by himself, other rappers even slap him while he's dancing and his butt covers almost the entire screen. The camera is supporting his movements with abrupt zooming. The lyrics say:

**Shake baby,**
**shake baby,**
**shake, shake, shake,**
**shake baby,**
**shake, shake, shake**

**Twerk baby,**
**twerk baby,**

**twerk, twerk, twerk,
twerk baby,
twerk, twerk, twerk**

Almost at the end of the song there are also female dancers shaking their booties. One girl in particular in twerking and her butt fills most parts of the screen. The lyrics referring to that specific scene say:

**Shake it like a dog,
shake it like a dog,
uh uh, shake it like a dog,
shake it like dog, uh!**

The real difference was the impact that Destiny's Child (the band that was responsible for Beyoncé's break through) had with the song *Bootylicious.* For the first time, in 2001, the perspective changed and it was not a man singing about female body parts and objectifying them. The song was from a women's perspective, encouraging themselves to be proud of their shapes. The interesting part of the song is when it recognises that it was clearly too early for the "conquest of the Butt", and the song is teasing with this acknowledgment. Almost like a diplomatic statement preparing the audience for what is about to come.

**Kelly, can you handle this?
Michelle, can you handle this?
Beyoncé, can you handle this?
I don't think they can handle this!**

**I don't think you are ready for this jelly
I don't think you are ready for this jelly
I don't think you are ready for this
Cause my booty too bootylicious for ya babe**

In fact it took another decade before the buttocks became the ultimate standard for beauty.
Still, singing and rapping about posteriors became more normal and acceptable, and each year more and more songs appeared.
Like in 2003 with the Ying Yang Twins' *Salt Shaker* and in 2014 Eminem's *Ass Like That;* which was a track also portraying voluptuous European and Asian women.

**The way you shake it, I can't believe it**
**I ain't never seen an ass like that**
**The way you move it,**
**you make my pee pee go**
**Doing, doing, doing**

Within its lyrics Eminem goes further by referring to famous celebrities, by paying them backhanded compliments about their behinds.

**Jessica Simpson, looks oh so temptin'**
**Nick I ain't never seen an ass like that**
**Every time I see that show on MTV**
**my pee pee goes**
**Doing, doing, doing**

**So Gwen Stefani, will you pee pee**
**on me please?**
**I ain't never seen an ass like that**
**Cuz the way you move it,**
**make my pee pe go**
**Doing, doing, doing**

The Jamaican rapper Sean Paul also released his song *Get Busy* in 2003. The lyrics as well as the clip brought –aside from the strong Jamaican slang– some of the island's culture, dance moves and body aesthetics. While this was happening in the spot light, the underground culture was already a few steps ahead. In 2000 the national recognition of twerking came with the song *Whistle While You Twerk* from duo Ying Yang Twins. Also in her 2005 single, *Check on It* Beyoncé sings about the famous dance move:

**Oh boy you looking like you like what you see**
**Won't you come over and check up on it,**
**I' don't let you work up on it**
**Ladies let em check up on it,**
**watch it while he check up on it**
**Dip it, pop ti, twerk it, stop it,**
**check on me tonight**

Finally, in 2006, with *Sexy Back* by Justin Timberlake the posterior breaks out of the hip hop and r&b scene. The song, in fact, has a rock attitude and as Timberlake revealed in an interview, the intention was to cover James Brown's song *Sex Machine* using the style of David Bowie and David Byrne.

In 2007 with her truly singular figure, Kim Kardashian and her family debuted their reality show, *Keeping Up With The Kardashians*.
While the whole family became famous, like a designer product, the actual star of the show was Kim's behind. Her ass was frequently used as a plot device, and in one episode she even X-rayed her body (fig. 3) to prove that her curves were real and that she didn't have implants: as it was popularly speculated at the time. It was also for the first time that somebody outside of the music scene was attracting this much attention with this specific body part. Then in 2010 Instagram was launched and it was just another platform for presenting Kim's already famous butt, which she of course used to her advantage. The picture of her and Black China (fig. 4)

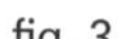
fig. 3

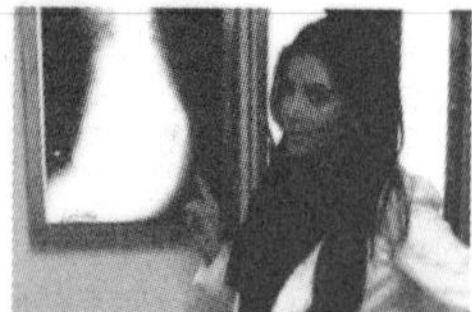

fig. 4

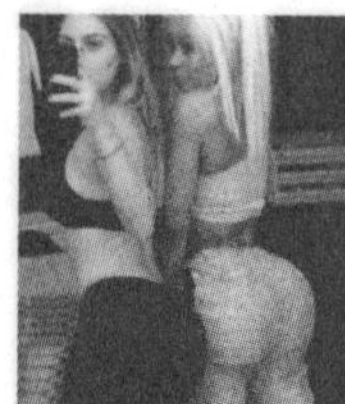

displaying their booties after working out generated over 600,000 likes. Instagram is the perfect platform for this type of self publicity and it launched many different famous booties. Its peculiarity is that it also allows the public to become famous. One example is Jen Selter, (fig. 5) a young girl who shaped her backside through sport, and who now has eleven million followers. We can now see 2011 as the official beginning of the "Booty Era". A Google trend research reveals in fact, that the interest in the word *twerk* peaked in November of that year. Twerking started to become popular and was adopted as a dance style.

fig. 5

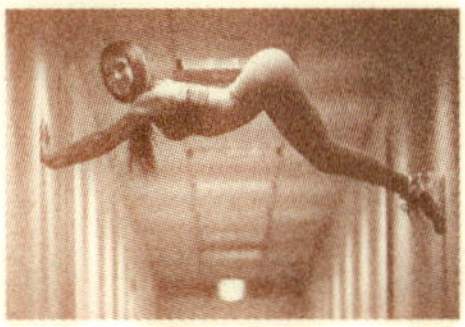

In the same year Nicki Minaj together with Big Sean released the single *Dance A$$,* the ultimate celebration of the big booty – this launched an even more exaggerated body type. Nicki Minaj, a Trinidadian–born American rapper, has the biggest posterior that the music industry has seen so far. As one of the most influential female rappers, she has positioned herself differently to others so far. She's claimed to be bi-sexual and in *Moment 4 Life,* she refers to herself as a "king" rather than a queen. Some of the lyrics of *Dance A$$* say:

**Kiss my ass and my anus,**
**'cause it's finally famous**
**And it's finally so, yeah, it's finally so!**
**I don't know, man, guess ass shots wore off!**
**Bitches ain't popping', Google my ass**

Twerking is probably the most popular dance move since the *Twist*[5] and it also became a part of live shows, like Australian rapper Iggy Azalea enacts in her performances. We can say that in 2013 the total "Bootyfication" of pop music happened. It seems like pop musicians worldwide,

5. The twist is a dance that was inspired by rock and roll music, popular world wide during the 60s.

were bearing their booties onstage or online. Miley Cyrus proved that a big butt wasn't necessary to became part of the movement and to attract attention. She achieved this by posting a video of herself twerking while wearing a unicorn suit. The same year she performed at the MTV Video Music Awards, twerking in a skin toned leather bikini. (fig. 6) Even though twerking was already around for 20 years, and many stars like Beyoncé used the word in their lyrics and performed it at live shows and in their music videos; it was only after Miley's performance the word become part of the Oxford Dictionary Online and runner up to selfie as word of the year. This break through is ironic since twerking clearly comes from Afro-American culture. After that, twerking become mainstream and it split from the music industry. The move was also adopted by wrestler Eve Torres (fig. 7) as a victory move against her opponents.

fig. 6

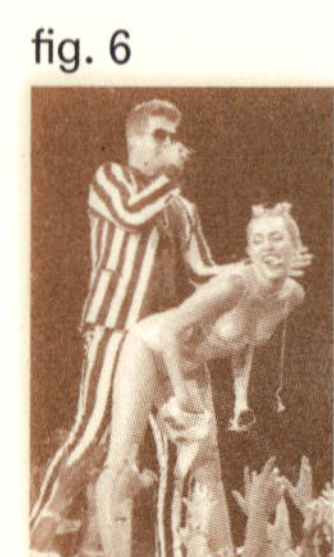

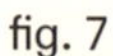

fig. 7

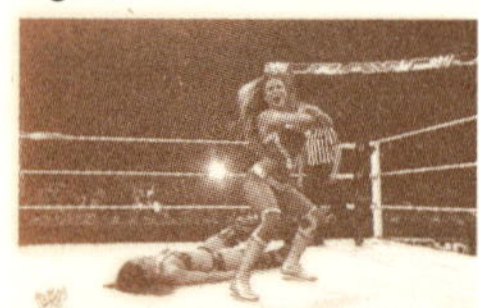

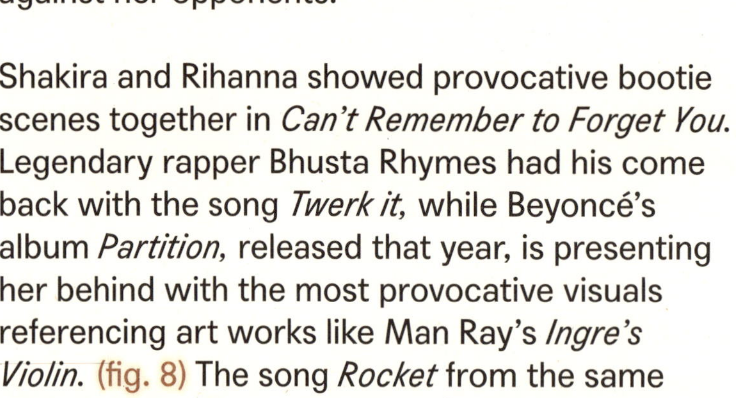

Shakira and Rihanna showed provocative bootie scenes together in *Can't Remember to Forget You*. Legendary rapper Bhusta Rhymes had his come back with the song *Twerk it,* while Beyoncé's album *Partition,* released that year, is presenting her behind with the most provocative visuals referencing art works like Man Ray's *Ingre's Violin.* (fig. 8) The song *Rocket* from the same album says:

fig. 8

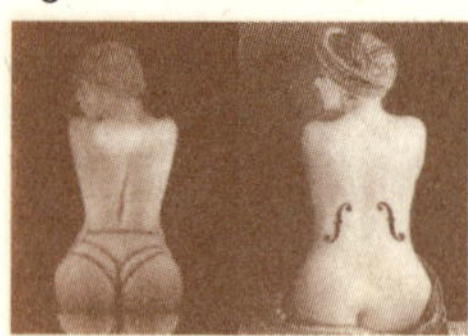

**Let me sit this ass on you**
**Show you how I feel**
**Will you watch me?**
**That's mass appeal**
**Don't take your eyes**
**Don't take your eyes off it**
**Watch it, babe, If you like you can touch it,**
**baby do you, do you wanna touch it, baby?**

New artists like Major Lazer became famous that particular year too. Their single *Bubble Butt* fitted perfectly into the scene and was another provocation. The most discussed element of it was the music video and its extraordinary plot. In the clip, three white girls are bored at home, when a giant flying Afro-American woman with an enormous behind lands next to their apartment. The giantess opens her mouth and metallic hoses snake their way into the apartment through the window. The extensions reach the girls posteriors and inflate them to an exaggerated size. Suddenly the walls from the apartment disappear and they find themselves in the middle of a night club. The whole club is filled with woman with gigantic asses and everyone is dancing and twerking. While most of the superstars are glorifying the epoch of the butt, others are creating ambiguous images, while criticising and playing with the phenomenon.

The rap collective Odd Future made a few controversial video clips using the butt in a completely different way. The video for the song *Rella* starts with a gigantic posterior of an African woman, but instead of the usual firm butt, this one is full of cellulite and it's almost painful to watch. This way of playing with the anti-aesthetic factor is also used in *Tamale* where Tyler, The Creator is jumping up and down on a oversized woman's behind while she laughs.

In 2014 Nicki Minaj dared to do what nobody had done so far. Almost 20 years after its first release, she created a cover version of the legendary song *Baby got Back*. In her own version, the song *Anaconda* took specific parts of the original lyrics and made them into the chorus.

**My Anaconda don't...**
**My Anaconda don't...**
**My Anaconda don't wants non unless**
**you got buns hun**
**Oh my gosh, look at her butt**
**Oh my gosh, look at her butt**
**Oh my gosh, look at her butt**
**Look at her butt (look at her butt)**

The rest of the lyrics were composed specifically for the song.

**Yeah, he love this fat ass**
**Yeah! This one is for my bitches with a**
**fat ass in the fucking club**
**I said, "Where my fat ass big bitches**
**in the club?"**
**Fuck the skinny bitches,**
**Fuck the skinny bitches in the club**
**I wanna see all the big fat ass bitches in the**
**mother fucking club**
**Fuck you skinny bitches.**
**What? Yeah. Ha–ha, ha...**

The video clip takes inspiration from the original one as Nicki is surrounded by curvy girls.
But in this version she's acting like a Madam, dancing with the women but also touching them to show her clear dominant position. The year of 2014 is also known for Jennifer Lopez's come back. Since she is now not the only curvy woman with a big behind, this song was a way to claim her title back. Together with Iggy Azalea and Pitt Bull she performed the song *Booty*. The clip was an attempt to win back her status and so she created extremely strong visual material.
The now 45-year-old singer dances in what looks like Vaseline or honey, saying "Throw up your hands if you love a big booty".

She also responded to Beyoncé's *Bootylicious* 13 years too late by singing: "It's safe to say that, this time around, the world is thoroughly ready for the jelly". In Pitt Bull's rap, her behind is crowned as the most influential off all.

**So much booty, she could supply the demand**
**I wanna take that big 'ol**
**booty shopping at the mall**
**I wanna pick it up and put that booty in my car**
**Baby your booty is a movie star**
**Oscar winner of the all...**

In the 2014 winter edition of Paper magazine, Kim Kardashian and her booty were featured on its cover. The issue had two different cover versions. The first showed her naked from behind, while the second was a remake of Jean-Paul Goude's photograph of Carolina Beaumont in 1976. (fig. 9) Goude's original, which was part of the book *Jungle Fever*, was provocative and fetishistic. Carolina stood naked in an acid blue room with a bottle of champagne in her hands and a glass positioned on her big behind: the remake has the same construction. Kim is not entirely naked but wearing a black glitter dress, she also has a glass on her butt and a bottle in her hands. (fig. 10) In both cases, the exact moment in which the bottle has been opened and a champagne ray is arching over both bodies and enters the glasses is captured. With this remake Goude has his come back. Even though not a lot of people were aware of the existence of the first version of the photograph, the cover was a big success and it even 'broke the internet'. In 2015, a side from the many new songs containing booty, Amy Schumer together with Amber Rose produced a meta-song about the whole phenomenon. The song is called

fig. 9

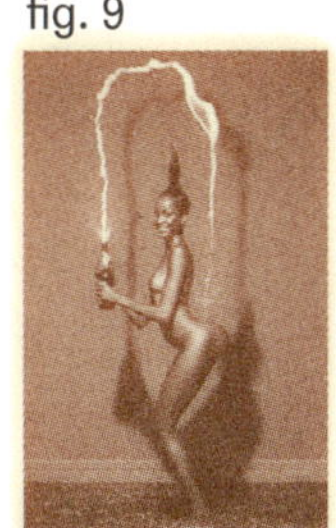

fig. 10

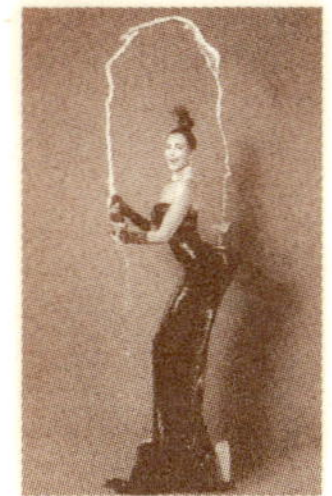

*Milk, Milk, Lemonade* and it says:

**I used to think that my tits was where it's at**
**Used to be concerned**
**that my booty was too fat**
**But now I know the truth**
**and that worry has been shot**
**Big booty's what they want**
**and big booty's what I got**

**Tits are old news if you know what I mean**
**All the guys love my fudge machine**
**Look me in the eye**
**Get your face in, don't be shy**
**You say you don't like asses**
**Cause I fart and break your glasses**

Also the song does not play around with words but gets straight to the point.

**This is where her poo comes out**
**This is where your poo comes out**
**This is where their poo comes out**
**This is where our poo comes out**

**This is what you think is hot**
**This is what you think is hot**
**This is what you think is hot**
**Talkin bout my fudge machine**

In the summer of 2016 a few particular music videos stood out because they were showing sport, which is often seen as the 'behind the scenes of the butt culture'. This particular aesthetic is a way to show the body in an extreme sexual way without being vulgar. Ariana Grande and Nicky Minaj's music video to the song *Side to Side* is a performed choreography on stationary exercise bikes. While Kanye West's clip to the

song *Fade* is shot in a Gym and shows a dance performance by Teyena Tylor. Both music videos show the 'hard work' behind a 'perfect' body and a 'perfect booty'. It is a celebration of the fitness aesthetics and the fact that it no longer needed to stay behind the scenes. It can be also used as a way to confront the audience with rumours about possible plastic surgery that celebrities might have had. Sport is shown as the way to get a good looking and healthy body.
In those videos we can admire the butt working out in different positions, like on a bike or during other sport activities. This sport revelation is also connected to the social network photography in which users – as well as celebrities– show themselves working out.

In the winter of 2016 the German magazine 032c published 11 spreads promoting Kanye West's fashion line. In the photographs Kim Kardashian and her sister Khloé are posing in the clothes of the new collection, contorting their bodies into aesthetic shapes with almost no face in sight. This is because both woman are of course completely recognisable by their butts. (fig. 11 – 12) The Kardashian's b-sides have become a brand, Kim's received an enormous amount of attention. Her butt may even be more famous than she is. These photographs went viral – of course – and the newspaper *Die Welt* wrote an article about them: "Kim wears models from Yeezy, the current collection of her husband Kanye, whose silent colours, straight cuts and simple materials, reducing the reduction itself; the impression of a brutal crude simplicity results from the refraction with the absolute artifice of a Kardashian body." The article explains that this aesthetic may tell us more about reality than it knows about itself. What has clearly happened

fig. 11

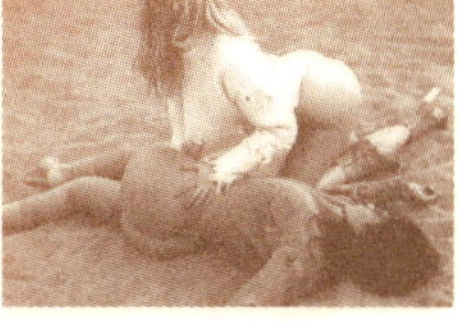

fig. 12

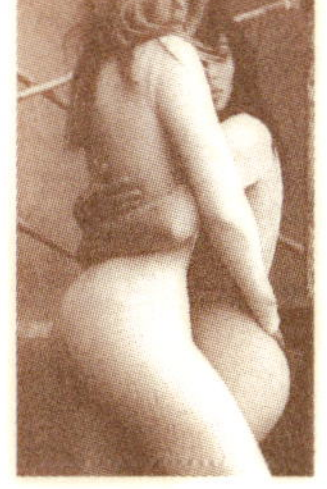

is that the butt was able to break out from the hip-hop scene and influence many different sectors of pop culture.

What started in songs through lyrics and clips can now be found on magazine covers, Instagram photography and so on. In *Resistance through rituals: Youth subcultures in post-war Britain*, Stuart Hall speaks about the transformation and re-signification, and about how re-evaluating life styles can take place because the original object-signs were positioned upon a divided society. However much of their preferred meanings attempted to mask that reality. What happens is not the creation of objects and meaning from nothing, but rather the transformation and rearrangements of what is given.[4] This is exactly what happened to the booty. Its original meaning represented in hip-hop has drifted away.

Not only did the content of those songs change, but once the booty left the music industry it become a decontextualised image for the masses with an uncontrollable meaning. The images are not only taken out of their original context but they are embedded in the context out our private lives, we see those images surrounded by familiarities and this creates a particular intimacy with them. Images don't belong to places anymore,[6] but they pop up on the screens of our devices, in our homes, and so they become intimate. Through the years the female buttocks have had different meanings and values. It was a way to integrate Latin and Afro-American beauty standards and their cultural values.

The booty also worked as an unifying tool for the Latin and Afro-American cultures. These two groups make up the biggest minorities in the U.S.A and have historically been rivals. Different ideals that are often fought over in gang wars can be united through similar body aesthetics.

6. S. Hall and J. Tony, Resistance through rituals: youth sub-cultures in post-war Britain, London, New York, Routledge, 2006, p.6

The 'big booty' represents both cultures, as both the Black and the Latin community fought for the same causes and the same acceptance of their body features. The butt serves as a common good for a glorious unification.

The material we are dealing with, both the images and lyrics are extracted from performances. Those performances designate a human action in which particular attention is paid to the executed communicative acts.[7] When this specific attention is put into a message it creates a certain 'poetic function' of the language. The performance is something creative and aware.[8] Most of the rap, R&B and hip-hop lyrics analysed are written in slang or pidgin, which is a simplified primary language with elements of others in it. This is not only a way for the musicians to stay close to their own cultures, but it is also a way to distinguish themselves from one another, to be different. Even if songs in slang or pidgin are mainstream they stay loyal to the identity of the performer and its first target group. The language choices are also valued according to aesthetic principles, that is, for the beauty of the formulation or pronunciation.[9] The image is in a certain manner the limit of meaning, when combined with text it creates a second level of information, a more direct one, that makes the intention of the whole message clear. When the butt left the music scene and became a pretty image, it lost its textual support and so its references.

7. J. Berger, Ways of seeing, Reissued as part of the Penguin Design Series, London, British Broadcasting Corporation, 2008, p. 23

8. A. Duranti, Linguistic anthropology, Cambridge textbooks in linguistics, New York, Cambridge University Press, 1997 p. 18

9. R. Bendix, In Search of Authenticity: The Formation of Folklore Studies, Madison, University of Wisconsin Press, 1997, p. 201

# The Background of the Non-Beautiful Venus

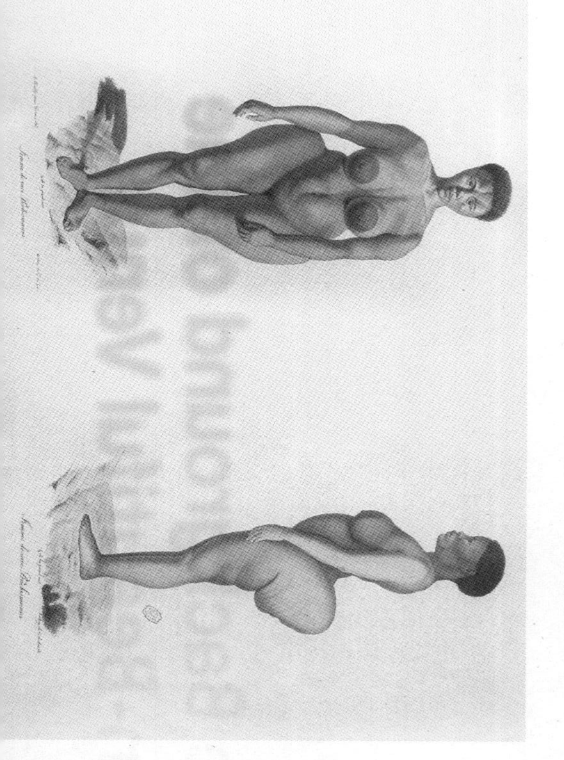

Venus Hottentot, Sarah Baartman,
Paris, 20th century

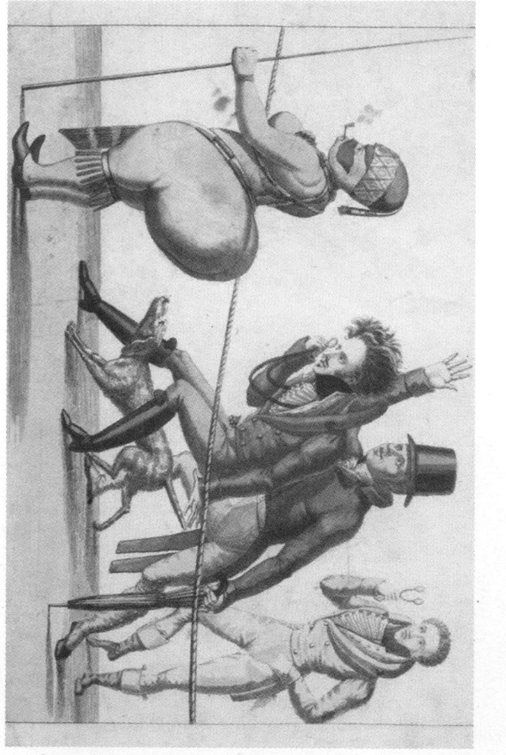

Venus Hottentot, Human Zoos,
London, 20th century

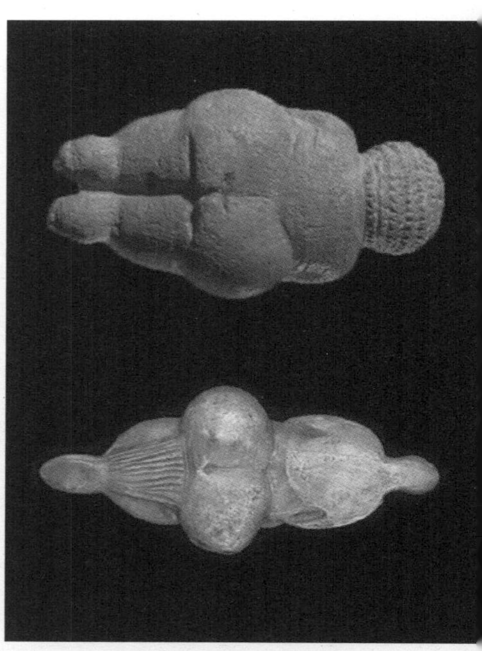

Venus Willendorf, 25.000 BCE
Venus Lespugne, 23.000 BCE

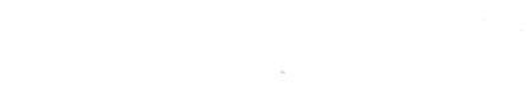

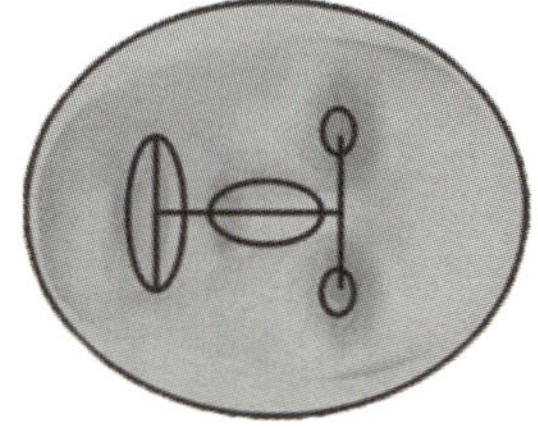

Study, Face Recognition,
Mariska Kret, 30.11.2016

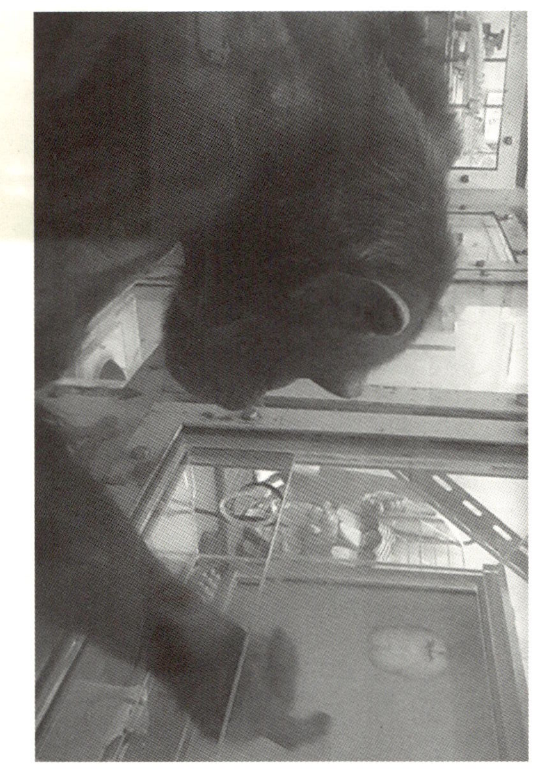

Study, Face Recognition,
Mariska Kret, 30.11.2016

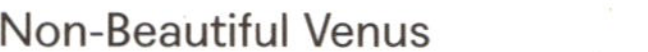

The buttocks also represent the primitive image of femininity, sexuality, fertility and lust.
We can find proof of this representation of female buttocks through objects that stretch back to early human history. Examples like the *Venus of Willendorf* (28,000 to 25,000 BCE) and the *Venus Lespunge* (around 23,000 BCE) show a fertility symbol that is concentrated around exaggerated female characteristics. (fig. 1) Both are statuettes around 15cm high and experts suggest that the figurines might have been intended as an example of the ideal body type. Among their special features and feminine shapes the exaggerated hips and buttock stand out.

fig. 1

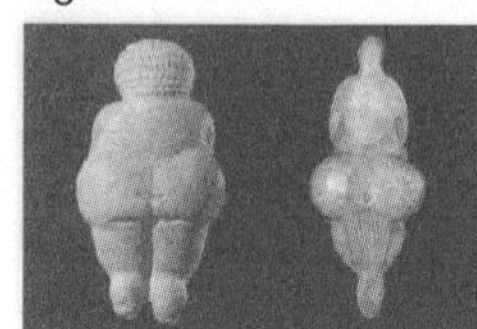

As the name suggests these figurines can be compared to the classical image of the "Venus" that followed many years later. Camille Paglia writes about the *Venus Willendorf* in *Sexual Personae* defining the statuette as "Our first exhibition from western art". She argues that the figure represents the laws of primitive earth-cults, in which the woman becomes an idol, an object and a Goddess. She also defines the Venus Willendorf as "un-beautiful by every standard" because "art has not yet found its relation to the eye".[1] Paglia argues that there is nothing beautiful in nature and that beauty is "our weapon against nature". This statement relates easily to contemporary beauty standards and plastic surgery that very often go far beyond anything natural. The 'perfection' that many want to achieve is only made possible by trying to interfere and change nature. This could also mean that art and media content are interfering with nature and create standards that are not real and can never be achieved by nature itself. Paglia also points out the lack of identity of the statuette, given by the absence of a face. She describes this feature as being a consequence of the culturally

1. C. Paglia, Sexual Personae, New Haven, Yale University Press, 1990 p. 87

primitive circumstances, which were far from a developed and cohesive society. Perhaps this lack of identity makes the image more universal? Her identity shifts from facial characteristics to body language, and creates an identity of its own. In a similar way this happens in music videos, in some scenes there is no face, the body becomes the main character. The body has been idealised over time and is represented as a collective universal language.

Individual identity does not only depend on facial features. We can find an example of that in a study conducted by Mariska Kret.[2] She's proved that primate monkeys, in fact, recognise each other by looking at their behinds. Their buttocks elicit the same level of recognition that faces do in humans. (fig 2 – 3) Their ability to be able to read buttocks is so nuanced that it's even possible for them to read other information like the fertility status of different females. "The primates focus on the body language becomes their main communication tool, making the buttocks the middle point of it".[3]

2,3. M. Kret, 'Getting to the Bottom of Face Processing. Species-Specific Inversion Effects for Faces and Behinds in Humans and Chimpanzees' Jouranl Plost, 30.11.2016 (accessed 5.03.2017)

Ironically today's ideal female beauty canons are similar to those that produced the ancient Venus statuettes, neglecting many different body trends from the many different epochs that followed it. The buttocks as an image for the Western masses is a constructed one that is made possible today only because of the different influences from the past. One of those influences derives from colonialism. In the Western Hemisphere dubious institutions called Human Zoos were introduced. As the curiosity for unknown exotic countries grew, travellers brought back to Europe plants, foods and animals that were then exhibited to highlight the planet's diversity: unfortunately

fig. 2

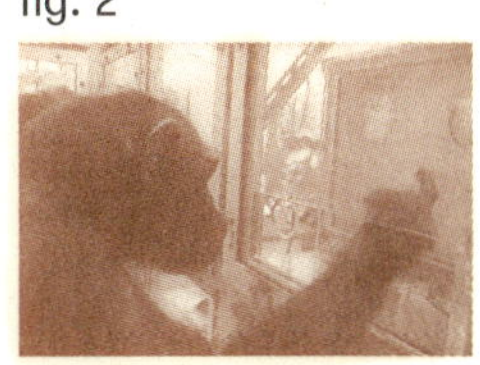

fig. 3

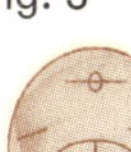

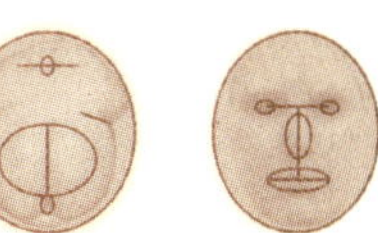

humans were also displayed. This 19th and early 20th century phenomenon, which was started in Mexico but was soon imported to some of the world's biggest cites like Paris, Hamburg, Antwerp, Barcelona, London and New York City. The diversity became entertainment, something to laugh and wonder at. Sarah Baartman, was the most famous Khoikhoi woman, who, due to her large buttocks, was exhibited as a freak show attraction in London and Paris. Originally she came from the Khoisan family from today's Eastern Cape of South Africa. Baartman was also known as the Venus Hottentot, (fig. 4) a Dutch word used to describe the people known as the Khoisan. Sarah Baartman performed in a skin toned and skin tight outfit that showed off her shapely body, for extra money the audience could touch her as proof that she was real.
Baartman died at the age 26 in 1815. Scientists then took her body and made a replica for the Paris Museum of Science where she was exhibited until 1974 with her brain, skeleton and sexual organs. This interest in the genitalia of racial exotics served the cultural agenda of early European ethnologists, as it enabled them to define racial differences that seemed to justify European colonial authority.[4] Even though South Africa's President Nelson Mandela requested for her repatriation in 1994, the French government only agreed to bury her body in 2002.

fig. 4

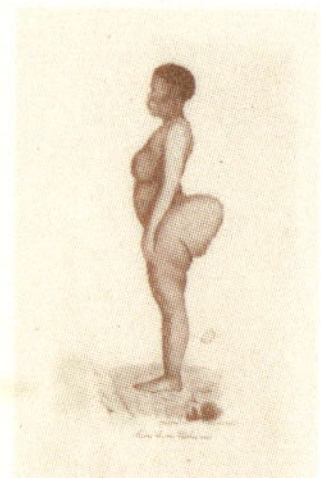

4. C. E. Forth and I. Crozier, Body Parts: Critical Exploration in Corporeality, Lanham, Lexington Books, 2005, p. 94

From this we can draw the conclusion that the *Venus Hottentot* – even though presenting a completely different scenario than the *Venus Willendorf* – is a non-beauty. She can be defined as such because she was brought to Europe to satisfy people's curiosity for the exotic.
She fulfilled the role of the different, not the role of the beauty, since her body proportions clearly

didn't fit within the canons of the Neoclassical age. She triggered horrifying reactions and satisfied the secret erotic fantasies of some men. The name "Venus" did not stand for beauty in this case. In fact it helped transform her into a symbol that stands for the submission of the colonised countries. Generally we can speak of a Western link to these such countries. This way a certain fascination for the exotic is created. The myth of African hyper-fertility expresses a legendary reproductive hardiness that dates from early encounters of Europeans and Africans during the Age of Exploration.[5] As John Hoberman explains, "Apart from reproductive capacity, Western interest in black female sexuality during the colonial period focused on genital anatomy and sexual drive. The nineteenth century perceived the black female as possessing not only a primitive sexual appetite, but also the external signs of this temperament". In pop-culture like in Human Zoos we can find the display of the human body. Both function with the idea of an audience. The big difference is that in the first case the main attraction was mainly given by the exotic. The audience wanted to fulfil its curiosity of the unknown. In the case of pop-culture, admiration plays a big role. The celebrities under the spotlight stand for beauty and perfection. They become the new standards of beauty cultures, standards that everyone wants to reach, and through globalisation these beauty ideals became universal. The big bottom might have been a curiosity in the nineteenth century, but now it is embedded in Western culture, and has become the new beauty standard.

5. C. E. Forth and I. Crozier, Body Parts: Critical Exploration in Corporeality, Lanham, Lexington Books, 2005, p. 93

# The Politics of Dancing, and Cinematic Framing as Cultural Expression

Documentray, Géneration Mapuka avec Les Tueuses de la Cote d'Ivore

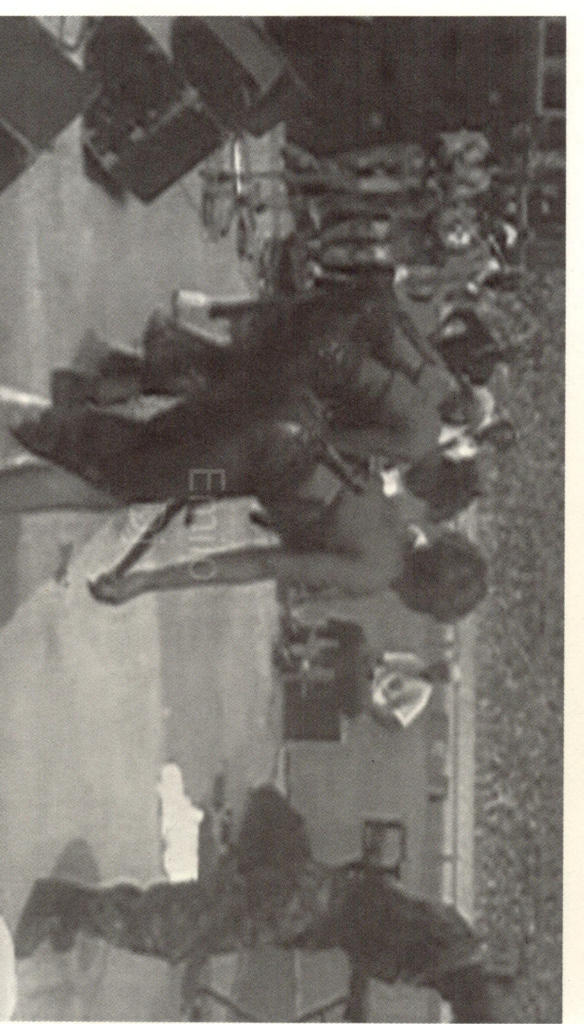


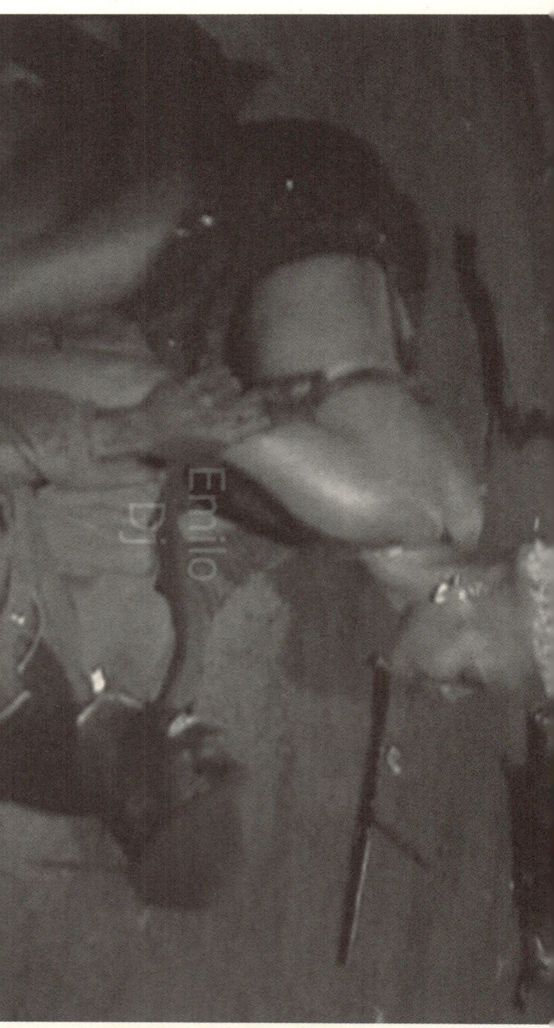

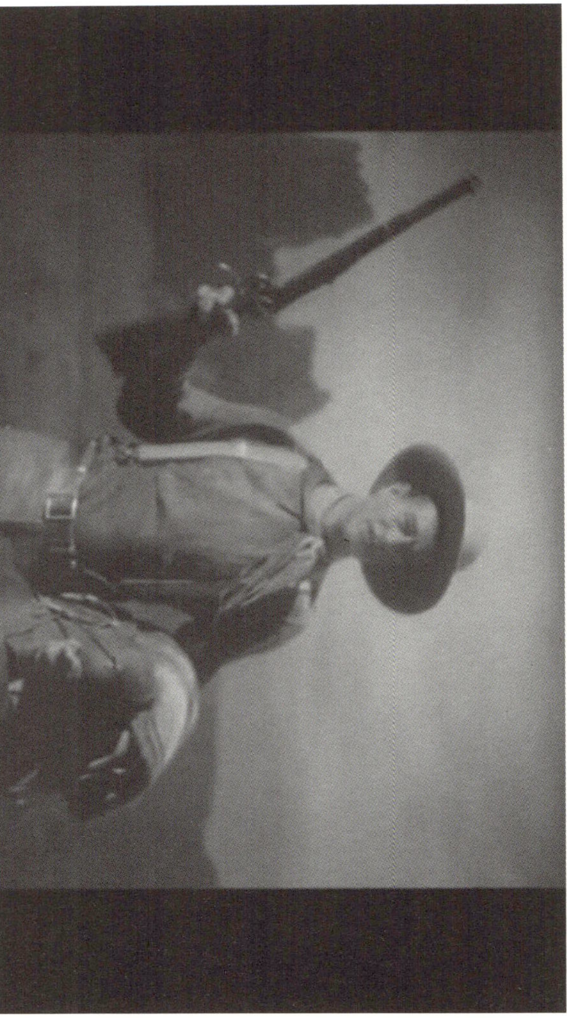

Stagecoach, John Wayne, Directed by John Ford, 1939

And God Created Woman, Brigitte Bardot, Directed by Roger Vadim, 1956

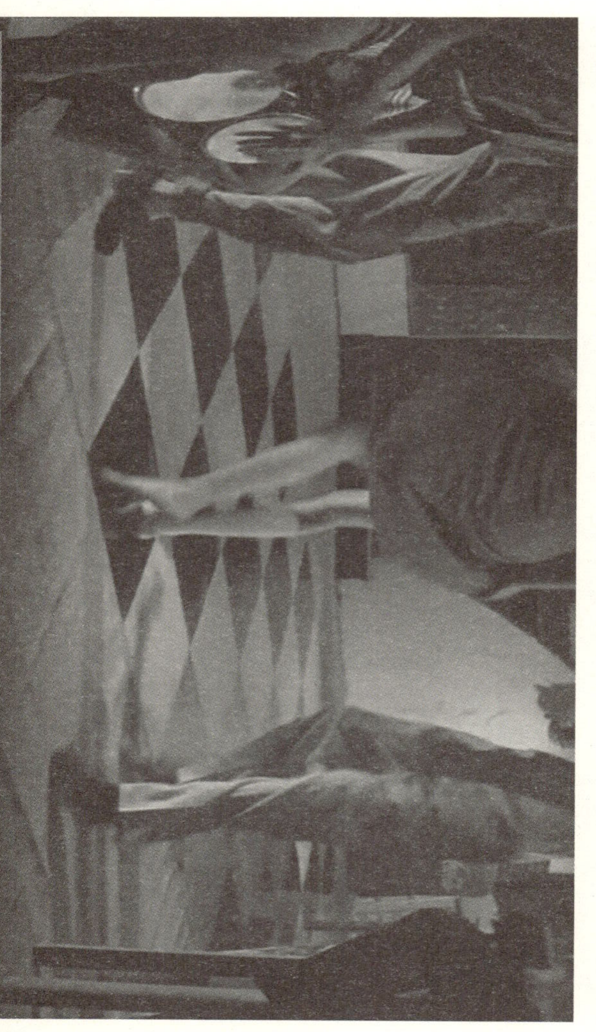

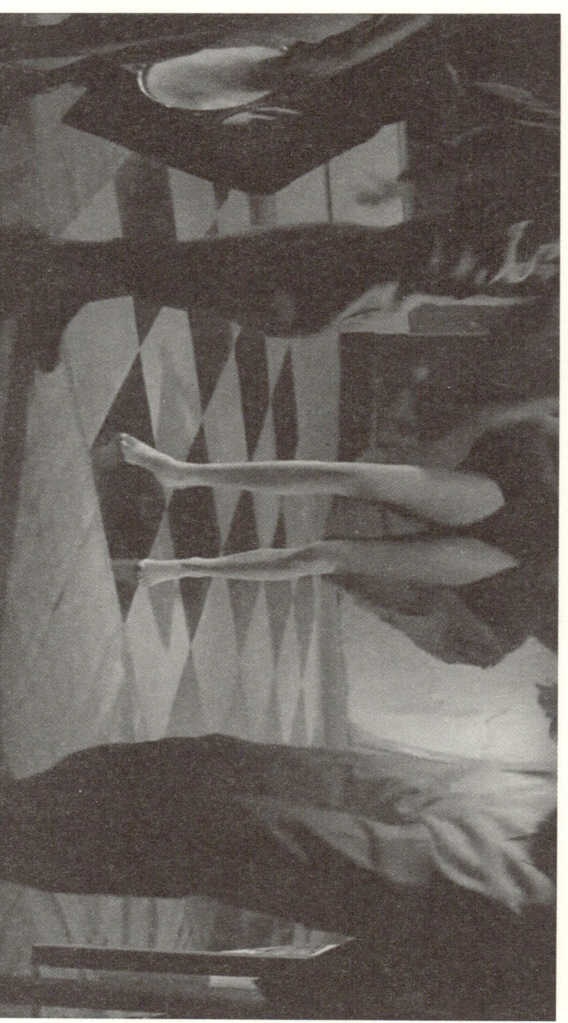

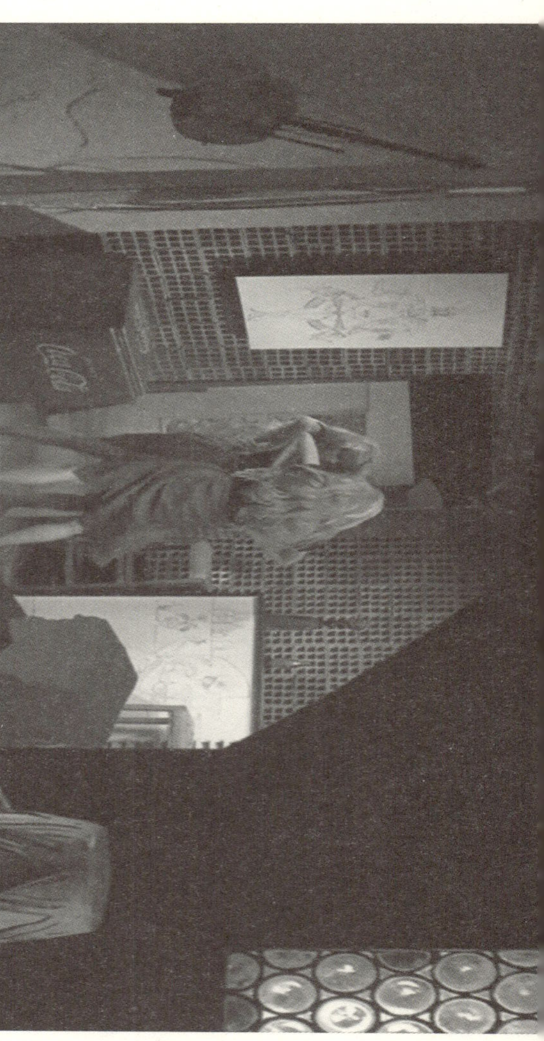

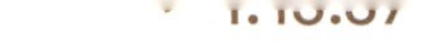

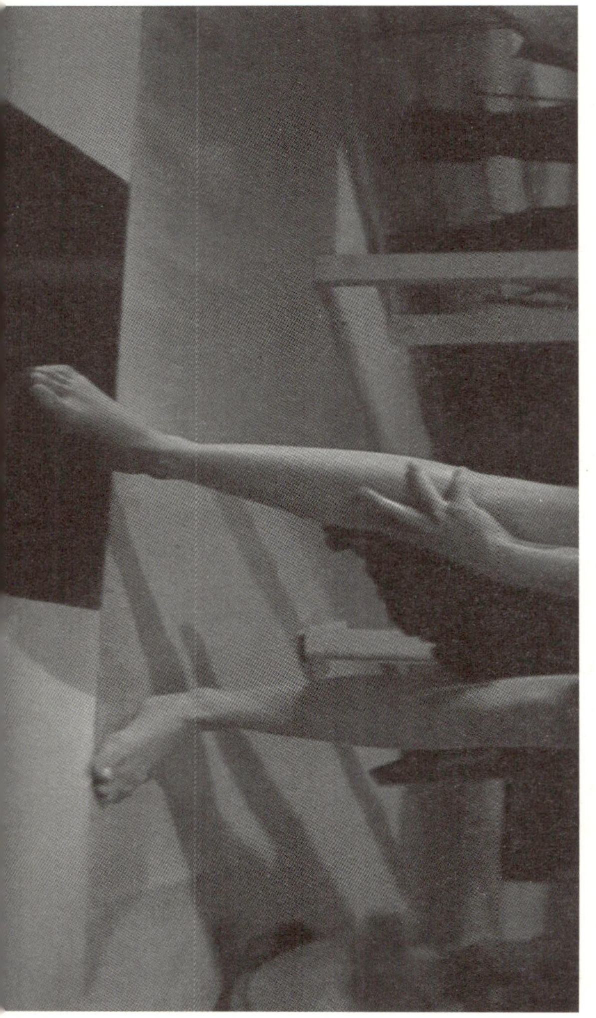

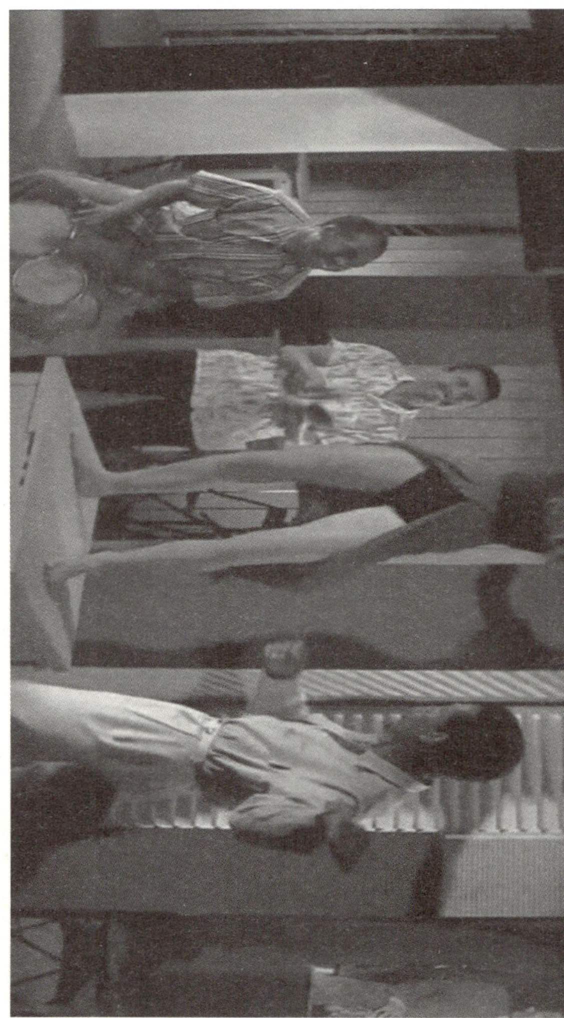

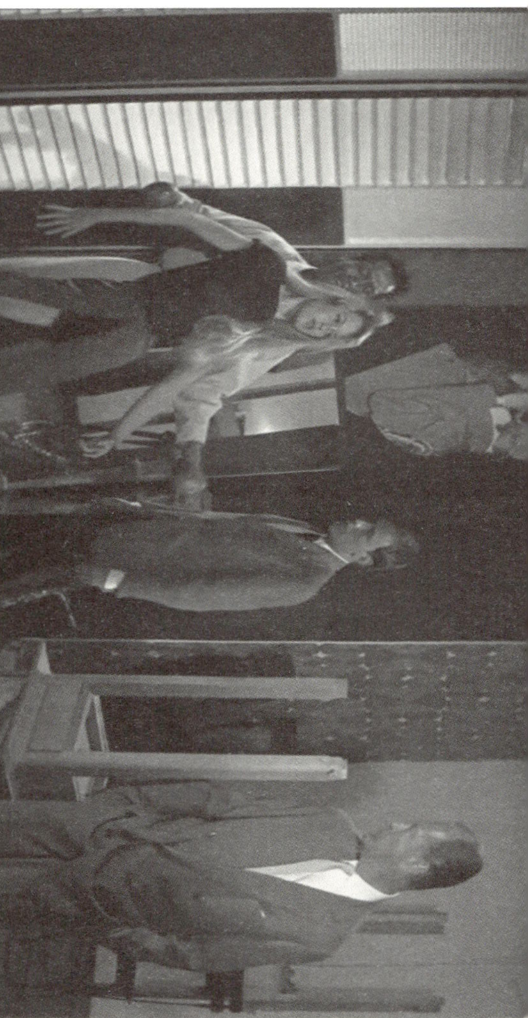

And God Created Woman, Brigitte Bardot, Directed by Roger Vadim, 1956

And God Created Woman, Brigitte Bardot, Directed by Roger Vadim, 1956

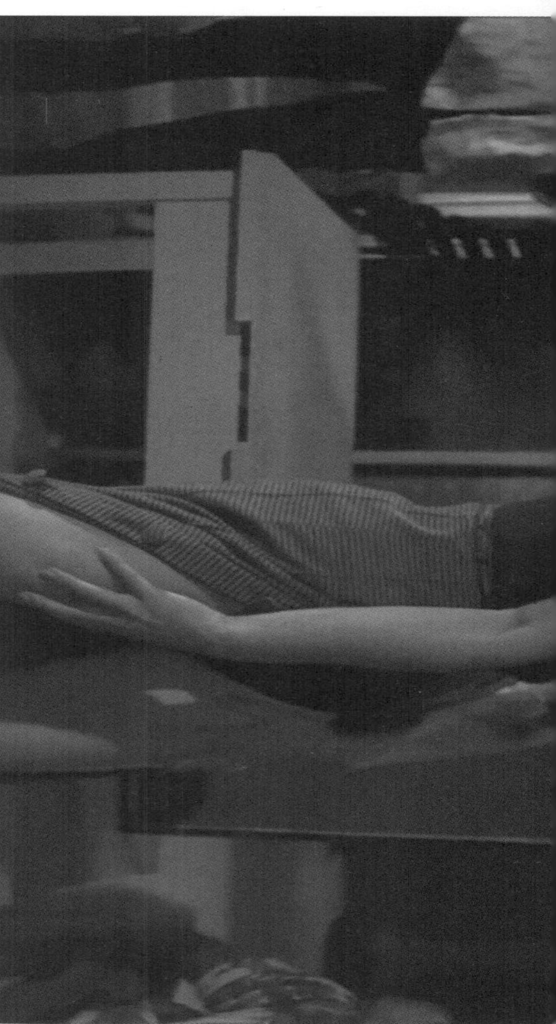

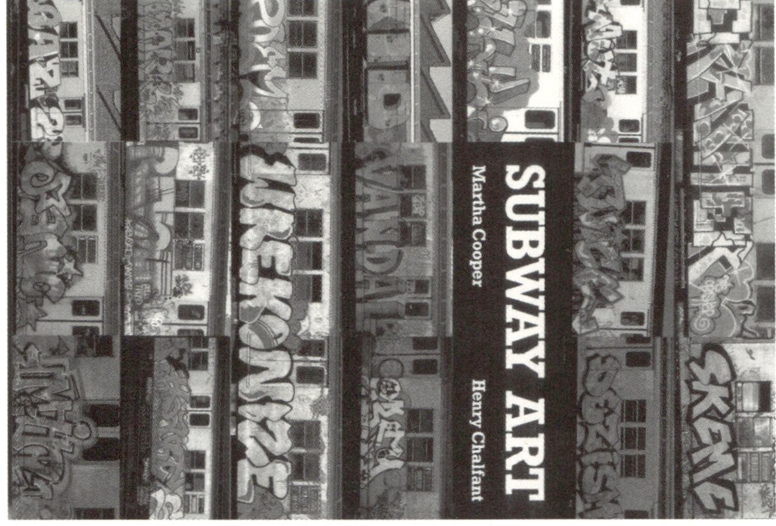


Subway Art, Martha Cooper, Henry Chalfant, 1984

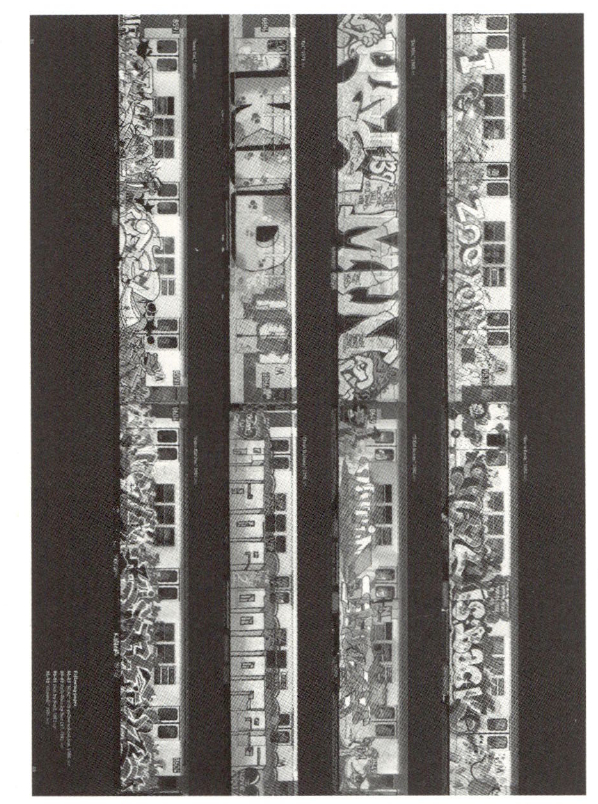

Subway Art, Martha Cooper,
Henry Chalfant, 1984

A fundamental part of the visual language concerning the booty is the moving image, especially the ones in music videos. The most obvious way of showing this body part is through dance. In fact, the focus on the butt goes hand in hand with the transformation of dancing in the last 50 years and the affirmation of twerking as a dance style. The Oxford English Dictionary's definition of twerking is: "A dance to popular music in a sexually provocative manner involving thrusting hip movements and a low, squatting stance." Even though twerking is a contemporary form of dance, it is an appropriation and reinterpretation of movements that were used by African tribes. The most similar tribal dance is the *Mapouka* from Ivory Coast. It literally means "la danse du fessier", "the dance of the behind". This performance by women, is executed while facing away from the audience, often bent over. The colonial settlers that first came to Africa perceived the indigenous population as simple and undeveloped. Their music and dance was seen as primitive and not worthy of understanding or emulation.[1]

Even though dance and music are primarily seen as entertainment tools they have an indirect and sometimes direct political function as the performance "generates feelings and relationships between people". Politics is inherently reflected in a culture and in its manifestation. Dance is a form of cultural expression, it is interwoven into the socio-political system, as well as in economics and even religious aspects of people's lives. Dancing goes hand in hand with our contemporary society. The acquisition and re-interpretation of exotic material is part of the integration of different cultures within the Western one. A big role is played by globalisation and by the multicultural societies we live in. Attitudes towards dance, the aesthetic values related to dance, and even the actual structures of the dances themselves are influenced by the political actions and thinking of a particular time in history. According to dance educator and anthropologist Sylvia Glasser, dancing needs to be understood in relation to a broad view of culture. "Culture is not only a set of symbols, values or beliefs of people, but also a response to circumstances".[2]

As Guy Debord puts it in *The Society of Spectacle:* "The spectacle is not a collection of images; rather, it is a social relationship between people that is mediated by images"[3]. What affirms a movement or a dance style is its repetition and its visibility. We can find both things in twerking. Twerking became mainstream around 2010, even though it was mentioned in song lyrics from the late 90s. From the 90s onwards we can now observe different ways of dancing in clips, but the fundamental difference lies in the framing of those movements. What changed is not only the position of the camera but also the duration of the scenes. While in the 90s there was mostly just a glimpse of butt, now it often becomes the main part of the scene.
For an extended time we can see the booty as the protagonist, like in an 'extreme close up'. While analysing the scenes and their repetition we have to take into consideration that dancing in cinema and in video clips, works only with the idea of a spectator. Every choreography and the framing of it is constructed for an audience. What we see, is part of a story and each angle adds something to the plot. The screen becomes a cage for the body and the French writer and critic Stéphane Bouquet explains that "one must

1, 2. S. Glasser, Is Dance Political Movement? Journal for the Anthropological Study of Human Movement, Jashm. Press Illinois, 1991 (accessed 12.04.2017)

3. G. Debord, The society of spectacle Berkeley, CAPress, Bureau of Public Secrets, 2013, first edition 1970, p. 2

get rid of the logic of scene, frame and position of camera, to substitute the logic of the setting in body".[3] Nevertheless the construction of frames reflects the narration.

3. S. Bouquet, Danse/cinéma, Paris, Capricci: [Pantin]: Centre national de la danse, 2012

In the years at the beginning of Wild West cinema in the USA the 'medium shot' was introduced. For the first time the 'medium close up' was enlarged to include the hips. The medium shot – in Italian also called *piano Americano*, the American shot – (fig. 1) was introduced particularly for western movies. This helped to follow the narration, since the pistols were hanging at the hips.

fig. 1

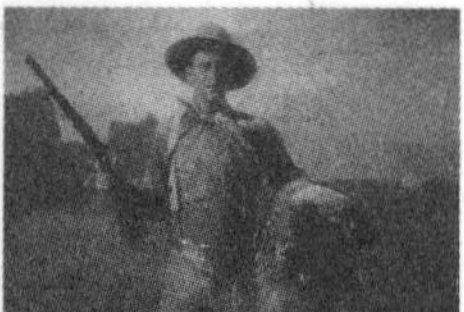

Similarities happened with dance. Frames changed and got lower in order to show the hips. In 1957 the French movie *And God Created Woman,* was launched in the US and pushed the boundaries of sexuality in American cinema. In the movie Brigitte Bardot is performing a particular dance in which she wears a wrap skirt. The framing includes her hips and shows her open skirt which exposes the body underneath to the viewer. While she is dancing to African drum music, she jumps on a table and her face is cut from the frame. (fig. 2) The focus lies entirely on her body making the face irrelevant for the duration of that particular frame. What at that time was a scandal, is common place in today's music videos. It seems that the face is not needed for specific moments in performance, and it is stronger when the focus lies entirely on the body. Also interesting is the choice of music and the African set in which Bardot's character lets herself go. The scene is also a kind of rebellion, she provokes through dancing and breaks free from the bourgeois surroundings she has married in to. Dancing and sexuality are strictly related

fig. 2

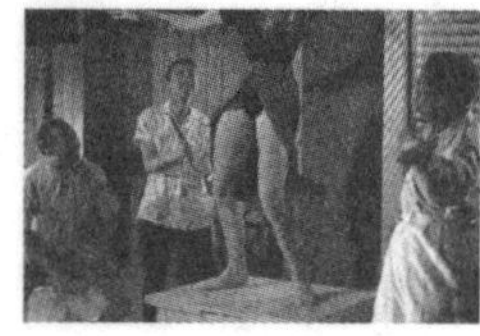

and in many movies and clips this sexuality is a way of self-expression. What makes twerking interesting is that, even though it might seem vulgar and shallow for many, it actually derives from neolithic sexual dances and celebratory rituals. Twerking was initially not intended for the male gaze. "If you go back to the neolithic dances, they were done to count time. They were cyclical. They were fertility dances in the sense of conception but also contraception".[4]
Even though twerking originates from a different background, the Western appropriation transformed it into a sexually provocative movement. Male attraction to this is just a logical consequence. The male gaze is also given by the way the female image works as an accessory. In many contemporary music clips women's appearances and performances have a purely 'decorative' function. Standing next to male singers and rappers, the prime function is to look beautiful and make the main performer look good: this role is also adopted by female performers. Nicky Minaj for example is often surrounded by female dancers while she acts and touches them like the male rappers would do. "Passivity, violability and lack of autonomy are sexual attractive characteristics in a female's representation".[5] From this we can conclude that there are different ways of performing. On the one hand the female image can be reduced to a passive decorative figure, on the other hand dancing can be a way of empowerment and also a way to be recognised. Representing a woman requires making decisions about all her visible physical features.[6] Women nowadays take this representation in to their own hands.

4. A. Hugill, 'Art & Feminism, An Interview with Fannie Sosa: On Twerking and the Commons', Berlin Art Link, 22.06.2015 (accessed 10.03.2017)

5, 6 J. Levinson and H. Maes, Art and pornography: philosophical essays New York, Oxford University Press, 2012, p. 278

Shakira for example is famous for her large hips and belly dancing skills. The way she is represented in video clips is highlighting those features, making her instantly memorable. The body acts as an unforgettably powerful tool, and the main advantage of the moving image lies within in the amount of people they reach and influence. Image manipulation and the appropriation of cultural references create a new context with a transformed meaning. The question we might ask ourselves is, does this re-interpretation harm the original reference? The answer lies in the paradox. The internet is the fastest mediation tool and makes it possible to transfer an enormous quantity of information to a large audience. While it's also amplifying the message, and helping make it become mainstream, it also shuts it down. Repetition is a powerful tool, but at some point it blinds us by taking the unexpected away, making the visual language become something worthless. As soon as a typology of images becomes part of our daily life we stop reacting to it. So what repetition does is shut down the initial message. Further more, repetition creates serial content and within this content it is easier to recognise similarities and behaviour patterns. We can therefore say that repetition creates anthropological material. This kind of material has an historical value because it documents the characteristics of people in a certain space and time. Photographer and anthropologist Martha Cooper dedicated her life to the documentation of the streets of New York City. Her material tells the story of the development of hip-hop. What she recorded in the streets, her repetition within the material, showed the first steps of hip-hop, the roots of this now billion dollar industry. Cooper's specific focus was on graffiti. Her book *Subway Art*, in collaboration with Henry Chalfant, shows a series of paint sprayed trains. Analysing this series, similarities can be found while differences in style can also be observed. (fig. 3) But what also happened is that the main customers of the book were graffiti artists themselves, and they started to use this book as a reference in order to inspire themselves and also to copy some of the content. Obviously the mediation of content inspires an audience to create similar content. The image is re-presentation, which is to say ultimately resurrection, and intelligible is reputed to lived experience.[7]

fig. 3

7. Rhetoric of the Image, Roland Barthes

# Plastic Surgery and Other Side Effects

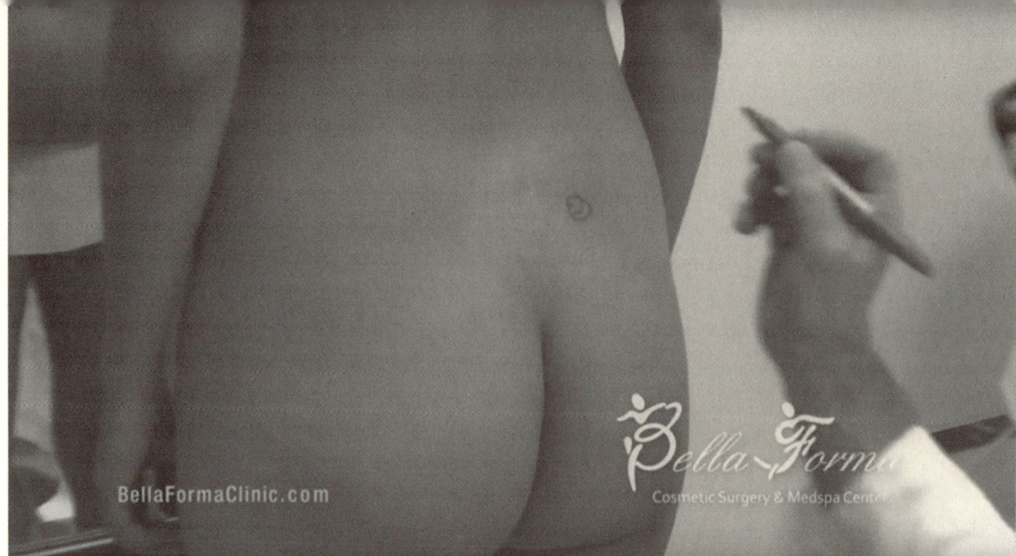


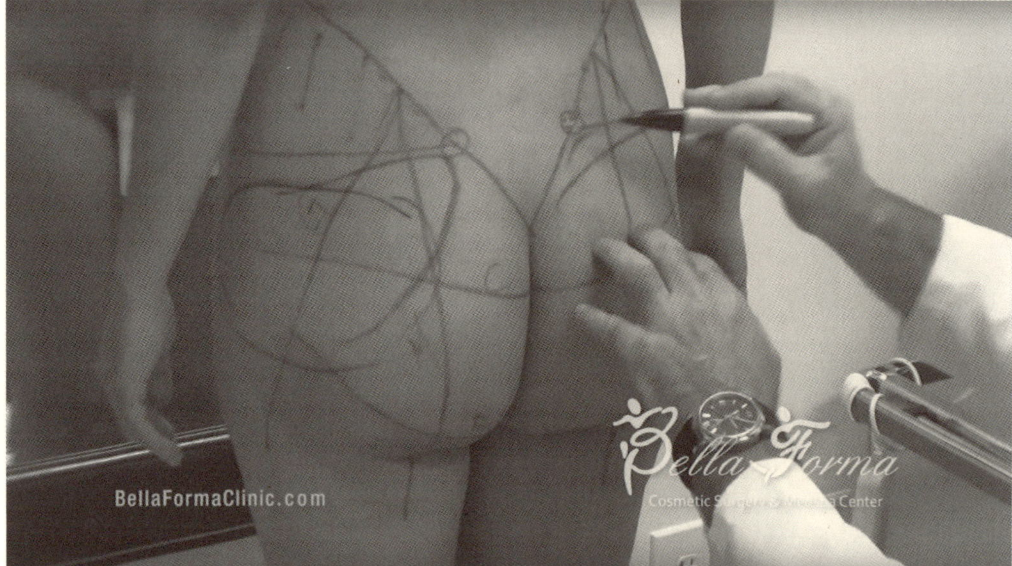


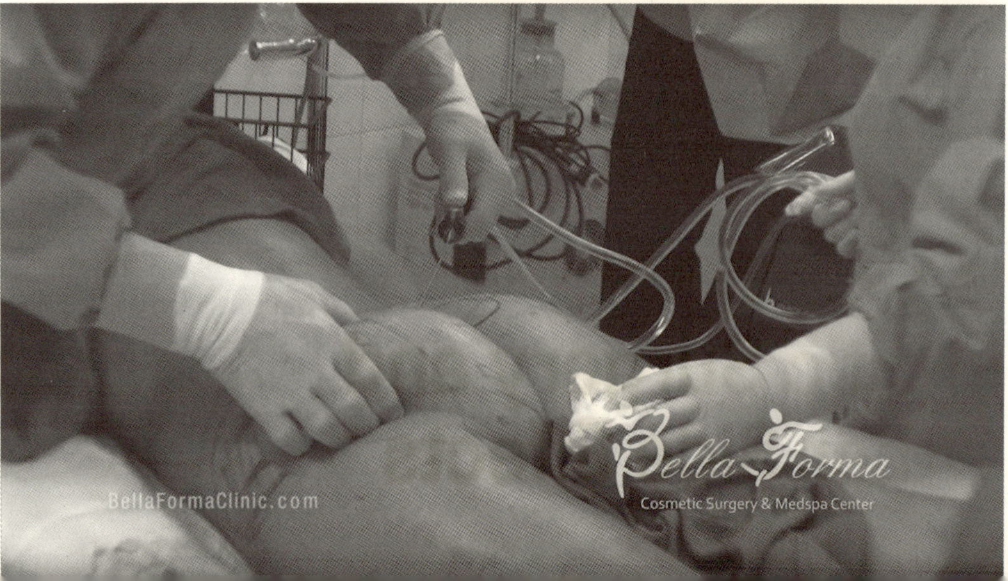


Gluteal Implant, Performed by Dr. Rajae Janho, 2014

▸ 13:39

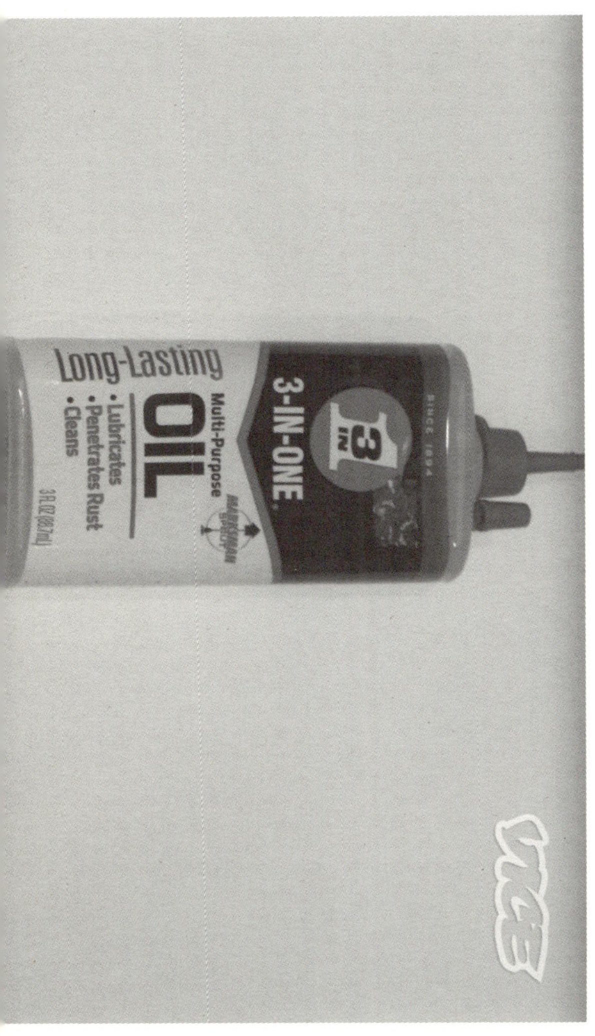


▸ 9:18

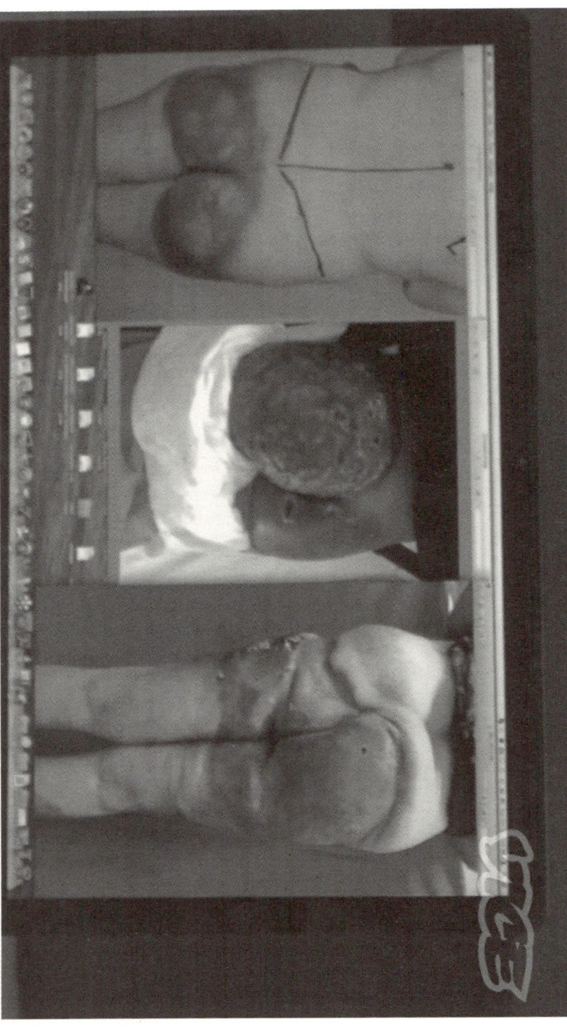


▸ 7:40

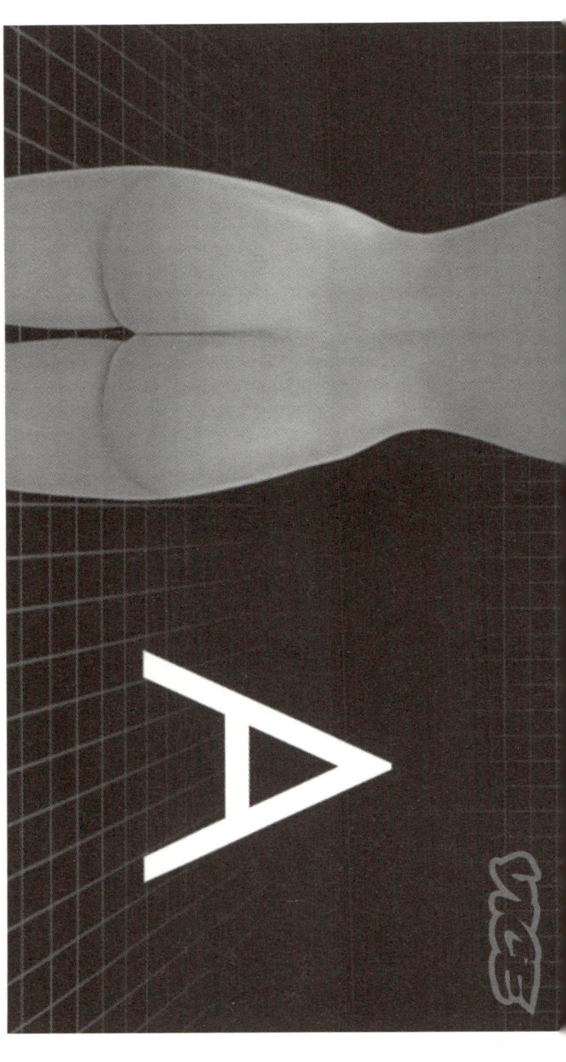




Vice Report, Buttloads of Pain: Ass Injections Gone Wrong, 2014

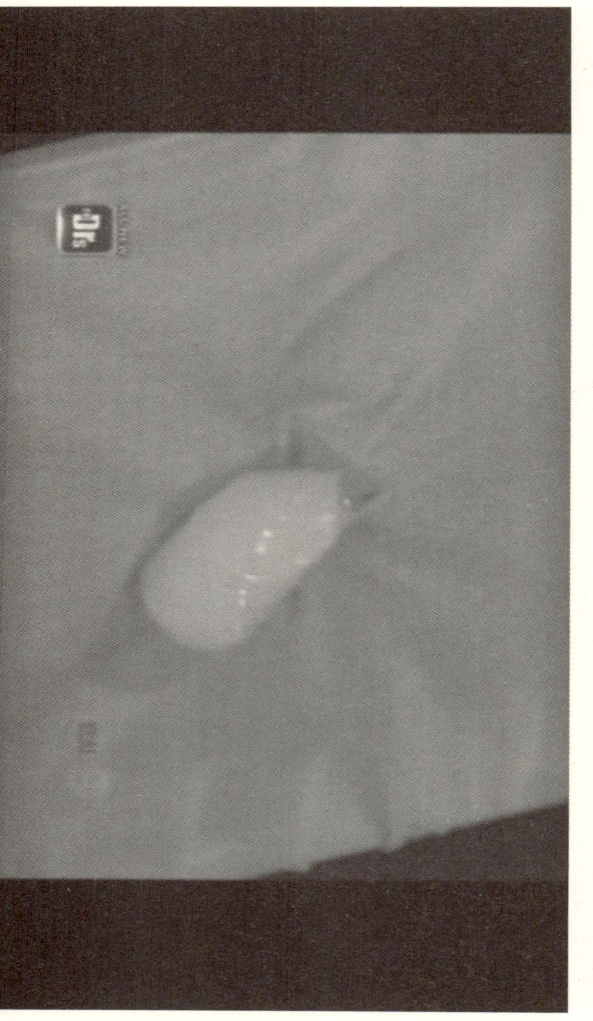

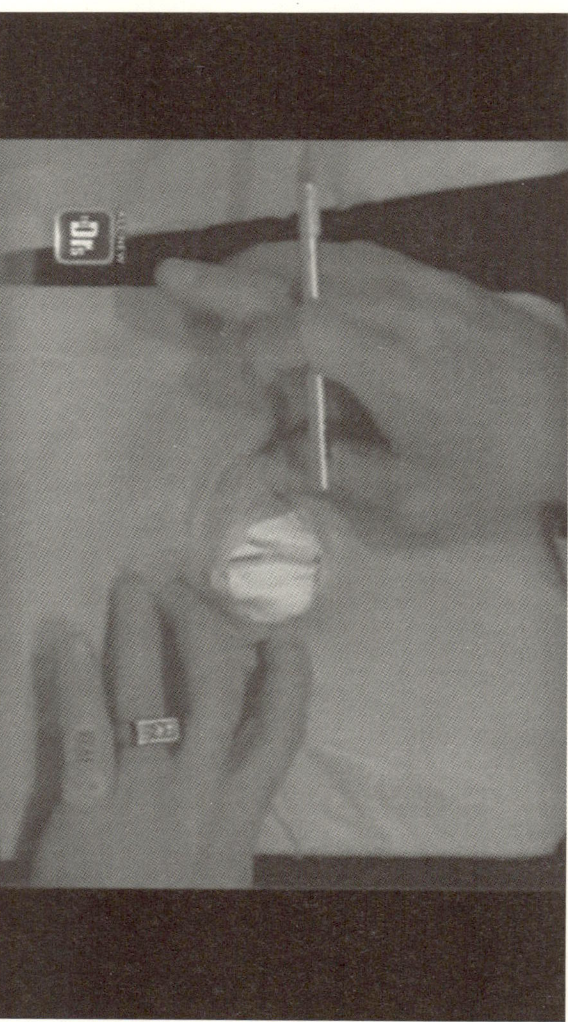

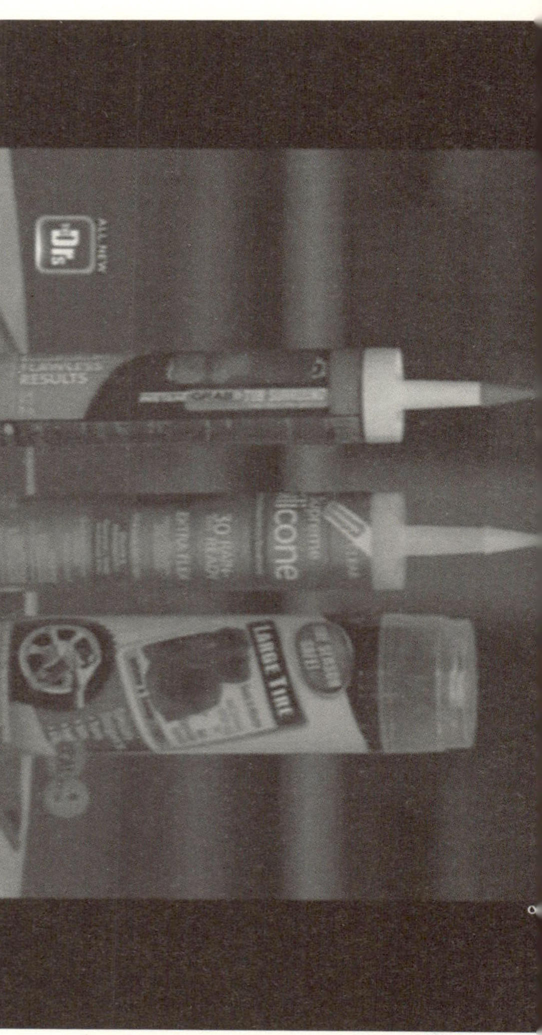
ALL NEW
LARGE TIRE

1:27

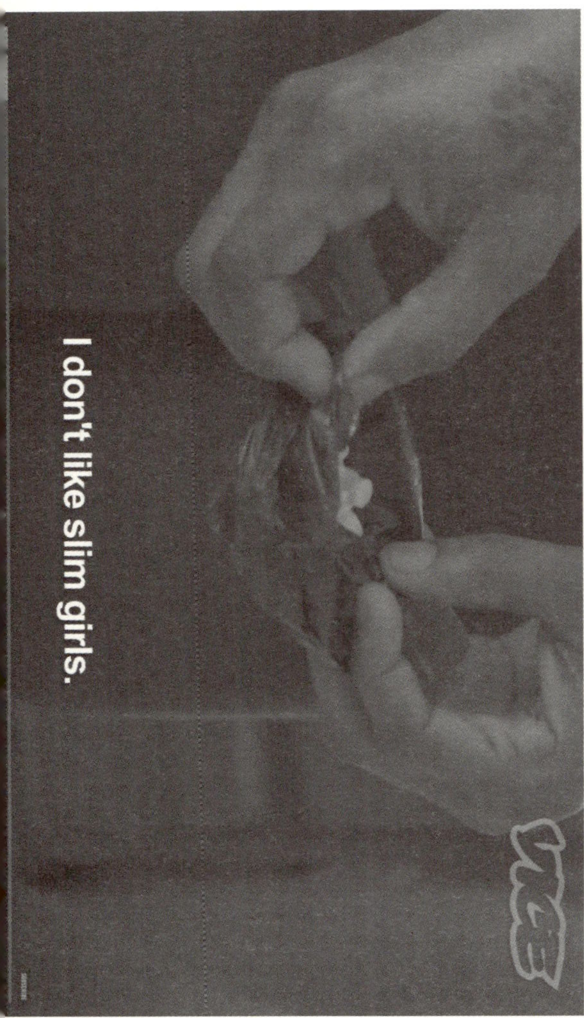


1:24

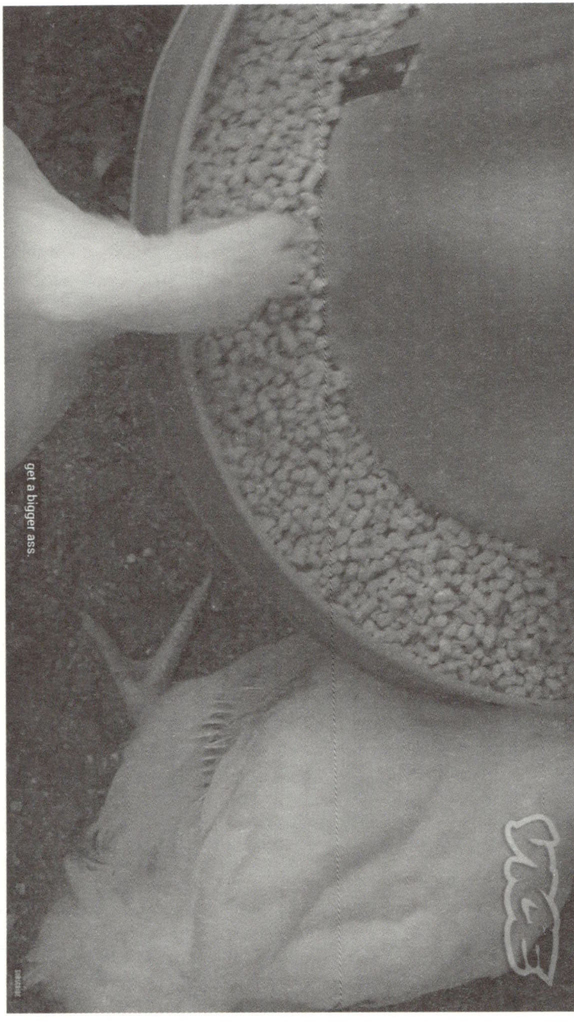


1:06

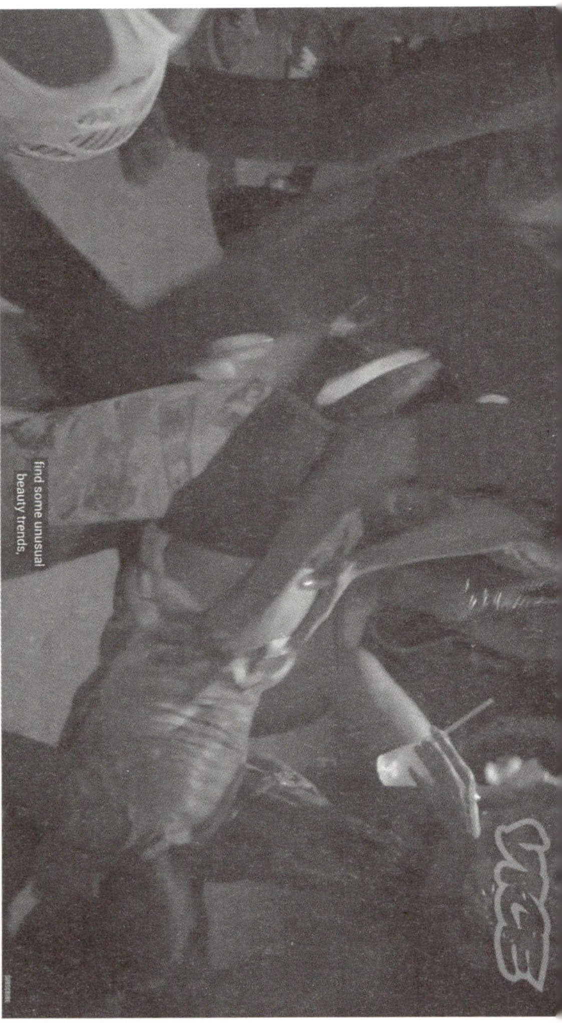




Caribbean Fashion Week,Vice Reports, 2012

Vice Report, Carebbean Fashion Week, 2012

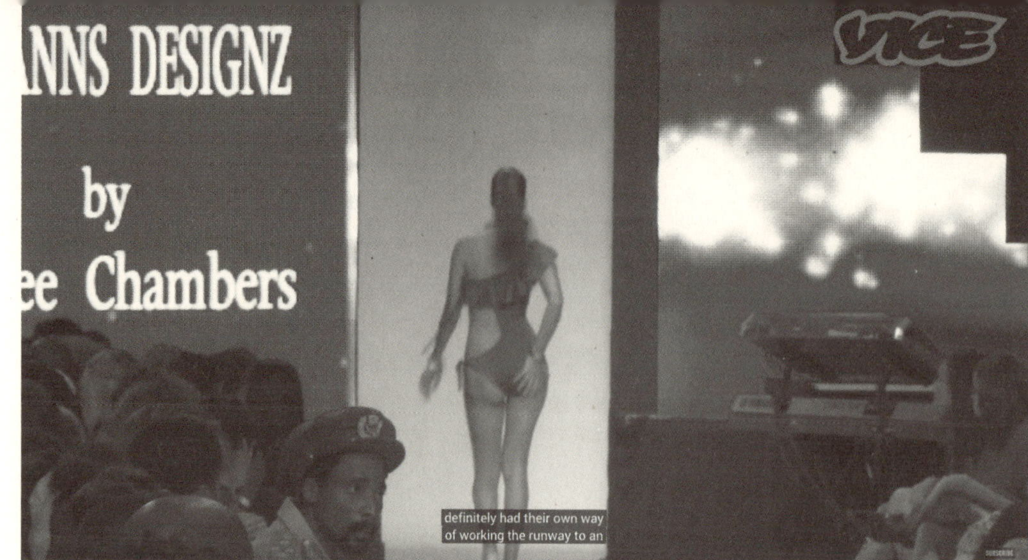


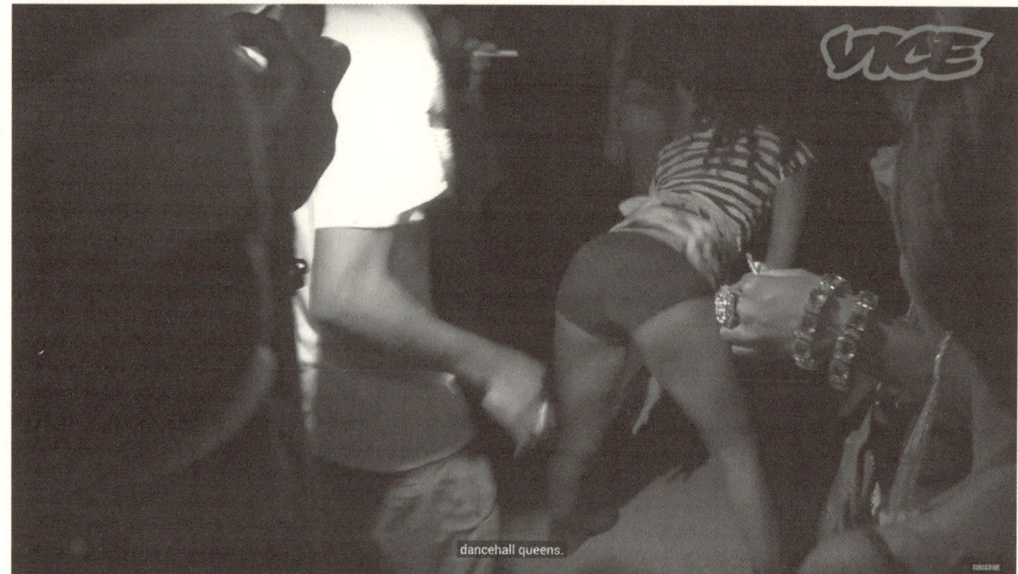


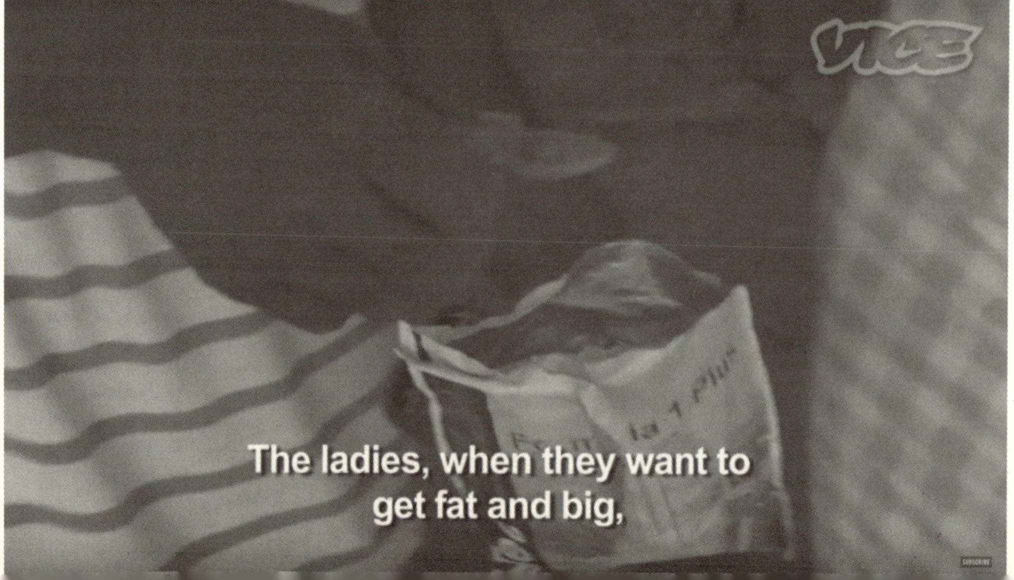

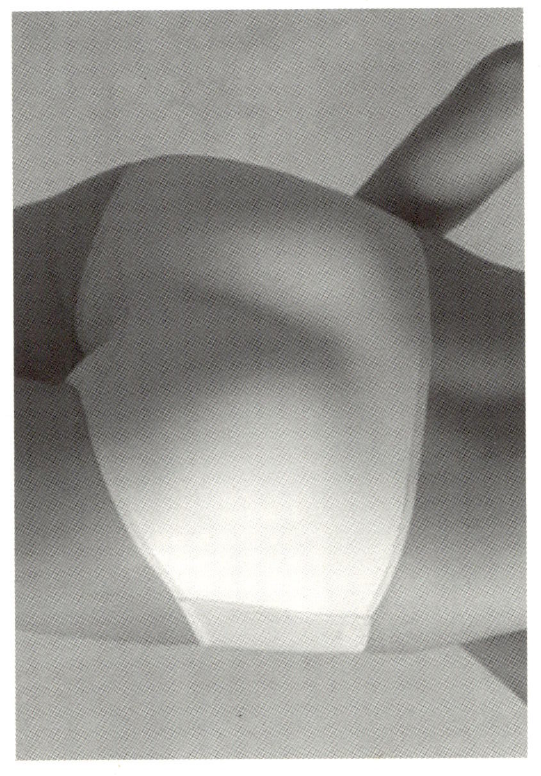

Buttock Push Up Lingerie, AliExpress $ 6.23

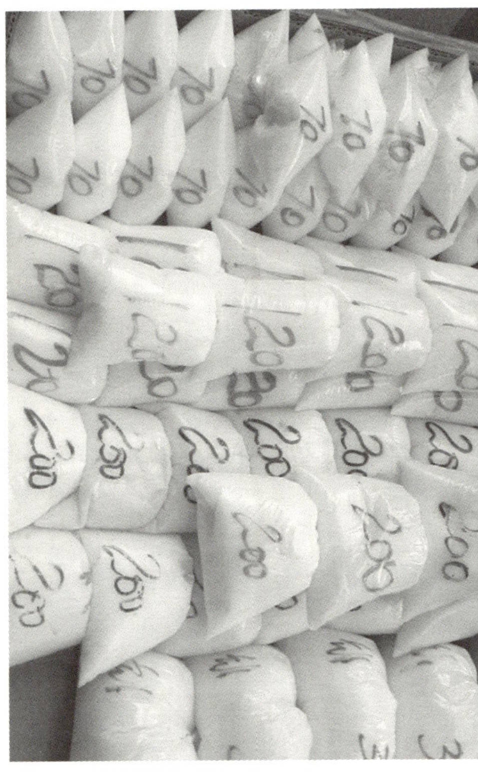

Chicken - pills

Since most of the celebrities are following the current "booty trend" the red carpets are filled with their nearly nude behinds. Also their Instagram profiles are full of pictures taken in bikinis from behind. And of course the music videos – where it all started– are loaded with an unimaginable amount of butt.
The butts are dancing, shaking, twerking and these shots are shown for an incredible length of time. In short there is a daily overload of butt in today's media and most of this material is created by the stars themselves. The paparazzo's time is over, as the celebrities today use social media and put most of the image production into their own hands. This self initiated image production and especially the huge amount of pictures it creates, has spawned complex relationships between image and reality. Sir-Mix-a-Lot was rapping about a healthy body, "Cause silicone parts are made for toys". But this phenomenon is now far from natural, and according to a 2015 report from the *American Society of Plastic Surgeons (ASPS)*, butt implants and lifts are the fastest growing types of plastic surgery in the United States.
This is because what the celebrities mainly do is motivate the rest of the world to start working out or take more drastic measures in order to have a nice b-side. The buttock-surgery trend had its boom in 2014, and on average, in the U.S. there was a buttock procedure every 30 minutes of every day. The most popular procedure worldwide is the buttock augmentation known as the Brazilian butt lift. It is a procedure that enhances the gluteal area providing an uplifted buttock profile. With this method it is common also to place a gluteal implant (buttock prothesis) inside the butt. The main goal is to resolve the patient's deformities of the gluteal region.
In 2005 alone, 14,705 procedures were performed

in the United States, an increase of 28% on the year before. Also Europe registered an enormous growth in buttocks surgery. In the summer of 2016 an article in Vice Magazine UK reported a 13% rise in fat-transfer operations. This means that fat is taken from the stomach or the thigh area and is squeezed into the buttocks: a procedure that is probably the safest, since it's working with body fat and not with silicones or other products.

Butt augmentation procedures are costly, approximately around $4,500 and obviously not everyone can afford them. This is where the real problem begins because people are not willing to give up on their dream of a big butt, so they throw themselves into the black market. While patients think they escape the fee, illegal injectors are earning large sums. What basically happens is that patients are injected with silicone intended to be used for metal or plastic lubrication. This kind of material can be found at any hardware store and costs around 5 Euros or Dollars for 300ml, (fig. 1) But these illegal procedures still cost a few thousand dollars. CNN's article "Black market butt injections: dangerous and deadly" by Liza Lucas talks about how often not even the environment of the operation is sterile. Many times the patients are treated in hotel rooms. The article talks about a case in which super glue and cotton balls were used to cover the injection holes to avoid the silicone to leak out. The article goes on describing the patients as ticking time bombs for the numerous side effects that can appear. Wilbert L. Cooper's report for Vice Magazine "Buttloads of Pain", describes some of the body's reactions to the injected foreign substances which include skin discolouration and necrosis. "The substances

fig. 1

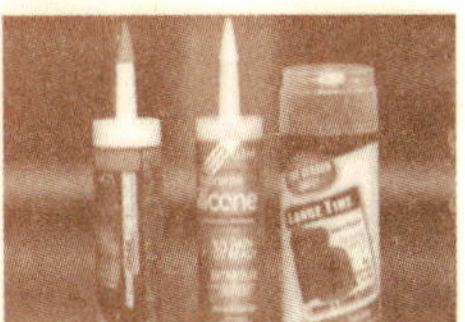

have also been known to migrate through the body and fuse themselves to organs, or enter into the bloodstream, spreading infection throughout the body and causing septic shock – which can led to the amputation of infected body parts, in the worst case death.” Deaths through illegal butt injections have, in fact, been reported in Alabama, Georgia, Pennsylvania, Nevada and New York, in the last year. Miami seems to be the city with the most butt injections and their practising plastic surgeon Dr. Costantino Mendieta[1] calls it “the heart of buttropolis”.

1.Specialist, Dr. Mendieta, Florida medical Association

While the U.S. has to deal with illegal butt injections, women in the Caribbean started a trend in which chicken pills are used in order to gain weight and increase the volume of their posterior. (fig. 2) “Woman take the chicken pills to increase the volume of their hips and bottoms. In our Jamaican culture, we love a girl that has a lot of shape.” Explains a young Jamaican interviewed for NPR’s article “Taking Surprising Risks for The Ideal Body”. The article explains that those ‘chicken pills’ contain arsenic that stimulate the appetite of the chicken. When taken by humans they trigger several side effects including diarrhoea and dermatitis, and since arsenic is a cumulative poison it can even build up in the body and cause cancer. Even though the government has banned the pill for chickens and humans, they are still available in farm stores and on the street. This trend started in the Caribbean islands around the 90s and has now also arrived in Europe. The Sun newspaper reported that “Thousands of British woman are so desperate for a bigger bottom they are risking their lives by taking pills designed to fatten up chickens.” These pills are incredibly easy to get, as they’re available on sites including *Amazon, eBay and Facebook.*

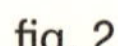
fig. 2

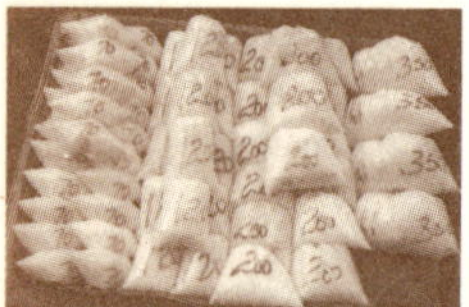

Of course lingerie is also adapting to the big booty, and fashion stores have started to sell silicon padded underwear. They are much the same as push-up bras, the 'Bum Enhancers' (fig. 3) – some filled with foam, some with silicon – create the illusion of a bigger behind.

fig. 3

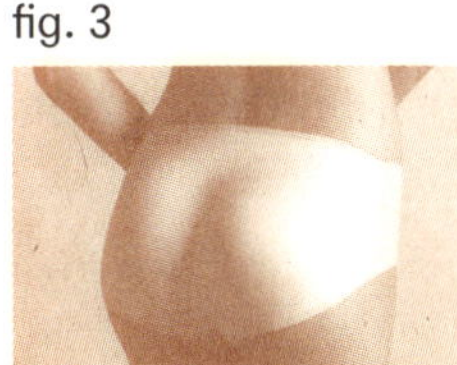

How far are people willing to go, in order to reach their ideal image of beauty? How powerful can an images be, in order to provoke such a strong motivation in people that they are willing to incorporate them in their own life and in to their own bodies? It seems like the fiction is so interwoven with culture that it has become part of it; furthermore the image is better than real life. It became a standard that everybody is trying to reach and nobody is able to keep up with, not even the producers of the image themselves. Images have the absolute power because they touch upon the personal ego.
Social networks created a battle field in which every one is basically looking for the same affirmation. Images help to reach this affirmation and for this attention people are willing to inject themselves with cheap silicon, to create the perfect picture and a social network moment. The price to pay is high, and while the photograph is immortal, the real butt will be eaten by the silicon and cause consequences that in the worst case can be death.

The image is the new beauty standard.
The problem is that we cannot trust the image.
The image is constructed, designed, manipulated and post produced–it is a surreal standard.
Further more, through plastic surgery, we now also question whether the photographed person is in fact natural or not? Plastic surgery is rising and cementing itself into contemporary culture.

This is connected to the impressive physical rejuvenations exhibited by media figures. These days surgery is associated with fame and success, and many celebrities had their break through after such procedures. Kim Kardashian's younger sister Kylie Jenner had a huge increase in popularity after having a massive face transformation. One main change was increasing the volume of her lips. Now she has a cosmetic line focused on lipsticks. Her 'new body part' was an investment that is now part of her brand. These examples give people the illusion that they could be more successful and have a better life if they 'improve' their physical appearance. For many, procedures, become the hope for a better life and to gain self confidence. Even though surgery is changing the physical appearance it also brings huge psychological consequences. Some patients may have symptoms of depression, anxiety or eating disorders.[2] What also needs to be taken into consideration is that many surgical procedures are related to a specific moment in fashion. The big booty is now trendy, before the attention was oriented towards bigger breasts. Changing the body because of a trend can bring huge psychological consequences, especially when the trend is not fashionable anymore and the damage done to the body is often irreversible.

2. V. Diller, 'A New Face: What Are the Psychological Risks?' The Huffington Post, 05.09.2011, (accessed 10.03. 2017)

# Conclusion

Starting with a dig into pop and internet culture the research focuses on the appearance of the female butt in today's media. Taking in to consideration that images exaggerate reality, we can observe how these take almost separate paths by becoming a world of their own. As the author and critic John Berger said: "Images don't belong to places anymore". Through the Internet and a myriad of digital devices we are able to see pictures every hour and everywhere. Pictures appear on screens in the private context of our homes, but also while we're traveling or waiting. They have become an active part of our familiar environment, therefore the relation with the images is more intimate than ever before.
The digital revolution also enlarged the power and influence of these images as they're now distributed worldwide.

The image is an excellent manipulative force, able to awaken desires and sell goods.
The butt is a body part that nowadays is constantly photographed, posted and shared.
It is one of the most mediated images of our times. It sells a product, a body part or more correctly an exaggerated version of it.
Those images – even though they are far from real – create a new beauty standard. The power of the image goes beyond simple influence, its ultimate power is the total integration into life.
But even though the image is an integrated part of our lives it isn't real. The real has been driven out of the reality. The image as a new beauty standard, is to have a standard than cannot be reached naturally in life. New images are constantly created and of course today everyone has the tools to manipulate their own pictures.
Our digital avatars are the perfect illusion created using images, they are the fetishist objects of

social media. Their colours are brighter than in normal life, the contrast higher and the butts firmer. There is an aesthetic intoxication coming from the images. Still many want to become the image. The fiction in our reality is taking the upper hand by creating a scenario in which people are willing to transform themselves and look like images. The body tries to become the image.
The body as an image is hyper reality, it is real and at the same time not. The butt is hyper reality and so are all the ideals that it stands for, they are tangible but at the same time fictional ideals.
In today's society we are no longer spectators,but actors in the performance, and actors increasingly integrated into the course of that performance.
This fiction is taking the upper hand by creating a scenario in which people inject themselves with cheap silicon, to have a moment of digital glory in order to produce their own image – the image of the perfect booty. While the digital version of the butt is immortal, the real one will be swallowed and eaten by the silicon.

This is the "Venus" of our time, she is not made out of prestigious materials, like marble or gold; she is cheap, like plastic and silicone. She will melt in the sun, she will be eaten by pain. The ultimate image of shame and discomfort, the image that nobody wants to see, nobody wants to post online. But there she is, the image of the Post Butt, she needs to be seen, she needs to be heard.

# Post-Butt

In the last chapters we saw the butt rising, becoming a zone of empowerment. While in a second moment mass culture and mainstream media transformed it into an object of plastic illusion. The butt stands out for being the democratic sex organ for excellence, pushing towards a new equality in all genres.
The butt is moulded flesh while simultaneously being political; it's the politics of integration, a genderless object of desire. It promises intimate equality, and sexuality without categories or taboos. The buttocks – masculine as well as feminine – assert themselves as the true star in today's media. The butt is viral, because of its deeply unifying sex appeal. A #belfie, or a butt selfie is the new selfie, an art of contortion performed on social media. The butt is technology, an omnipresent image on our daily screens, a viral phenomenon of our digital lives. The optimisation of new media and information transmission made this possible. The cult of the butt is re-injected and celebrated by all identities and styles. It goes beyond genre, the new unisex, as personal as it is political.

The butt is feminine power, with it Kim Kardashian made plus size fashionable and redefined feminism. It is the new symbol for diversity and self-confidence, yet every picture of it looks the same. The butt is claimed sexuality but also the celebration of fertility and is therefore family friendly.

Every perfect butt needs the perfect fit, a body-condom that attaches to the curves. The butt is fashion, it tells a fluid story of contemporary culture. It stands for fitness apparel and represents the sports culture that goes with it. The tight fitness pants are the

perfect way to show body shapes.
We are living in the re-incarnation of the 80s or rather the explosion of sports. The muscular buttock, indicates a control of itself and its owner's life. It is the protagonist of sport campaigns, the muscular rump acts as an identity for the triumph of the workout over prior biological offerings. The butt does not revolt against filiform thinness, neither has the world refused the model measurements. While many are obsessed with the big booty, the mini-ass continues to exist. It to, has more attention now as it walks down Victoria Secrets catwalks.
It stands for the girly pop look, connected to the 60s rock culture and fashion icon Jane Birkin.
Globalisation has found its representative, the perfect object. The butt. It is influential and for sale. It comes in many shapes and colours and it's genderless.

## Books

**Art and pornography: philosophical essays**
Maes Hans, Levison Jerrold, 2005, ISBN 978-0-19-874408-5

**Danse/cinéma**
Bouquet Stéphane, Capricci : Centre national de la danse, Paris, 2012, ISBN 978-2-918040-49-1

**Envisioning information**
Tufte Edward Rolf, Graphics Press, Cheshire, Connecticut, 2013
ISBN 978-0-9613921-1-6

**Empire of illusion: the end of literacy and the triumph of spectacle**
Hedges Chris, National Books, New York, 2009 ISBN 978-1-56858-437-9

**From bananas to buttocks: the Latina body in popular film and culture**
Mendible Myra, University of Texas Press, Austin, 2007 ISBN 9780292714939

**Image music text**
Barthes Roland, ISBN 8601300008257

**Jeff Koons**
Koons Jeff, Taschen Angelika, Amman Jean - Christophe
Taschen, Köln, 1992 ISBN 978-3-8228-9351-7

**Linguistic anthropology: a reader**
Duranti Alessandro, Wiley-Blackwell , Malden, MA, 2009
ISBN 978-1-4051-2633-5 978-1-4051-2632-8

**L'occhio del Novecento: cinema, esperienza, modernità**
Casetti Francesco, 1. ed. Studi Bompiani, R.C.S. Libri, Milano, 2005
ISBN 978-88-452-3484-2

**Post/porn/politics: symposium/reader: queer - feminist perspective on the politics of porn performance and sex-work as culture production**
Stüttgen Tim, Berlin E - Books, 2009, ISBN 978-3-933557-76-6

**Representation**
Stuart Hall, Los Angeles, Milton Keynes, Sage
The Open University, 2013, ISBN 978-1-84920-563-4 978-1-84920-547-4

**Resistance through rituals: youth subcultures in post-war Britain**
Hall Stuart, Routledge, London, New York, 2006 ISBN 978-0-203-35705-7

**Schiavi della visibilità**
Perna Tonino, Soveria Mannelli, Rubbetino, 2014 ISBN 978-88-498-4066-7

**Sexual personae. Art and decadence from Nefertiti to Emily Dickinson**
Paglia Camille, Yale University Press, New Haven, 1990 ISBN 978-0-300-04396-9

**Styles of radical will**
Sontag Susan, 1st Picador USA ed, New York, 2002
ISBN 978-0-312-42021-5

**The image society: essays on visual culture**
Gierstberg Frits, Oosterbaan Warna, Dijck van José
NAi Publishers, Rotterdam, 2002, ISBN 978-90-5662-284-8

**The medium is the massage: an inventory of effects**
McLuhan Marshall, Fiore Quentin, Agel Jerome,
HardWired, San Francisco, 1996, ISBN 978-1-888869-02-6

**The perfect crime**
Baudrillard Jean, Verso, London, New York, 1996, ISBN 9781859840443

**The Society of the spectacle**
Debord Guy, Bureau of Public Secrets, Berkeley, CA, 2013 ISBN 978-0-939682-06-5

**The visual culture reader**
Mirzoeff Nicholas, Routledge, London, 2010 ISBN 978-0-415-25222-5 978-0-415-25221-8

**Visual culture**
Jenks Chris, Routledge, London ; New York, 1995, ISBN 978-0-415-10622-1 978-0-415-10623-8

**Ways of seeing: based on the BBC television series with John Berger**
Berger John, British Broadcasting Corporation and Penguin Books, London, 1990
ISBN 978-0-14-013515-2

## Articles


**Affen erkennen einander am Hintern**
ORF, 30.11.2016 http://science.orf.at/stories/2812383/

**À l'époque des zoos humains**
CNRS Le Journal, Charline Zeitoun, 25.08.2015
https://lejournal.cnrs.fr/articles/a-lepoque-des-zoos-humains

**Art and Pornography**
Tate, Lily Bonesso, 2.4.2015
http://www.tate.org.uk/context-comment/articles/art-and-pornography

**Art & Feminism, An Interview with Fannie Sosa: On Twerking and the Common**
Berlin Art Link, Alison Hugill, 22. 07. 2015,
http://www.berlinartlink.com/2015/06/22/artfeminism-an-interview-with-fannie-sosa-on-twerking-and-the-commons/

**Black market butt injections: dangerous and deadly**
CNN, Liza Lucas, 24.06.2015
http://edition.cnn.com/2015/06/24/health/deadly-butt-injections/

**Der angeprollt - edle Populismus in den USA - Donald Trumps Amerika: Was uns der nackte Hintern von Kim Kardashian sagt**
Welt, Mara Delius, 20.11.2016
https://www.welt.de/kultur/article159602822/Der-angeprollt-edle-Populismus-tin-den-USA.html

**Estetica del gergo. Come una cultura si fa forma linguistica**
La Ricerca Folklorica, Sanga Glauco, 04. 1989
http://www.jstor.org/stable/1479127?origin=crossref

**Five Things You Might Not Know About Egon Schiele**
An Other, Gillian Hopper, 12.11.2014
http://www.anothermag.com/art-photography/4096/five-things-you-might-not-know-about-egon-schiele?utm_source=fb&utm_medium=social+&utm_campaign=dazed

**Getting to the Bottom of Face Processing. Species - Specific Inversion Effects for Faces and Behinds in Human and Chimpazees**
Plos, Mariska E. Kret, 30.11.2016
http://journals.plos.org/plosone/article?id=10.1371/journal.pone.0165357#pone-0165357-g001

**How J. Lo's Ass Changed the World**
The Huffingtonpost, Erica Kennedy, 25.5.2011
http://www.huffingtonpost.com/erica-kennedy/how-j-los-ass-changed-the_b_586226.html

**Is this the first Instagram masterpiece?**
The Telegraph, Alastair Sooke, 18.1.2016
http://www.telegraph.co.uk/photography/what-to-see/is-this-the-first-instagram-masterpiece/

**New Statistics Reflect the Changing Face of Plastic Surgery - American Society of Plastic Surgeons Releases Reports Showing Shift in Procedures**
https://www.plasticsurgery.org/news/press-releases/new-statistics-reflect-the-changing-face-of-plastic-surgery

**Pills 'for fattening chicken' - Thousand of British women are so desperate for a bigger bottom they are risking their lives by taking pills designed to fatten up chickens.**
The Sun, Jane Hamilton, 12.02.2011
https://www.thesun.co.uk/archives/news/367290/pills-for-fattening-chicken/

**Sugar? Sure, but Salted With Meaning - 'A Subtlety, or the Marvelous Sugar Baby' at the Domino Plant**
New York Times, Roberta Smith, 11.5.2014
https://www.nytimes.com/2014/05/12/arts/design/a-subtlety-or-the-marvelous-sugar-baby-at-the-domino-plant.html

**The Big Problem With Kim Kardashian's Butt Photos Nobody Is Talking About**
Get Mic Daily, Derrick Clifton, 13.11.2104t
https://mic.com/articles/104188/the-big-problem-with-kim-kardashian-s-photos-nobody-is-talking-about#.SAOxElYnz

**Wait - How Many People Got Butt Implants Last Year?**
Shape, Kylie Gilbert, 01.03.2016
http://www.shape.com/lifestyle/beauty-style/wait-how-many-people-got-butt-implants-last-year

**We're Officially in the Era of the Big Booty**
Vouge, Patricia Garcia, 9.9.2014
http://www.vogue.com/1342927/booty-in-pop-culture-jennifer-lopez-iggy-azalea/

**Why Are So Many More British Woman Getting Butt Implants?**
Vice, Josh Surtees, 26.11.2014
https://www.vice.com/en_us/article/uk-butt-implants-240

**Why Smart Woman Are Killing Themselves with Illegal Butt Injections**
Vice, Wilbert L. Cooper, 04.06.2015
https://www.vice.com/en_ca/article/why-women-are-getting-underground-butt-injections-456

**You Will Never Want An Illegal Butt Injection After Watching 'Buttloads Of Pain'**
The Huffingtonpost, 25.01.2014
http://www.huffingtonpost.com/2014/01/16/illegal-butt-injection-video_n_4611838.html

## Documentaries

**Buttloads of Pain: Ass Injection Gone Wrong**
**Vice Reports, 2014**
https://video.vice.com/en_us/video/buttloads-of-pain-ass-injections-gone wrong/56054419b4d863da4a6a19ae

**Caribbean Fashion Week, Dance Hall and Skin Bleaching**
**Vice Reports, 2012**
https://www.vice.com/en_us/article/caribbean-fashion-week-full-length

**Dr. Constantino Mendieta on The Doctors**
**Discussing Illegal Butt Augmentations, 2014**
https://www.youtube.com/watch?v=a1SzswXQKXM&t=1s

**Fashion Week Internationale - Colombia Fashion Week:**
**Ass Implants and Couture, Vice Reports, 2011**
https://video.vice.com/en_us/video/colombia-fashion-week-ass-implants-couture/
55b25b20091d63551dfee831

**Génération Mapouka avec Les Tueuses de la Cote d'Ivoire**
https://www.youtube.com/watch?v=OdLDJA8m2_8

**Gluteal Implant, Buttock Implants by Dr. Rajae Janho, 2014**
https://www.youtube.com/watch?v=mey6wMkFdBA&t=1s

**Rio Fashion Week, Ass Shaking and Transsexual Supermodels**
**Vice Reports, 2012**
https://www.vice.com/en_us/article/rio-fashion-week-part-3

## Movies

**And God Created Woman, 1957**
Directed by Roger Vadim, Starring, Brigitte Bardot,
Curd Jürgens, Jean-Louis Trintignant

**Stagecoach, 1939**
Directed by John Ford, Starring, Claire Trevor, John Wayne

Songs (in order of appearance)

**Shake Your Moneymaker, Elmore James, 1961**
https://www.youtube.com/watch?v=vn77rGEV6XM

**KC and the Sunshine Band, Shake Your Booty, 1976**
https://www.youtube.com/watch?v=xWxLc555sgU

**Fat Bottomed Girls, Queens, 1978**
https://www.youtube.com/watch?v=VMnjF1O4eH0

**Da Butt, E.U. 1989**
https://www.youtube.com/watch?v=Ypcs4c7ihSo

**Baby got Back, Sir Mix-a-Lot, 1992**
https://www.youtube.com/watch?v=kY84MRnxVzo

**Rumpshaker, Wreckx-n-effect, 1992**
https://www.youtube.com/watch?v=XfUdTXs8FWI

**Shake Yaa Ass, Mystikal, 2000**
https://www.youtube.com/watch?v=Vb2mnDp68S0

**Ying Yang Twins, Whistle While You Twurk, 2000**
https://www.youtube.com/watch?v=15PQvqsaBG8

**Bootylicious, Destiny's Child, 2001**

https://www.youtube.com/watch?v=lyYnnUcgeMc

**Salt Shaker, Ying Yang Twins 2003**
https://www.youtube.com/watch?v=aJEzl31zL-I

**A** Like That, Eminem, 2014**
https://www.youtube.com/watch?v=um4-d7VzZiE

**Get Busy, Sean Paul 2014**
https://www.youtube.com/watch?v=oPQ3o14ksaM

**Check on It, Beyoncé 2005**
https://www.youtube.com/watch?v=Q1dUDzBdnml

**SexyBack, Justin Timberlake, 2016**
https://www.youtube.com/watch?v=3gOHvDP_vCs

**Dance A$$, Big Sean, Nicki Minaj, 2011**
https://www.youtube.com/watch?v=pn1VGytzXus

**Moment 4 Life, Nicki Minaj 2011**
https://www.youtube.com/watch?v=D7GW8TYCEG4

**Work, Iggy Azalea, 2013**
https://www.youtube.com/watch?v=_zR6ROjoOX0

**Wrecking Ball, Miley Cyrus, 2013**
https://www.youtube.com/watch?v=My2FRPA3Gf8

**Can't Remember to Forget You, Shakira & Rihanna, 2013**
https://www.youtube.com/watch?v=o3mP3mJDL2k

**Twerk it, Busta Rhymes, 2013**
https://www.youtube.com/watch?v=j47MYli8pj4

**Partition, Beyonce, 2013**
https://www.youtube.com/watch?v=pZ12_E5R3qc

**Rocket, Beyonce, 2013**
https://www.youtube.com/watch?v=sAz2bRy8-L8

**Bubble Butt, Major Lazer, 2013**
https://www.youtube.com/watch?v=wO89_H7GqaQ

**Rella, Odd Future, 2013**
https://www.youtube.com/watch?v=fN-xq7t6pKw

**Tamale, Odd Future, 2013**
https://www.youtube.com/watch?v=OxlJLz9M8hQ

**Anaconda, Nicki Minaj, 2014**
https://www.youtube.com/watch?v=LDZX4ooRsWs

**Booty, Jennifer Lopez & Iggy Azalea, 2014**
https://www.youtube.com/watch?v=nxtlRArhVD4

**Milk, Milk, Lemonade, Amy Schumer, 2015**
https://www.youtube.com/watch?v=HeiSx5MNDvg

**Side To Side, Ariana Grande, Nicki Minaj**
https://www.youtube.com/watch?v=SXiSVQZLje8

**Fade, Kanye West**
https://www.youtube.com/watch?v=IxGvm6btP1A

**Onomatopee 137.1**
**Post-Butt. The Power of the Image**

Author, research and graphic design: Melani De Luca
Editor: Pernilla Ellens
Editorial advice: Freek Lomme
Research and design advice: Joost Grootens, Gert Staal, Simon Davies, Arthur Roeloffzen, Delphine Bedel
Proofreading: Josh Plough
Introduction: Charlotte Van Buylaere
Translation of manifesto: Megan Dinius
Printing: Printon, Tallin Estonia
Edition 2: 1000